GOD, FAMILY and SEXUALITY

edited by

David W. Torrance

The Handsel Press Ltd
The Stables, Carberry, EH21 8PY
Scotland

British Library Cataloguing in Publication Data:
A catalogue record for this publication is available from the British Library
ISBN   1 871828 32 5

Typeset in 11 pt. Garamond

Printed by B.P.C. Wheaton Ltd

This book developed out of a study group commissioned by the
Scottish Order of Christian Unity: it included members of
the Anglican Church, the Church of Scotland,
the Free Church of Scotland, the Christian Brethren,
the Methodist Church and the Roman Catholic Church

CONTENTS

FOREWORD

The Very Revd Professor Thomas F. Torrance
President, *The Scottish Order of Christian Unity*

Today there is a tendency to smooth away all concrete Christian dogmas into vague theism or a vaguer pantheism, and to flatten out the firm lines of Christian ethics into pious sentiment. It is a tendency which must be strongly combated. The foundation of our faith is not only that 'God is love'. It is still more the tremendous historical fact that 'God so loved the world that he gave his only begotten Son: that whosoever believes in him should not perish but have everlasting life.'

That was a statement made by Lord Tweedsmuir, John Buchan, sixty years ago in an address he gave to an assembly of world churchmen in Montreal, when he was Governor-General of Canada. He went on to point out that "there is today a general loosening of moral sanctions", and insisted that "we cannot shut our eyes to the fact that there is a good deal of moral anarchy abroad, and that the social discipline, which insisted upon a certain standard of conduct, has been gravely weakened." "This is partly due", he thought, "to the importance acquired by the mere mechanism of life through our scientific developments. And it is partly due to the popularizing of half-understood philosophic ideas about the right of each man to self-realization and the development of his personality."

If John Buchan were with us today, he would surely repeat what he said in 1937, and reinforce his call for moral and social reform, without forgetting that "the Gospel is concerned primarily with spiritual redemption, not with social reform." "At the same time", he added, "while it is wrong to pin Christianity down to any social formula, it is most necessary that the Christian spirit should interpenetrate our public life."

That is what some of us in *The Scottish Order of Christian Unity*, together with others not in the Order, are concerned with in the preparation of this book which is devoted to *the Christian family*. The moral and social situation is now rather more serious than it was in 1937, especially after the so-called "swinging sixties", with the revelling of people in erotic music, and the widespread sexualisation of human life and thought not least as fostered by the media. We are in need of deep moral and spiritual renewal. We believe that we must listen again to the Words of Jesus, and let them speak directly to us in our day with all their pristine divine force. In this book a group of Christians from various churches have cooperated in working out ways in which the teaching of Christ may be allowed to exert again in our private and social life the power of the Holy Spirit which originally gave shape to the Christian Church, and redemptively transformed the moral culture of the ancient world. Today this means that we have to allow the teaching of Jesus to bear directly upon the ethical implications of genetics in society, and not least upon the popular emphasis upon sexual and social mechanisms, together with the naturalistic philosophy of self-realisation and self-fulfilment which have been steadily interpenetrating education and corroding our family and public way of life.

In this volume the authors seek to face new conditions and new questions, and to offer the kind of spiritual and moral guidance which so many of our 'social counsellors' today seem unable to give. We are certainly concerned in *The Scottish Order of Christian Unity*, as in *The Order of Christian Unity* in London, with the kind of moral rearmament that comes from a profounder sense of the majesty and purity of God, but throughout we are concerned with the redemptive power of the living Voice of God which we hear in the Holy Scriptures and with the healing force of the Gospel.

It is my prayer that this work will be widely used in the spiritual and moral renewal of our family and social life today.

PREFACE

The aim of the Scottish Order of Christianity Unity, according to its Charter, is to seek "to realise and defend essential Christian ethics... especially in family life...". In pursuit of this aim, the SOCU in 1994 appointed a Study Group to consider the whole area of the Christian Family and related sexual matters in so far as these from the Christian point of view are under challenge today.

The members of the Study Group were the Revd William D. Brown (Secretary of the SOCU), Lady Brigid McEwen, Revd Professor Donald McLeod, Revd David C. Searle, Professor David Short, Revd Jock Stein, Revd Mrs Margaret Stein, Revd Howard Taylor, Revd David W. Torrance (Chairman of the Group), Revd Professor James B. Torrance. The Revd Dr R.B.W. Walker (Treasurer of the SOCU), helpfully joined the Group *ex officio*. Notes on the Contributors, along with a message from Lady Lothian, patron of the SOCU, are at the end of the book.

Papers were presented by various members of the Study Group. Others who had specialised in a particular area were also invited to contribute. Each paper was discussed by the group. Suggestions and constructive criticisms were made and in the light of these each paper was revised. This book is presented as a corporate contribution. This does not mean that there are no differences of opinion among those contributing or among members of the Group. There is however a remarkable consensus of agreement on the whole thrust of what is here offered. In the end each contributor is solely responsible for what he or she has written. Likewise, this book should not be read as reflecting the opinions of all members of the SOCU, who, although coming from different church disciplines, remain remarkably united in their understanding of Christ and of Scripture.

As editor I would like to thank each contributor and each member of the Study Group all of whom whether contributing a paper or aiding in discussion have helped greatly in the production of this volume. I give my special thanks to the Revd Dr R.B. Walker for much help in the checking and correcting of manuscripts and to my brother the Very Revd Professor T.F. Torrance and to his son Dr Thomas Torrance for technical help in this age of word processing.

It is our prayer that this book may stimulate readers to think more deeply in a biblical way about the issues raised: that it may encourage them to seek to understand more clearly what God may be saying to us and that it may help the churches and other Christian organisations in their work and witness.

David W. Torrance
North Berwick, 1996

INTRODUCTION

In recent years and throughout Western countries changes have come about in society's understanding of marriage and family life. These changes continue. Peoples' hopes and expectations of marriage and family life are changing. Living together without the normal obligations which marriage imposes has become socially acceptable. Many no longer look on marriage as necessarily involving a life-long commitment. The understanding of man-woman relationships has changed. There is a greater emphasis on individual and personal fulfilment rather than on commitment to a marriage partner and to family. Consequently the relationship of parents and children has changed.

Many things have brought about these changes. Women have greater financial independence, society is more mobile than formerly, people move and settle far from their place of early upbringing, the restraining influences of the extended family are less, expectations and hopes have been raised through the public media and through advertising. Alcohol plays a large part in the break-down of marriage. Gambling and drugs contribute. Above all the decline in the practice of the Christian Faith has deeply affected the understanding of marriage and family life.

Despite the fact that all this challenges the Christian understanding of marriage and family life, the Church in the West has had little impact in stemming the tide. Often the churches have manifested uncertainty about what to say or what attitude to adopt in the present crisis situation. Their position has been rendered more difficult by some within the churches being themselves influenced by changing secular attitudes.

All Christians need to examine afresh the teaching of Scripture and its relevance for today and together to seek to understand what God is saying in the present situation. This requires courage and faith and the discipline of seeking to be faithful to God's revelation of himself in Christ through his Word.

One of the great challenges confronting the churches concerns the relevance of God's Word for our generation. Can Scripture speak relevantly today with regard to marriage, divorce and family life? Can Scripture guide us effectively concerning sexuality and homosexuality and the other practical needs and issues facing society today? The Scriptures were written long ago. In their form if not their content they have been culturally and socially conditioned. They were relevant for the age when they were written. Society today is vastly different from what it was in Bible times. Is Scripture a relevant and practical guide to present day issues?

In Part 1, the concern is with the Bible as the Word of God, its authority and its relevance for today. God is himself in Jesus Christ the authority of scripture. The Bible is the place of meeting between God and men and women. It is the place where as men and women we hear God speaking to us in our need, for our help and salvation. Both contributors seek to demonstrate "how the Bible continues to be relevant, despite its cultural distance. Scripture enables us to see, or at least to glimpse, human reality as it is truly ordered in, and by, Christ... The Christian life is inseparably connected to the Word of God. It is God's Word that evokes faith and orients it. Our vocation as Christians is to live out and witness to the Word of God in all that we say and do. In being called to be the Body of Christ, the Church is called to embody God's Word.... Scripture. in all its diverse literary forms, may profitably be taken up in every time, place and situation, as we seek to conform our lives to Jesus Christ: the Way, the Truth and the Life".

In Part 2, attention is focused on marriage, divorce and family issues. Very often today statements on the doctrine of marriage have laid considerable stress on the order of creation and little stress on God's covenant of grace and on redemption. Marriage, so it is argued, belongs to the natural order as created by God. In failing however to stress God's covenant of grace and redemption and therefore the centrality of Christ with reference to marriage, the churches have found it difficult to answer the often repeated question of secular society, "What is natural?". Is it natural for two people to be committed to the same partner for life? Or is it natural for two people to be committed to each other in marriage just so long as love continues? Is it natural for a single person to remain celibate? Is it natural for two people who have an homosexual orientation not to be approved of, both within the Church and society, when they seek to express that orientation? The Bible interpreted in the light of Christ has much to say on these issues.

The Bible stresses one covenant of grace which embraces not only the Church, but all mankind and all creation. Jesus Christ has lovingly gathered up and fulfilled in himself all God's purposes of redemption and creation. Creation and the natural order are important as that which is of God. We cannot however separate or seek to understand creation apart from redemption in Christ, nor yet redemption apart from creation. This is Paul's argument in chapters one of both Ephesians and Colossians. God "purposed in Christ.... to bring all things in heaven and on earth together under one head, even Christ" (Ephesians 1:10). We can only rightly understand creation and the natural order when we do so in Christ. Without Christ or apart from Christ we misunderstand creation and the natural order. Marriage and family life can only rightly be understood in the light of God's purpose for them in Christ. Only in His light can we understand their true place in creation. In this context marriage between God's people in the Old Testament is always understood as rightly taking place within God's covenant of grace. It is patterned on it, embraced within it and sealed by it. In the New Testament the marriage of God's people is embraced and sealed by Christ. Christian marriage is "in the Lord". The chapters on Marriage and Divorce stress the centrality of Christ and thus the unity of redemption and creation.

The chapters on Cohabitation, the Christian family, Childlessness, and Singleness are each concerned to highlight the centrality of Jesus Christ and the important bearing of grace and redemption on these practical issues.

In the chapter on Fertility, Contraception and the Family a Catholic point of view is presented. Many in the main stream Protestant churches have perhaps too easily accepted and welcomed the contribution of medical science in this sphere. Whereas the introduction of the contraceptive Pill has been followed by an increase in promiscuity and unwanted pregnancies, which Christians everywhere deplore, they have generally wished to argue that it is the immorality that is to be condemned rather than contraception. The problem is a difficult one and remains. Readers of this book are being encouraged to ponder what is so ably presented.

In Part 3, attention is focused on Sexuality. Societies through the centuries have wrestled with the issue. With its many aspects and widespread implications for marriage, family life, society and Church, it is a burning issue today.

God has created us as spiritual/physical, spiritual/sexual beings. We are created and called to live and act in an integrated way as whole people living in the wholeness of loving relationships with one another. Yet few people seem to enjoy that continuous wholeness of being and relationship with others that God wants where there is complete harmony between our spiritual and physical nature. Why is that?

Our sexual instincts are God given. In themselves they are holy and good. God has created them pleasurable for our good and the welfare of society. Yet as all history indicates they all too often, in the way that they have been used, degrade and enslave human nature and corrupt society. What has happened? What would God have us do?

Each contributor has written out of the depth of their experience and understanding, and presented a biblical position.

Perhaps few issues generate more heat and passion today than that of homosexuality. It calls for considerable thought and understanding and much love and compassion toward those who are so orientated. We have much yet to learn about this complex issue, as is clear from the chapter on *Homosexuality - Predisposing Factors.*

The very suggestion that people who have been homosexual for years can be healed, can arouse not only in society but also at times in the Church, strong hostility. The suggestion of healing suggests on the part of the homosexual abnormality, lack of wholeness or even illness. Sadly, people with a homosexual orientation can even feel threatened or criticised by the suggestion. We assure them of our love and share the pain of those who are struggling to remain celibate. Much work has been done, however, pastorally and in the way of healing, in the U.S.A. by "Pastoral Care Ministries" of which Leanne Payne is President, and in the U.K. by "Maranatha" co-founded and directed by Dennis Wrigley. It is out of considerable experience and success in this field that Dennis Wrigley and Dr Linda Stalley have written here on this subject in the final chapters. Even so, we recognise as they do that many people live with a range of disabilities, and deserve our love, our understanding and our prayers.

David W. Torrance

Part I   THE WORD OF GOD

Chapter 1   THE AUTHORITY OF THE BIBLE

David C. Searle

There are many questions being asked today about truth, morality and human behaviour. Television plays, films, magazines, chat shows and theatre constantly question traditional values. Very subtly they portray new ways of thinking and have been bringing about a major change in western attitudes. As a result, many people are absorbing new standards without realising the radical change in their ideas of morality.

Take as an example the change of attitude towards marriage. A few years ago, it was generally accepted that when a man and woman married, it was for life - "until death do us part". Because it was held that faithfulness to marriage vows was a first priority, husbands and wives stuck together through bad times as well as good, and they refused even to consider ending their relationship.

However, almost like a morning mist, such a view of marriage has all but disappeared. Instead of fidelity to marriage vows being a first priority, a new goal of living has emerged: people today are looking for self-fulfilment - their quest is to 'find' themselves. The talk now is all about being an 'authentic person', and if a marriage partner appears to be inhibiting the other's progress towards discovery of his or her 'true self', then the relationship is regarded as deserving to be ended without any further ado.

This massive shift in attitude has profound implications for our understanding of truth. Morality and indeed all human behaviour had been seen in the past as being governed by divine laws. These laws were to be found in the Scriptures of the Old and New Testaments. The earlier approach of fidelity, responsibility and duty was actually based on the Bible's clear teaching. It was accepted that the Ten Commandments were given by God for our security and happiness. Moreover, it was also considered that God was to be reverenced and his laws ought to be obeyed simply because they were his laws. Jesus Christ was understood as having come to fulfil the Old

Testament. Therefore the Christian Bible was accepted as the supreme authority in all matters of faith and conduct.

But with the new way of thinking, the Bible's authority and relevance has been increasingly questioned. People are saying that a book written centuries ago for a nomadic tribe of shepherds has nothing to say to men and women living in a modern world. The argument goes that times have changed. We now live in a global village. We are learning that different nationalities have different religions and different ideas about morality. Therefore we are learning that truth is what a particular society believes. For an ethnic group of one religion, truth will be very different from truth for another group with another religion. Truth is flexible and is what works in any situation.

It is not difficult to see how the Bible's authority is quickly undermined by this way of thinking. From time immemorial, Christians (following the faith of Old Testament believers) have been certain that there are absolute values of truth, beauty and goodness which can never change. These values emanate from God himself and cannot be disassociated from the Person of God. They are reflected in the Bible and are revealed fully and finally in Jesus of Nazareth. The book you are reading now is based firmly and squarely on this understanding of Holy Scripture.

As we draw towards the conclusion of the twentieth century and face a new beginning with a new century, can we still believe the Bible and base our lives on its teaching? What about the objections to its authority so many people are making? These are questions which we must seriously consider for they will affect very deeply what we believe, and let us remember, what we believe will shape the way we live.

What is the Bible about?

Christians believe the Bible is the Word of God and that all scripture is given by inspiration. That does not mean that those who wrote the Bible became like word processors with some mystical divine fingers prompting them to press each key to tap out a message straight from heaven. That is not the way God works.

Let's begin with the *Old Testament*. God is speaking through his dealings with various people and with one nation in particular whom he chose to be the means of his self-revelation. The life of Abraham may be taken as an illustration. Abraham heard a call from God. God spoke and Abraham obeyed. Through Abraham's obedience, an intimate relationship grew up between him and God until this man became known as "the friend of God".

Through his experiences of God's goodness to him and through the promises and help God gave him, Abraham learned certain things about God. This learning process was part of his everyday life and continued right through his life. The story of Abraham preserves for us in a wonderful way the important things he came to understand about God.

However, this was not a process that began or ended with one man. It was a learning experience that had begun with our first parents and which continued, generation after generation. God was gently and graciously showing a little more of himself to men and women. He was teaching them to trust him. He was unfolding to them the difference between good and bad, true and false, the lovely and the unlovely.

This process can be seen quite clearly in the ongoing story of the Old Testament. God used his dealings with Abraham, Moses, Deborah and countless others. He also used historical events such as the deliverance of the Hebrew slaves from Egypt and their journey through the Sinai desert. He used a complex system of ceremonial laws which became established in ancient Israel. He used sermons which prophets preached to the people. He used poetry and wise sayings recorded by different people in praise of himself. The Old Testament is the record of this process through which God showed his people what he himself was like and what he expected of them.

But there is something missing in the Old Testament. No one can read the Jewish scriptures carefully without quickly realising that there is constantly an expectation of a great event which has not happened but which is promised. This is true generally of the Bible from Genesis to Malachi. Everything we read is characterised by *promise*. The mood is prospective - looking forward to Someone who is still to come. That brings us to the second major part of the Christian Bible.

The *New Testament* is significantly different from the Old Testament in one important way. While the Old Testament is characterised by *promise*, the New Testament is characterised by *fulfilment*. The Gospels tell the story of the birth of a special Baby, and then give an account of his life, his ministry, his death and resurrection. The rest of the New Testament tells the story of the rapid growth of the Church which he founded.

In the New Testament, as in the Old, the process of God showing himself to men and women continues. But more, in the New Testament that process comes to a glorious climax as the very nature and likeness of God is seen in the face of Jesus Christ.

How can an ancient book like the Bible be true for today?

It is obvious that throughout history there have been enormous changes. Men and women have made massive strides in their understanding of the world of nature and the nature of the world. We have progressed from travelling on horseback to space age rockets. Our knowledge of the universe is expanding all the time. Giant steps forward have been taken in the fields of medicine and science. Life in Europe today is hugely different from the way it was a few hundred years ago.

These changes have caused some people to ask how a book written so long ago can have anything of value to teach modern people. We know so much more than they did about the world we live in. We have discovered more about the natural resources of our environment than they ever dreamed of. We know far more than they knew about the functioning of the human body and about the conception and birth of children. Surely our superior knowledge means we have outgrown an old book which is centuries old!

We should remember, however, that there are certain things which have not, and indeed cannot, change. I mention only some of these.

First, from the very beginning of the Church and until today some things can happen when the Bible (either the Old or New Testament) is faithfully preached or read by people in their own homes. Hardened sinners who have been opposed to God are completely changed. This has happened on countless occasions indicating that there is a power in the Bible to transform human lives. It has been said that arguments can always be refuted, but no one can deny a transformed character. The Bible itself and the history of the Church provide us with the most compelling evidence of this transforming power of scripture.

Second, the Bible reveals to those who hear its message or who read it and hear what it has to say, a God who never changes in his holiness, love and compassion towards men and women and whose saving grace is boundless. People's perception of God certainly changes. But God never changes. He always remains faithful to himself and to his own nature, and to his will to save.

Third, human nature has not changed and the spiritual needs of men and women have not changed. We all have a problem with our behaviour. There is a built-in bias which is inherently selfish. That is why there is so much unhappiness and cruelty in the world. For all our brilliant progress, human nature has not changed. We may be able to control and harness the elements. But we cannot control or harness the selfishness of the human heart.

There are more prisons in Britain today than ever before in our history. There are more children in care today than before. There is more fear from robbery and crimes of violence (including sexual assault) than there has been within living memory. At every level of society, the fatal flaw in human nature can be clearly seen. The answer to all human need has ever been found and is being found in God in Jesus Christ, who reveals himself in scripture.

Fourth, in spite of all the new ideas that truth is relative (that is, the belief that what is true for me living in Scotland might not be true for an Indonesian living in Java), the absolutes of good and evil, truth and falsehood, beauty and ugliness have not changed. No one would deny that different nations have slightly different perceptions of these things. But there is an underlying uniformity about absolute values which are self-authenticating and confirm that they do exist. These values are absolute because God himself never changes.

Fifth and most important of all, the Bible is true for today because it is God's book. God the Father has inspired it. Its great subject and content is God the Son and it is understood only through the illumination of God the Spirit. God alone can reveal God. Only he gives the Bible its authority and ability to meet every human need in every generation. The Psalmist puts it like this: "For with you is the fountain of life; and in your light we see light".[1]

Whether a man is dying of leprosy in Palestine 2000 years ago, or whether a woman is dying of cancer and being given radio-therapy in a modern hospital, their spiritual needs remain the same. The grace of God to bring them comfort and consolation in the face of death also remains the same. That is why the Bible still speaks with the same power today as it has always had. The truth it reveals is eternal truth.

What is the relationship of the Bible to God himself?

The great central fact of the Christian faith is a Person, and that Person is himself called the Word of God. The reason why the early Church accepted the authority of the Old Testament scriptures was that Jesus Christ himself accepted their authority and saw himself as fulfilling them. He claimed that he had come, not to abolish the Old Testament law, but to fulfil it. He constantly referred to the Old Testament prophets as speaking about himself and the events of his birth, ministry, death and resurrection. It was the relationship of the Old Testament to Jesus Christ which left no doubt at all in the minds of the first Christians of its authority as the Word of God. They understood (as we have seen in the previous section above) that God himself was its authority.

We also know that the apostles whom Jesus Christ appointed and who were the founders of his Church (himself being the chief cornerstone), used the Old Testament scriptures as their source of authoritative preaching about him. Moreover, their apostolic teaching was realised by the early Church to be an unchanging testimony about Christ. That teaching was gradually preserved in those writings which we now call the New Testament. Even though the books of the New Testament came chronologically after the Church had been founded and had spread across the Roman world, the Church quickly took the apostles' writings as her doctrinal norm. The early believers received these writings as the divinely given witness to the event of Jesus Christ who had broken into human history as Saviour, Lord and King.

Christians understand the Bible as God's means of divine revelation. 'Revelation' means 'unveiling' in the sense of drawing back the curtains to show what has been concealed behind them - a portrait, for example. In the Bible, therefore, we have the record of God revealing himself. But God is not only showing men and women what he is like. He is giving himself to them. That self-giving came and goes on coming with all the impact of his holy presence.

While there is a gradual unfolding of this mysterious divine presence - so that in the book of Genesis we have only a partial record of God's self-disclosure - we must not think that in Genesis God was only partially present. Such a thing would be impossible for the Lord of Glory! Always when he came to people, he came to them as the holy God of grace; it was his whole self that was in action in visiting them.

Nevertheless, we can safely say that the record of this revelation of God, for example in Genesis, was at first partial. The record was only finally complete when the apostolic testimony to Jesus Christ was complete. That record is, of course, the Christian Bible.

Can anyone understand the Bible?

The Bible is not always an easy book to read and understand. There is a story in the New Testament which illustrates this. An Ethiopian was travelling in his chariot reading an Old Testament scroll but was baffled by what he was reading. A Christian called Philip heard him reading Isaiah 53 and asked him if he knew the meaning. The Ethiopian admitted he didn't and so invited Philip to explain the words to him.[2]

That is why this book has been written. Each chapter endeavours to give an explanation in modern terms of various aspects of the truth of scripture. It has been written by those whom the Church has recognised as having a gift of teaching. This gift comes from the Holy Spirit and is God's way of enabling people of each generation to understand the relevance and meaning of the Bible for today.

This does not mean that those without any special training or gift cannot read and understand the Bible. Everyone can take up the Bible and read it, praying that the Holy Spirit will open its words to their understanding.

In the Bible we read of God's love for the world and his desire to reveal himself to each of us and to save us. When we read it and are ready and willing to receive his grace, the Bible is the place where we will meet him and hear him speak. Even so, all of us need help in our reading so that we can understand what the Bible is saying and so share more fully in God's grace.

Different genres of Scripture

Scripture has to be interpreted with skill and care. It contains various kinds (genres) of writings such as history, biography, law, poetry, sermons, prophecy, memoirs, visions and didactic letters with concentrated doctrinal and ethical teaching. While we all have the privilege of opening our Bibles in the privacy of our homes (too few exercise this great privilege), we also need teachers to guide us in our understanding of the great themes and messages of God's truth.

We cannot interpret historical chapters, for example in 1 and 11 Samuel, in the same way we would interpret Hebrew poetry, for example in the Psalms. Similarly, we cannot interpret prophecy such as that in Isaiah in the same way that we would interpret Paul's letter to the Romans. These different kinds (genres) of writing must be respected and carefully understood according to appropriate ways of interpretation.

The skill of interpreting the Bible has a technical name. It is called *hermeneutics*. Those who study hermeneutics learn how to follow the golden thread that runs through the Bible as the record shows more and more of the truth about God, beginning with the early chapters of Genesis and continuing through to the Revelation of Jesus Christ - the last book of the Bible. They learn how to handle all the various kinds of writing. They also learn to build 'bridges' between the 'then and there' of Bible times and the 'here and now' of modern times.

Conclusion

It is the prayer of those who have worked to produce this book that readers will be aware that it contains eternal truths which are given to us in God's special book, the Bible. Also that readers will realise that the writers have sought to interpret scripture carefully and to build 'bridges' between what the Bible *meant* when it was first written and what it *means* for us today.

We would urge readers to go back to the Bible for themselves, to study the wonderful stories and teaching contained there, asking for the help of the Holy Spirit to understand the truths of God's grace in Jesus Christ. As we read the Bible, we need to pray that God himself will meet us in its pages and will himself enable us to hear what he is saying and to obey him in our daily living. It is in this way that ordinary people can make a significant contribution to society today and act as lights shining in a dark place. May God be pleased to bless this book to that end.

[1] Psalm 36:9
[2] Acts 8:26ff.

Appendix: THE BIBLE:
ITS RELEVANCE FOR TODAY

Kevin J. Vanhoozer

A. Introduction: the case for biblical irrelevance

My topic, at first glance, appears to state either a nonsense or a truism. Surely the Word of the eternal God, of all words, would be timelessly relevant? That the Creator of the cosmos could be behind the times is a fantastic notion, the invention of a proud race indeed. But of course, my topic is neither silly nor redundant. For the real issue concerns the nature and locus of the Word of God. Where, when and how does God speak to his people today? Can we take the Bible as the Word of God? If so, how can we use it in discussions concerning such contemporary issues as euthanasia, genetic engineering, the ecological crisis, artificial intelligence, and the like? And, in particular, does Scripture still have anything important to say to us about marriage, the family and sexuality?

1. The irrelevance of texts in general: literary and philosophical arguments

a. Cultural relativism
"The problems of our own time are very different from those of biblical times; how then can material from that very different biblical situation be decisive for our problems."[1] Two centuries and more of biblical criticism have struggled to overcome historical distance. The ugly ditch, however, is deep: an ancient text may have a different meaning, or no meaning at all, in our time and culture.[2] We might call this the 'modern' problem of relevance: the Bible's meaning is difficult to recover and may be out of date.

b. Reader-response criticism
The newer reader-response approach to interpretation finds the road to textual relevance blocked at the other end. It is not only the text that is suspect, but the reader. All readings are situated in particular sociopolitical contexts and involve a struggle for power; there is no 'innocent interpretation'. "Biblical scholars have been slow to awaken . . . to the realization that our representations of and discourse about what the text meant and how it means are inseparable from what we *want* it to mean, from how we *will* it to mean".[3] Interpretation is about making the Bible

meaningful rather than discovering its own intrinsic meaning. Is the price to be paid for making the Bible relevant thus to read it as if we had authored it? If so, then the cost is too high. The Bible will ultimately be *less* rather than more relevant if it is unable to challenge our interpretations of it. Radical reader-response criticism makes the text a nose of wax and invites the reader to tweak.

c. Deconstruction

Jacques Derrida, by declaring the author irrelevant to interpretation (hence the 'death' of the author), effectively saps texts of their strength and denies to texts their say or say-so (authority). The text is a doomed attempt to fix meaning because writing, unlike speech, is an endlessly shifting play of signs that are empty and infinitely changing (*différence*). Texts take on new significations as they enter into new contexts and interact with other sign systems. There is, accordingly, nothing to hang onto. Or as Derrida has put it: "there is nothing outside the text".

Recent literary theory and deconstruction therefore pose what we might call the 'postmodern' problem of textual relevance. It is not simply that textual meaning is out of date or difficult to recover because mired in the past (cultural relativism); it is rather that texts have no determinate meaning to bring to bear on the present (semantic relativism). Of course, the urge to find meaning dies hard. What actually happens in radical reader-response criticism and deconstruction is that meaning is not found but constructed. Unlike Patristic allegory, however, there is no rule of faith (or charity) to check interpretation. The new allegorizers manufacture a plethora of readings, taking special delight in those interpretations that make the text mean other than what it says.

2. The relevance of the Bible in particular: exegetical and theological arguments

The next three arguments have one trait in common: they question the relevance or sufficiency of the Bible on the basis of their view of God (e.g., on an understanding of how God relates to the world, how God may be known, how God acts). Each of the three arguments undermines the claim that the Bible is God's Word by revising, or reducing, Trinitarian orthodoxy.

a. God the Father: Lord of history or immanent presence?

"We can no longer accept the supernaturalistic picture of the way God relates to the world, nor the notion of salvation history that follows from it". Many contemporary theologians believe that, in order to be modern, they must reject the Bible's obsolete worldview. Revisionists object to a storyline that is hopelessly supernaturalistic. Bultmann commented famously that the three-storeyed picture of the cosmos assumed by the biblical authors is an example of primitive mythology that modern persons cannot accept. More recent revisionist theologians find the notion of a God that acts to save here and there in history, but not everywhere and at all times, both ethnocentric and exclusivistic. If the Bible is to have any continuing relevance, it will be only as a myth, model or allegory of some symbolic truth about the universal love of God.

b. God the Son: God's Word is Jesus Christ

According to James Barr and John Barton, God simply does not speak as the Bible represents it. The Bible is only a very human attempt to understand God's revelation in Christ. "What is written in the Bible, with rare exceptions such as certain prophetic oracles, is presented as human words about God, not as words of God to man."[4] The Bible is a book of human, not divine, wisdom. "The biblical text mediates not information or opinion but encounter."[5] Though they acknowledge the Bible as the 'classic model' for understanding God, they reject one of its most important themes: namely, that God is a speaking God who has committed his Word to certain authorised writings. What, then, does it mean to believe in Christ if not to believe in the biblical witness to Christ? How can one state the Gospel apart from the explicit formulations in Scripture?

c. God the Spirit: the autonomy of the third person

Both those on the theological left and the theological right have recently appealed to the Holy Spirit as a source that supplements, or perhaps corrects, the Bible. It is the Spirit, not the Word, that keeps the Gospel relevant. The Bible lacks 'material sufficiency': it does not even address, much less provide answers for, today's questions. It is the Spirit, after all, who will lead us into all truth.[6] A number of postmodern theologians have appealed to God the Spirit as their basic paradigm for understanding God's relation to the world. The problem, as I see it, is that this is a Spirit cut off or 'deregulated' from the Word. It is a conception of Spirit that owes more to Hegel and Hinduism than to Scripture. According to Scripture, the Spirit is the Spirit of the Father and the Son, not an independent itinerant evangelist of some other Gospel. The main difficulty in appealing to the Spirit apart from Christ is that we forego the criteria with which to distinguish the divine from the demonic. And indeed, this may be where the relevance of the Bible comes into its own in our confused times.[7]

Postmodern philosophy and theology alike thus conspire to marginalize the Word in favour of the Spirit, understood as the presence of God in the world today. According to the philosophers, meaning is a product of the interpreting community. According to the theologians, the Word of God describes not the text nor its referent, but the community's encounter with the text. What meaning and truth there may be in texts is, on this postmodern account, a function of the reader's aims and interests rather than the author's. Such an exchange of roles is both ironic and tragic: for if relevance must be *made* rather than *discovered*, then all the text can bring us is what we already know. The Bible can thus be neither revelatory nor relevant.

B. The meaning of relevance and the relevance of meaning

1. The meaning of relevance

Something is relevant insofar as it has a bearing on a certain problem or task. The Bible, obviously enough, is not relevant to just any human enterprise (e.g., making a kite, splitting the atom). On the other hand, it may be relevant to activities that its human authors never envisaged (e.g., making a nuclear weapon, splicing human genes). In the dictionary, 'relevance' occupies a position between 'relativism' and 'revelation'. This lexical fact is also an index to our problem: how to reconcile the Bible's cultural and historical *relativity* with the claim that it is also *revelatory* of God. Nevertheless, this will be my claim: that the Bible is of permanent relevance in any and all discussions about the Good and the True. Indeed, a more than passing acquaintance with the Bible is not only relevant, but indispensable, for human well-being and for knowing God.

a. Doctrinal relevance: the True

Postmodern thinkers distrust reason's pretension to stand above culture in order to see reality, or the text, from a 'God's eye' point of view. Knowledge is always 'interested': always socially conditioned, never absolute. For these postmodern masters of suspicion, theories and facts alike are always relative - relative to some point of view.

Ludwig Feuerbach's thesis that all God-talk is really talk about ourselves, projections of our own ideals and dreams, has become a near-universal principle in postmodernity.[8] For the non-realist, all important distinctions - true/false, good/bad, beautiful/ugly - are human projections and constructions rather than reflections of the way things are. What is Truth? According to Richard Rorty, truth is simply what is good for us to believe, here and now. Language and interpretation for Rorty are matters of *coping* with reality, not copying it. Rorty sentences the reader to a life of allegorizing, without hope of parole.

> "Dogmatics measures the Church's proclamation by the standard of
> the Holy Scriptures... Should a dogmatics lose sight of this standard,
> it would be an irrelevant dogmatics."[9]

In the postmodern world there is no standard, only opinion - no dogma, only *doxa*. Postmodern interpreters may be able to teach the Bible new, politically correct, tricks, but this makes it less relevant, not more. For the created order - the divine Author's intention - is really there, whether or not it is acknowledged. In commending sound doctrine, then, the Bible is relevant in three respects: first, it preserves the question of truth as a live, and urgent, option; second, it witnesses to what is genuinely other and leads us to encounter him who is the truth. Lastly, the Bible provides norms for correct speech and thought about God, an invaluable service, since God-talk is too powerful a form of speech to be let loose without criteria.

b. Ethical relevance: the Good

"Without knowledge of God there is no knowledge of self" (Calvin). It is only in coming to know God in Scripture that we come to know ourselves. Doctrine - true teaching - is relevant because it shapes the way we conceive, and live, our lives. The apostle Paul's indicative statements are the ground of the imperatives that typically follow them. However, the Bible's relevance for determining the Good is chiefly a matter of communicating a worldview, rather than of laying down the law with moral universals.

It is modern thinkers who tend to equate the relevant with the universal. Indeed, 'morality' refers to the modern quest for universal criteria by which an action is considered right or wrong. Postmodern thinkers are, by and large, contextualists: what counts as good is relative to a particular situation and learned by participating in a particular community. 'Ethics' refers to the different conceptions as to what the aim or goal of action should be. The difference between morality and ethics is just the difference between norms or rules on the one hand and goods or goals on the other. Whereas modern philosophers (e.g., Kant) formulate universal moral principles, postmodern ethics are multicultural and pluralistic. Multiculturalism presents two distinct problems for those who proclaim the relevance of the Bible: first, it suggests there are many legitimate ways to read the Bible. Second, it suggests that there are many legitimate conceptions of the Good. "If it's good for you" is often the irrefutable justification of interpretations and lifestyles alike.[10]

That the Bible is read by a plurality of cultures is an incontestable fact. One of the growing trends in contemporary hermeneutics is so-called "cultural exegesis".[11] This approach encourages people to draw on their own cultural identities in their reading of the Bible. The question is: does multiculturalism imply cultural and semantic relativism? Are there in Scripture a plurality of goods? meanings? theologies? I shall take a mediating position in this debate between universalists and contextualists and argue that Christians learn to discern the eternal Good by participating in specific contextual - namely, *canonical* - practices. The Bible gives us ethical aims before it gives us moral rules.

The basic issue concerns the 'realism' of meaning, namely, whether there is a discernible author's intention that fixes the meaning of the text, and whether there is a discernible Author's intention that fixes the meaning of life. If we aim to recover the author's intention, we stand a better chance of recovering the Christian vision of the Good, namely, life with God through Jesus Christ. We may find that what is most relevant in Scripture for diverse readers and cultures are not the moral rules but the ethical aims, not only its laws but its larger picture of abundant life.

2. The relevance of meaning

a. How hermeneutics may hinder

A text of which one can make no sense is of no help to anyone. The immediate problem is the distance between past and present. The old hermeneutical question was: What did Scripture originally mean? That question has now been displaced by another: What does Scripture *now* mean? The distance between past and present has to be spanned in both directions: I have to be able to get back to the past in order to exegete, but the past has got to be able to get to the present in order to be relevant. Hermeneutics is the bridge between past and present, between 'what it meant' and 'what it means', between 'meaning' and 'significance'.

Two immediate questions about the hermeneutical bridge come to mind: first, is there anything in the biblical text worth bringing across? Can we find permanent, transcultural truths and values in Scripture given its cultural conditioning? Second, even if we want to get across the bridge, can we? Given all the baggage we are already carrying (viz., our biases and interests), how can we return to the original message?

b. How hermeneutics may help

My basic thesis can be stated in a formula:

biblical relevance = revelatory meaning + relative significance.

The rest of this paper shall be spent unpacking this hermeneutical equation.

E. D. Hirsch, the literary critic, draws an important distinction between 'meaning' and 'significance'.[12] The meaning of a text is the sense that its author intended. To say 'what it meant' is to describe past communicative action: meaning 'accomplished'. The meaning of a text does not change, for what is done is done. Meaning, therefore, is 'accomplished' by the author. 'Significance' is Hirsch's term for the relation a text's meaning has to some other context than that envisaged by the author. A text's significance, unlike its meaning, can change from context to context and is therefore relative. Think of significance as meaning 'applied', as not *intending* meaning but *extending* it. Significance thus refers to the way in which the author's meaning bears on the concerns of the present-day reader.

Can meaning - what is said and done - become dated? Need the pastness of meaning imply irrelevance? Hirsch acknowledges that some texts can become insignificant. But dated meanings usually have a very narrow scope; that is, they do not treat universal human themes but are overly tied to particular situations (i.e., the insignificant meaning may be one that was once *too* relevant).[13] There is no such problem of dated meanings with the Bible, for its meaning is *revelatory*. Scripture mediates God's self-disclosure in the history of Israel and in the life of Jesus Christ. The meaning is revelatory because it discloses a referent, Jesus Christ, who is himself the self-disclosure of God. However, while the meaning and referent of the text - God's self-disclosure in Jesus Christ - are revelatory, the significance of the text is relative, for the *same* meaning may be brought to bear on different situations in *different* ways. Make no mistake: 'relativity' is one of Scripture's perfections. For a revealed meaning, a divine-human word, can speak to (viz., be of significance in) *all* times and places.

C. Relevance or relativity: the Bible as revealed Word

My formula for biblical relevance raises an important question concerning the nature and locus of the Word of God: is the Word of God to be identified with the *meaning* of the Bible or with its *significance*, or *both*?[14] Did some parts of the Bible used to be the Word of God but are now no longer God's Word to the Church? Alternately, can God say anything new if his Word is tied to the biblical texts? If the Bible, the supreme rule for the faith and life of the church, is a document from the past, does that mean that the church lives from its past, or that God, having revealed himself once for all, has since retired, like the God of the Deists, to the periphery of human history?

1 Meaning and interpretation: does the Bible have a determinate meaning?

The first condition for biblical relevance is that the Bible has a determinate revelatory meaning. Biblical relevance and revelation alike are undermined by the claim that its meaning is indeterminate. We might call this the problem of hermeneutical insufficiency. The Bible, it is argued, needs to be supplemented by something else; on its own it cannot be the Word of God to us.

With regard to content, it is claimed that the Bible does not even address, much less provide answers for, today's questions. Something other than the text of Scripture is needed to make Scripture relevant. What else? Historical-critics want more information about 'what actually happened' or about the history of the text's composition. Some literary critics, on the other hand, believe that meaning is incomplete without a reader whose interpretation produces sense by fusing horizons. In the next section I shall argue that Scripture itself provides light for determining where the Word of God is to be found in Scripture, and guidance as to how to interpret its significance. I shall resist the notion that there is a Word of God independent from Scripture, a Word that can be used to discriminate which parts of Scripture are to be considered relevant and authoritative and which are not. Decisions about the significance of Scripture must be shaped by our study of the meaning of Scripture.

Need God's speaking today imply that he has something new to say? Can the significance of the text ever be considered revelatory, that is, God's new Word for us today? My hermeneutical model of biblical relevance suggests that the new thing God says is always (and only) a matter of applying or extending the meaning of the Word written. God may bring the Bible's meaning and its referent to bear in our situation in new ways, but it remains the selfsame Word.

2. Scripture and Tradition

Not everyone identifies God's revelatory Word to the church with a definitive past fact, a matter 'for the record', so to speak. Some look instead to the ongoing tradition as the locus of God's Word. R.E. Brown distinguishes between literal meaning (what a passage meant to its author), canonical meaning (what it meant to those who first accepted it as Scripture), and what it means today in the context of the Christian community.[15] In our postmodern climate, the latter meaning is lording it over the others. What is often taken as authoritative and relevant, therefore, is not Scripture itself, but rather the community's interpretation of Scripture, informed by reason and experience: Tradition.

3. Scripture and Spirit

Others appeal to the Spirit of God as over against the Word written. The Spirit, not the Word, will lead us into all truth. To anyone with Reformed sensibilities, the current tendency to deregulate the Spirit from the Word, to open up the canonical windows and let the Spirit blow where it will, is most disturbing. This is especially so when some suggest that the Spirit of God is said to be involved in the world in a revelatory and salvific manner that has nothing to do with Christ. Word and Spirit have here been prised apart.

My account of biblical relevance depends on recovering the hermeneutical bond between Word and Spirit: *Spirit is tied to Word as significance is tied to meaning.* The special role of the Spirit is to bring out the significance of the Word written. The meaning of Scripture is revelatory and fixed by the canonical context; but the significance of Scripture is relative and open to new situations. What must be noted, however, is that the Word of God for *today* (significance) is a function of the Word of God in the *text* (meaning), which in turn is a witness to the living and eternal Word of God in the *Trinity* (referent).

D. What it meant: texts and contexts

How can we appropriate biblical texts from so remote a historical distance? I believe that the contexts which help us determine 'what it meant' can also help us to 'recontextualize' it, that is, to determine the significance of the biblical text for a a different context.

1. Fixing meaning

According to Kirster Stendahl's celebrated distinction, it is the task of Biblical Theology to describe 'what it meant' and for Systematic Theology to decide 'what it means'.[16] Those who care about biblical relevance will want to show how to move from the one to the other. It is now time to redeem my earlier claim that the Bible provides its own contexts for facilitating this move. Between the contexts of author and reader stand a number of *textual* contexts that, I believe, help us in extending biblical meaning towards the present. My goal in what follows is to avoid reducing the Bible either to a mere human word from the past (meaning without significance), or to an all-too human word for today (significance without meaning).[17] The Bible ultimately confronts us not only with a horizon from the past, but with a horizon from the future - with an eschatological horizon that charges our present with meaning, relevance and hope. Scripture is relevant because it is the indispensable means for being instructed in the wisdom of God and thus in the highest good for humanity.

2. Levels of textual context: extending the meaning to today

Against the claim that the Bible needs to be supplemented by something else, I believe that Scripture is its own best context for interpretation.

a. Historical-linguistic

The meaning of a text has to be one of the possibilities that the author could have intended. Otherwise we risk anachronistic interpretations which, far from challenging us, confront us only with ourselves. 'What it meant' is a function of what the author could have intended to say, and this is established by determining historical parameters. The text itself, however, is the best evidence for reconstructing the author's original context.

b. Generic

Every text is a kind of something, a particular kind of communicative act. What makes a text history rather than fiction, or warning rather than promise, is a matter both of authorial intention and generic convention. Again, it is the text itself that is our best guide as to what the author is doing.

A literary genre (= kind) is not only a communicative but a cognitive strategy. Each genre represents a particular kind of thinking about and experiencing of the world. Like maps, different literary genres represent the world in different ways. One has to know what kind of map one is reading. Genre is of great significance, I believe, for an appreciation of biblical relevance. Not only is it vital for interpretation that one recognise literary genre, but genres contain a depth of wisdom and power that often outlasts that of its component parts. Meaning is genre-bound, and this exposes the shortcomings of proof-texting. Literary genres do not merely yield data about God, but rather ways of seeing, processing and organising the data into meaningful wholes. The Christian worldview is built up and encouraged by the several word-views of the various biblical genres.

c. Narrative

Narrative is an excellent example of how literary genres carry their own type of relevance. A good story will provide all the clues one needs to follow its plot from beginning to end. Narratives therefore travel well; they make good candidates for transcultural communication. How large a story do we need in order for the Bible to be its own interpreter? The biblical story reaches back to the beginning of time and forward to its end. To a large extent, human understanding is 'storied'. We fit new discoveries and facts into the framework of familiar stories. The biblical story displays a way of viewing God, the world, and ourselves. Far from being a private or esoteric worldview, the Bible "offers a story which is the story of the whole world. It is public truth".[18]

d. Canonical

'Canon' means 'rule' or 'measuring rod'. On one level, this refers to the Bible as an authoritative list of books that together make up God's Word. But Brevard Childs has recently argued that canon plays a hermeneutic role as well. For Childs, the canonical context allows us to describe the significance of a particular biblical text in light of the Scriptures as a whole. Childs speaks also of "canonical intention" to signal the Scripture's concern that future generations of readers be able to read it with profit as a norm for the community. To some extent, then, the question of 'what it means' is implicit in the Bible. Does this mean that the canonical context changes the *meaning* of the OT so that we can read it as a witness to Christ? No. The NT does not change the meaning of the OT but explains its significance and renders its referent - God's gracious provision for Israel and the world - more specific through the name "Jesus Christ".

Because the future-oriented concern of the Bible is part of its intention, exegetes do not have to invent ways for the Bible to speak to the present. Taken as a whole, the canon shows us what in the Bible is only culturally (or even theologically) relative (e.g., the Levitical laws, animal sacrifice).[19] Nevertheless, I do not wish to imply that some parts of the Bible are no longer God's Word to the Church, only that they may no longer be *imperative* words. Commands to the ancient Israelites about cloth-making may no longer be directives to us, but they can still be instructive. It would be a mistake to confine the notion of the Word of God to the imperative mood only and not to the indicative as well. The Bible's testimony to past covenantal arrangements (e.g., circumcision) are also part of its continuing witness.[20]

Two further points about the significance of the canonical context: first, for all the talk of distance between ancient and modern, contemporary readers share the same historical condition as that of the NT authors and canonizers, namely, a position 'between the times' - that eschatologically charged situation of 'already' and 'not yet'. The second point follows from the first: the world of the canonical text should not be mistaken for the original historical context. The canonical ways of viewing the world often criticize the prevailing world views: many kings of Israel and even the disciples are often the subject of unflattering portraits. The canon subverts the world of the reader, ancient and modern alike, for the biblical world is a world where the old things are already passing away.

3. A realism of meaning

All interpretation involves presuppositions on the part of the reader (so Bultmann). A naive realism of meaning is thus out of the question. We can never simply identify our interpretations with 'the' meaning of the text, full stop. On the other hand, the Bible would be irrelevant if readers encounter only themselves when they come to the text. The critical realism I have here defended, however, affirms that textual meaning (and reference) is really there to be grasped (or missed), independent of our reading. Only if meaning is prior to our reception of it is there something to be extended into our present and applied to our problems. We may not have perfect knowledge of this meaning, but we can attain provisional knowledge. 'What it meant' is relevant for us today because it constitutes the authoritative witness to the reality of God in Jesus Christ. The canon represents a cloud of earthly witnesses to the meaning and truth of God's gracious provisions for humanity in Jesus Christ.

E. What it means: the present-day significance of the Bible

How can we extract what is normative for today from what was culturally conditioned in Scripture? Is there some hermeneutical key that would allow us to make the magical move from 'what it meant' to 'what it means'? Yes: Scripture itself. As we have seen, genre, story and canon all work to extend 'what it meant' beyond its original situation in the past. Today, the major divide in interpretation is between those who believe that the biblical text be interpreted in the light of the contemporary context and those who believe that contemporary experience should be interpreted in the light of Scripture. It is the difference between those who believe that textual meaning is revelatory and superior to any situated interpretation and those who are unable to distinguish the text from the history of its effects.

1. A popular solution: separating wheat from chaff

One popular way to span the culture gap is to distinguish transcultural principles from their cultural incarnations. One locates these principles by searching for signs either of multicultural validity (e.g, an appeal to the created order) or of monocultural validity (e.g., reference to Levirate marriage). To what extent is a command tied to cultural practices specific to the ancient near east, or to the first century, but not to today?[21] For instance, the OT law tells house-builders to build parapets around their roofs. That was a culture-specific rule directed at people who live in flat-roofed houses. But the principle - to make visitors to one's house safe - is one that crosses the culture gap. Today we put fences around swimming pools.

My concern with this strategy of pulling out the so-called 'universal principles' from Scripture it that it ultimately renders the Bible more abstract, and thus more difficult to bring to bear on particular situations. In what follows I will put forward an account that handles the universal-particular relation a bit differently.

The Bible is neither a collection of eternal truths nor a set of moral proof texts. Much unnecessary trouble has accompanied the attempt to lift out permanent theological or moral truths from Scripture without attending to their larger literary and canonical contexts. Yet it is precisely the story as a whole which is more valuable for Christian ethics than any principle we might abstract from it. Indeed, not only the story, but all the literary genres of Scripture serve what is ultimately an ethical purpose by shaping the way we view God, the world and ourselves. Moreover, the canon itself helps us on our way as we journey from meaning (what it meant) to significance (what it means).

Consider the universal appeal of Shakespeare: "Great art can bring men of different convictions together by translating, as it were, their different vocabularies into a tangible experience that incorporates what they mean".[22] As C. S. Lewis says, stories allow us both to 'taste' and to 'see'. Story is neither abstract truth, nor is it bound to particulars, as is empirical experience. It rather partakes of both. Story, and the other biblical genres as well, represent not so much an alternative to the 'Bible as eternal truths' approach but a more sophisticated version of it. Again, the problem with the former approach is not that it appeals to truths, but that it does so by extracting them from the literary form which is their indispensable (and authoritative) expression. In great literature, universal truths come in concrete forms. The Bible, similarly, functions as what literary critics call a 'concrete universal'. Theology's task is to make as conceptually explicit as possible the truth that is implicit in the Bible's many literary forms.

2. Scripture interprets Scripture: the case for hermeneutical sufficiency

"The Bible cannot be the exclusive means for deciding all ethical issues. As it stands, it is insufficient. We need more - more information, more guidance."[23] This objection to the sufficiency of Scripture runs counter to the Westminster Confession: "The infallible rule of interpretation of Scripture is the Scripture itself".[24] The recent Pontifical Biblical Commission's document on biblical interpretation similarly affirms this principle.[25] My thesis, once again, is that *the Bible's meaning, illumined by the Spirit, is a sufficient criterion for determining its significance*. It is now time to redeem this vital claim.

a. Tota scriptura

To acknowledge the Bible as Scripture is to acknowledge its overall unity and authority. The biblical texts, woven together by narrative, form a 'metanarrative': a coherent and comprehensive perspective that articulates, in story form, the Christian worldview. The Bible, through its diverse genres, offers a number of different, though compatible, literary lenses on which it maps reality. Taken as a whole, the Bible indicates what was only of limited cultural (or religious) significance (e.g., animal sacrifice). The *whole* story - the canonical narrative - is an indispensable aid for sorting out what was only temporarily authoritative for the people of God and what is timelessly authoritative.

b. Sola scriptura

To affirm *sola scriptura* is to acknowledge that the Bible is the *controlling* story of one's worldview. *Sola scriptura* does not mean that the Bible is the

Christian's only resource, but rather that it functions as the 'rule' for discriminating between the various stories humans tell in the search for self-understanding. It means that, while the Bible may not address every ethical question we could raise, we must nevertheless consider all our questions in the light of the larger, bigger questions which Scripture does ask (and answers).

3. Forming evangelical character: canonical competence

It is not enough to exegete the text. We need to exegete the world too. The present-day world too should be incorporated into the biblical metanarrative. The Bible will be relevant only when it is 'followed' from canonical page into contemporary practice. Moreover, the Bible is relevant not only as a source of universal norms but as a *resource* for training people in all righteousness.[26] By training us to see the world in particular ways, Scripture trains us to perceive what is truly natural (i.e., in accord with the Creator's will). To understand God's Word fully means not only having correct information or propositional knowledge about God, but also good judgment; it means knowing how to *act* biblically in a given situation. Scripture is not a mere storehouse of moral principles but a means of visioning the world, and the good, as God sees them. The Bible's diverse forms of literature express the kind of individual and corporate life that best fits God's created order, and so nourishes our hearts and imaginations as well as our minds. Theology - the interpretation of the world in the light of the Word - is ultimately about knowing how to live to the glory of God.

a. Canonical practices

The relevance of the Bible is ultimately not a function of the community's use of Scripture but of Scripture's own canonical practices. I have argued that the Bible itself anticipates an extension of its meaning into new situations:[27] "We learn ethics from a story by allowing its way of seeing the world to become our own symbolic structure of meaning".[28] The many biblical texts together communicate God's ordering and reordering of creation not only propositionally, but in ways that enable us to experience it, and to reproduce it, as well. The biblical interpreter is like an apprentice who learns a craft - the craft of theology - from his master. Whether the Bible is relevant depends partially on whether its interpreters are competent.

b. Phronesis: right practical judgment

"Set your minds [*phronein*] on things that are above".[29] *Phronesis* or practical reason pertains to thought about human action. Aristotle speaks of it to refer to judgment rather than knowledge, to deliberation rather than calculation. *Phronesis* involves making judgments for situations *where there are no universal rules*. A person with right practical reason grasps at once both the principle and the particular situation.

The literature of the Bible helps to educate our moral sensibilities by shaping our imaginations to see the world christocentrically. "The primary way we learn goodness from the Bible is by making the story of the Bible the interpretive framework through which we view all of life".[30] Here I agree with the narrativists about the character-forming power of story. Yet I wish to incorporate the other literary forms of Scripture as well. Each biblical genre serves as a pedagogue that teaches us not only what to say about God, but when and where to say it, and under what conditions. The Scriptures are our school wherein we learn the grammar, and the reflexes, of faith. The biblical text gives us not only propositions but a set of practices, practices that train us to discern the will and wisdom of God.

Abstract principles are not enough. What does it *mean* to love God and neighbour? Israel's law shows us what it meant in their situation. Jesus' parables show what it means in another. Divine wisdom is incarnated in a person and inscribed in a text. Theology's task is to render explicit the implicit know-how underlying the diverse canonical books. In sum, the canon trains our ways of seeing the world and orients our ethical judgments. In so doing it yields not absolute but adequate knowledge - light enough to take the next step.

The context-specific nature of the Bible is a help rather than a hindrance in our attempt to span the cultural distance. For while the cultural situations in the Bible are specific, the *phronesis* or practical wisdom that we glean by indwelling these situations is not. By dwelling in the world of the text, we learn how to practise faith - a skill that we can transfer to our world. We thus gradually achieve a kind of theological and ethical competence. For instance, though Israel's context included the social structure of slavery, we learn that Israel was to free all slaves every seven years.[31] Within the system of patriarchy, we learn that Israel was to protect the rights of women.[32] The canon helped Israel to create a counter-culture. The cultures of Israel or first-century Palestine are not authoritative for us, but the canonical counter-cultural wisdom is.

c. Discipleship as recontextualization

Biblical hermeneutics and theology are ultimately spiritual exercises whose goal is to produce faithful disciples. The competent interpreter is one who can follow the logic of the biblical story and put it into life today. That is, the disciple, the one who follows the Word, is also able to recontextualize it.

Determining textual significance is a matter of recontextualizing meaning, of applying meaning to new situations. Contextualization is already a concern of the biblical authors. Indeed, the very relation of the OT and NT is a case study in contextualization. The authors of the NT had to answer the question of what the OT means in the light of the Christ event. Jesus himself told the travellers to Emmaus in Luke 24 that the law and prophets spoke of him. And, just as Jesus' story is a retelling of the story of Israel, so the story of the Church - as yet unfinished - is a retelling and prolongation of the story of Jesus' ministry, death, and resurrection.[33] The apostle Paul, for instance, understood his own existence in the light of the story of Jesus: "I have been crucified with Christ".[34] This suggests that the

Bible is most relevant, not when we bring it into our context, but when we fit our context into Scripture's.

Canonical competence refers not to the formulation of some transcultural set of principles (*theoria*), but rather to the ability to respond to God fittingly in our particular time and place (*phronesis*). Those, like Paul, whose minds and visions are shaped by the biblical story and the other canonical practices will develop a Christian *habitus* - a cognitive disposition, a practical skill, and an orientation of the soul. It is the Holy Spirit, however, who ultimately incorporates us into Christ through the mediation of the written Word. The letter of the text is material with and through which the Spirit works. Insofar as canonical competence is a form of Christian discipleship, it is the Spirit's work.

4. Forming evangelical culture: cultivating Christ

Is there such a thing as a biblical culture? Can we cultivate biblical wisdom? The canon, illumined by the Spirit, educates our religious affections. The final goal of biblical interpretation is to let the Word and Spirit shape the way we see the world. For only by reading, and dwelling in, the world of the biblical text will we come to see the world as it really is: as held together in Christ.

a. Rendering the evangel

Biblical hermeneutics leads to ethics and to discipleship: the disciplined effort to live well with others in God's creation. The literary styles of the Bible lead to Christian lifestyles. The Word generates not only ways of seeing but ways of *being* in the world. The *euangelion* has transformative power (significance) because it first has informative content (meaning). The Gospel is a freeing Word not because it is a magical word but a meaningful one. Christian freedom should be tempered by the wisdom that comes from dwelling in the biblical texts. Canonical competence is a matter of knowing how to render the Word of God in the contemporary world in one's speech, thought, and life. In the words of Lesslie Newbigin, the church ought to be "a hermeneutic of the Gospel".

b. Rendering our eucharist

When the Church, in the power of the Spirit, performs this word in wisdom and discernment, then it becomes a witness to Christ and a cultivating influence in the world. The Church is that community of the Word's followers which not only proclaims but *embodies* the wisdom of God. Such is the measure of Christian witness: not only to proclaim the *euangelion* of freedom in Christ, but thankfully to put this freedom into practice. The response to God's grace (*charis*) should be thanksgiving (*eucharist*): the canonical *euangelion* begets a *eucharistic culture,* where everything we do is an expression of our thanks for the gift of freedom in the Spirit. The Bible will be seen to be relevant whenever the Church cultivates and 'enculturates' the Gospel story.

F. A practical illustration: homosexuality

Homosexuality is an appropriate case for a study of how the Word of God has relevance for today. It is one thing to claim that Paul does or does not condemn homosexuality. That is an exegetical question. It is quite another thing to claim that, whether or not Paul condemns homosexual behavior, his teachings do not apply to us today. That is a hermeneutical issue, an issue of how 'what it meant' bears on 'what it means'.

1. Hermeneutical arguments

a. A hermeneutics of cultural sensitivity: "The Bible is irrelevant"
    Some make the hermeneutical point that the Bible never talks about homosexuality as we know it today. Loving and permanent same-sex relationships were never within the biblical 'horizon'. Some argue that Lev 18:22 (and 20:13), and 1 Cor 6:9-11 are prohibitions of cultic prostitution or pederasty. That prohibition is no more universal than the ban on cutting one's beard in a certain way.[35] Others claim that Paul imposed Jewish customs and rules on non-Jewish readers. Still others say that Paul, in Rom 1, is talking about heterosexual men and women who act unnaturally by engaging in same-sex activities. *Physis* refers not to a universal natural law, but to the personal nature of the pagans in question (e.g., to their proper sexual orientations). What all these interpretations share is the conviction that the Bible says nothing that is relevant to the debate about homosexuality today.
    In response, we might note the following points. First, the overall context of Lev 18-29 is not only cultic, but moral. Indeed, it appears that moral concerns even predominate the passage. Moreover, though child sacrifice is mentioned in 18:21, no one argues that that is a culturally relative matter. Is it really conceivable that Israelite society could have tolerated child sacrifice (or homosexuality) if they could have been disinfected of their Canaanite and cultic associations? Furthermore, the Bible's observations about greed, drunkenness, adultery and so on are also time-bound and uninformed by the latest psychological, sociological and biological data. Is Scripture in an inferior position on these issues too? Those who are inclined to say yes should be prepared to accept the consequences, for this line of argument cuts both ways. If what the Bible says about sex is culturally conditioned (and thus relative), why not the love of God as well?

b. A hermeneutics of nature: "It's just the way I am"
    Perhaps the most powerful argument to justify homosexual behavior is to claim that it follows from one's nature: "This is who I am". To be sure, this appeal could be used by other social types, including racists and kleptomaniacs, to legitimate their behavior. Moreover, an explanation of an activity is not the same as its justification. Nevertheless, this is an important objection, and it brings the issue of the Bible's relevance to contemporary society to the boiling point. For it demonstrates that the crux

of the matter is over *who we say we are*. It is not so much that the Bible is relevant, but that it is, to many, repellent. For to accept our identity as those who are created and redeemed in Christ, as people whose life "is hid in Christ", requires us to give up many of the attractive lies we tell about ourselves. It requires us to surrender our 'glittering images' in order to grow into him who is the very image of God.

Paul introduces the subject of homosexuality in Romans 1, a passage which is about the consequences of not acknowledging God as Creator. Homosexuality serves Paul's purpose of showing how the creature's impulse towards self-glorification leads to self-destruction. Note the parallels: God and truth have been exchanged for creatures and lies, just as the natural has been exchanged for the unnatural. Homosexual intercourse is characterized by Paul as *para physin* (contrary to nature). What then, from a biblical perspective, does it mean to call an activity "natural"? The category "natural" admits of at least three senses:

1. The 'physical' natural: a biological regularity. "Natural" could refer to that which we find in the physical world. The natural is a regular physical happening. For some, only this level of reality is relevant, for all other levels are ultimately illusory. This is the *biological* level of nature, and it is of no particular moral significance.

2. The 'social' natural: a habitual regularity. "Natural" can refer to types of learned behaviour that have become 'typical', to that which happens regularly (but not through causality so much as through habit). The cultural relativist claims that the patterns of social behaviour we see in the Bible are "natural" only in this sense of being typical of one group at a particular place and time. On this view, then, the "natural" is a cultural product. Many today, for instance, believe that gender and sexuality are not biological givens so much as *sociological* constructs.

3. The 'theological' natural: an intentional order. Finally, the "natural" can refer to something that is in accord with the Creator's intention. It is important to distinguish the natural from the normal. It may one day be 'normal' that married couples divorce, but that would not make divorce "natural".[36]

This third sense of natural merits a closer look. The theological natural refers not to what is but to what ought to be (or better: to what is *in Christ*). Many of the arguments over the morality of homosexual activity appeal to the causes of homosexual orientation. At present, there is no consensus among scientists as to whether homosexual orientation is due more to biology (our first sense of "natural"), to social conditioning ("natural" in the second sense) or to some combination of the two. For my purposes, this does not really matter. For I am distinguishing the explanation of an act from the morality of an act, the ground of a particular kind of behaviour from its goodness. Homosexual orientation is, in and of itself, morally neutral, though willingly cultivating it is not. Regardless of how one comes to have a homosexual orientation, the ethical question is: how does homosexual activity fit into the larger picture of God's intentions for the human creature? How does this way of being in the world fit into the Christian metanarrative?

2. Sexual ethos in the Scriptural metanarrative

One should not be forced to choose between particulars and principles when discussing the relevance of the Bible for today. On the one hand, some of the particulars may have no parallel in our day. Paul may not have had in mind precisely the kind of homosexual relationships that many today now champion. On the other hand, free-floating eternal principles are distinctly unhelpful when it comes to making concrete decisions. Love may be a Christian virtue, but if abstracted from the particular ways in which it is embodied in the NT it can be made to mean almost anything.

The approach I am commending attempts, therefore, to hold particulars and principles together by attending to the way in which the Bible's meaning is mediated by its literary forms. There is a certain amount of information that we need to know which the Bible gives us: that we are created beings, that we are fallen, spiritually disfunctional beings, that God has identified himself with the human plight, entered into history, and saved us. As Lesslie Newbigin puts it: the dogma is the story. But Scripture is not merely a handbook of information. It is also a training manual that aims, in conjunction with the Spirit, at producing wisdom and righteousness in its readers. In short, the Bible seeks to render Christ to its readers and its readers to Christ.

a. The ethos and ethics of Genesis

The move from text to context, from biblical hermeneutics to contemporary ethical debates, is best made by letting Scripture shape our understanding of God and of what it is to be human. What is the place of sex in Scripture? What is the *ethos* - the general spirit or attitude - that characterizes the Bible's treatment of sex, and how does it bear on contemporary ethics?

The biblical view of sexuality should not be reduced to moral prohibitions. The prohibitions against homosexuality only make sense against an overall sexual ethic and an overarching vision of what is good for humanity. With regard to sexual ethics, the Bible affirms heterosexual marriage as the good. The Bible's overall position on matters sexual is shaped by a positive vision of the good (e.g., by ethics) rather than by negative prohibitions (e.g., by morality). That is, the Bible's *aims* for sexuality precede its rules. Christian ethics aims at the good life with and for others. Homosexual activity runs the risk of being not only immoral but unethical, insofar as it pursues the wrong aim for human beings and, in so doing, hurts oneself and others.

The Genesis account is therefore valuable, not only for its explicit commands about sexuality, but above all for creating the overall *ethos* for sexuality together with the specifications of its authoritative form. Genesis affirms that reproduction is good,[37] that male and female complementarity is good,[38] and that sexual intercourse between a covenanted man and woman is good.[39] Genesis gives what we might call the 'design plan' for sexuality. It explains how sexuality is supposed to function. The activities of our bodies must fit the way we were made. This is not merely an argument from biology to morality. On the contrary, the Bible views biology and morality together, just as it views body and soul together. We are not simply neutral sexual beings, but male and female, and we honour God when we honour our male-female complementarity. Men and women are made to find sexual fulfilment with each other.

Within the biblical ethos of monogamous marriages, the only legitimate alternative is celibacy. What distinguishes celibacy from homosexuality is that it operates within the ethos of heterosexual monogamy. The celibate affirm that heterosexual marriage is good for them now, or might be later, if they could find a partner, or that it was formerly (when they were married), or that it would be if they had not decided to devote themselves to Christian ministry. Homosexual practice, on the other hand, says that there is another expression of sexual activity that is *good*, or by implication, that heterosexual marriage is not good for them.

What harm is there in two people expressing their sexuality in another way? Here we have to consider what is good for the community, as well as for the two individuals. Homosexual activity is a denial in practice of the good instituted by God from the beginning. If all sexual relationships are morally the same so long as they are qualified by love, mutuality and fidelity, then the uniqueness of heterosexual marriage is undermined.

Paul in Romans 1 stays true to the ethos of Genesis. If we believe that Paul was right about God and humanity, then it is difficult to fault his logic concerning homosexuality. Paul's statements about God, humanity and homosexuality represent a coherent account of the created order: "We cannot fault Paul's appraisal of homosexual behaviour without denying the theological vision that informs his understanding of God and humanity".[40] In refusing God's 'authorial' intention for creation, then, we violate our own natures.

b. The meaning and significance of sex

Our understanding of a being's good, of that which leads to its flourishing and completion, is intrinsically connected to our understanding of that being's nature. This understanding is found in Scripture's revelatory meaning - the first half of my equation for biblical relevance. The Bible is relevant in helping us understand aspects of the created order that transcend those open to empirical investigation. The Bible makes us wise unto *creation*.

It is difficult to argue that homosexual activity advances the good of heterosexual unions, of the church, or of the larger human community. Of course, it is biologically possible for two men to enter into some kind of sexual relation. But even a loving relationship between two men fails to illustrate the nature of the relation between God and his people, as marriage is supposed to do. The husband-wife relation, a relation of unity-in-difference, better pictures the relation between Christ and his church.[41]

Ethics has to do with the orientation of our freedom and the orderings of our loves. Human love cannot operate correctly apart from God's love; and God's love has ordered the world. Love itself is ordered "in accordance with the order that it discovered in its object".[42] That is, love acts *for* a being only on the basis of an appreciation *of* that being. We will not know how to pursue the good for a being until we know what *kind* of being it is. The Bible, as the story of the origins, orientation and destiny of humanity, is supremely relevant, for it tells us who we are as well as what, and how, to love wisely. Love is Christian when it is properly oriented to God's created order. It is not merely a coincidence that classical Christian descriptions of love so often invoke the theme of 'wisdom'. Wisdom too is a matter of discerning how things fit together for good in the created order. It does not require a strenuous exercise of Christian wisdom, I believe, to see that sexual relations between two males lacks fittingness.

G. Conclusion: the Word of God and the vocation of humanity

This brief case study of homosexuality has, I trust, demonstrated how the Bible continues to be relevant, despite its cultural distance. Scripture enables us to see, or at least to glimpse, human reality as it is truly ordered in, and by, Christ. Seen with the spectacles of faith (Calvin), we realize that one's sexual orientation does not really indicate what a person truly is. The claim that one's sexual orientation indicates what a person is stems not from the biblical story but from a cultural myth. According to the prevailing cultural story, we must act according to who we are in order to realise our potential and to achieve our good. There is nothing wrong with this logic. But the premise - that who we are is a matter of our sexual preferences - is mistaken. While we are sexual beings, our being should not be reduced to its sexual dimension. But this is what conceiving of one's identity as 'gay' does. However much the media may proclaim otherwise, having sex is not essential to anyone's being.[43] Who and what we truly are as human beings does not depend only on what we do. We are at best co-authors of our being. Our true identity is rather a function of our relation to the covenant God and to one another.

The Christian life is inseparably connected to the Word of God. It is God's Word that evokes faith and orients it. Our vocation as Christians is to live out and witness to the Word of God in all that we say and do. In being called to be the Body of Christ, the Church is called to embody God's Word.

Our English word 'relevant' comes from the Latin *relevare* "to lift or raise up". It is also related to the term 'relieve', which means "to assist someone in difficulty". The Bible only relieves when it is taken up. It is only when we take up our book and walk that its message will be brought to bear on life today. The Bible is relevant because when taken up it relieves: it provides guidance, mitigates tedium and frees from distress. Scripture, in all its diverse literary forms, may profitably be taken up in every time, place and situation, as we seek to conform our lives to Jesus Christ: the Way, the Truth and the Good Life.

[1] Barr, *Bible in the Modern World* {London: SCM, 1973] p. 10.

[2] Ibid., p. 39.

[3] *The Postmodern Bible* (Yale University Press, 1995) p. 14.

[4] John Barton, *People of the Book*, p. 56.

[5] Ibid.

[6] John 16:13

[7] See Ronald Hall, *Word and Spirit*, for an analysis of how Reformed understanding of their relation is crucial for responding to modernity and postmodernity.

[8] Ludwig Feuerbach, *The Essence of Christianity.*

[9] Barth, *Dogmatics in Outline* [London: SCM, 1949) p. 13.

[10] We would do well to remember that it is possible to be too relevant. Something may speak so specifically to a particular situation that it has virtually nothing to say to another. What passes for relevance is often merely fashion. To be shiningly relevant is to occupy centre stage on the present horizon. But it is also to be limited to the horizon of the present.

[11] Cf Daniel Smith-Christopher, ed., *Text & Experience: Towards a Cultural Exegesis of the Bible*, 1995.

[12] Hirsch, *Validity in Interpretation* (New Haven, Yale: 1967). See also his "Meaning and Significance Reinterpreted", *Critical Inquiry* 11 (1984) 202-24.

[13] One way to make dated texts relevant is to allegorize them. Such a saving of the text comes at too high a price, however, insofar as allegorizing puts textual and intellectual integrity at risk.

[14] Of course, the prior question is whether the Bible should be identified with the Word of God in the first place or whether it only becomes the Word of God here and there, now and then.

[15] R. E. Brown, "'And the Lord Said?' Biblical Reflections on Scripture as the Word of God" *Theological Studies* 42 (1981) 3-19.

[16] Stendahl, "Biblical Theology", *Interpreters' Dictionary of the Bible.*.

[17] I shall resist the temptation to define the Bible's relevance by appealing to its eternal principles, though there is, I believe, a place for a judicious appeal to such transcultural norms.

[18] N. T. Wright, *The New Testament and the People of God*, p. 42.

[19] The history of revelation is an indispensable aid in sorting out what was only temporarily authoritative for the people of God and what is timelessly authoritative.

[20] Indeed, the passages concerning circumcision remain relevant to our understanding of our present practice of baptism.

[21] One has to decide whether the surface command applies only to the particular historical context (in which case the underlying principle can be applied differently today), or whether the surface command is normative. William Larkin assumes that, unless the text indicates otherwise, we should assume that the (cultural) forms are as authoritative as the (canonical) content (*Culture & Biblical Hermeneutics*, p. 316). What we need is criteria for recognizing the non-normativeness of certain forms. In other words, we assume that the biblical word is a word for us unless there is canonical evidence to the contrary (e.g., the context of a passage may limit its application [such as celibacy in 1 Cor 7:8]; subsequent revelation may limit its application [e.g., food laws]).

[22] Wayne Booth, *The Rhetoric of Fiction*, p. 141.

[23] This statement is not a direct quotation so much as a composite sketch of a commonly held objection to the relevance of the Bible. The implications of such an objection for the doctrine of God are serious and far-reaching, though beyond the scope of this essay.

[24] W.C.F. I,9.

[25] "The most sure and promising method for arriving at a successful actualization is the interpretation of scripture by scripture" (*The Interpretation of the Bible in the Church* ed. J. L. Houlden (London: SCM, 1995, p. 84).

[26] 2 Tim. 3:16.

[27] Deut.6:4-9

[28] Bernard Adeney, *Strange Virtues*, p. 88.

[29] Col.3:2

[30] Ibid., p. 85.

[31] Deut.15

[32] Deut.21:22

[33] George Lindbeck coins the term "intratextuality" to describe the process of reading the Bible in such a way that the Word "absorbs" the world. Intratextual interpretation lets the story become the interpretive framework for the reader's exeprience, rather than vice versa. See his *The Nature of Doctrine* (Philadelphia: Westminster Press, 1984).

[34] Gal.2:20

[35] Lev.19:27

[36] To distinguish between the world as it is and the world as God intended it to be is, of course, to invoke the distinction between creation and Fall.

[37] Gen.1:28

[38] Gen.1:27; 2:23

[39] Gen.2:23-25

[40] Marion Soards, *Scripture and Homosexuality*, p. 26.

[41] Ephes.5:31-32

[42] Oliver O'Donovan, *The Resurrection of Moral Order*, p. 26.

[43] Human sexuality is a broader matter, and does not have to be expressed by sexual activity.

Part 2   THE FAMILY

Chapter 2   MARRIAGE IN THE LIGHT OF HOLY SCRIPTURE

David W. Torrance

Introduction

In seeking a Biblical doctrine of marriage it is helpful if we follow the example of the Reformers and seek to consider not simply individual passages of Scripture but the whole Word of God. They continually endeavoured to understand the Scriptures as a whole and interpreted passages in the light of each other, and in accordance with the divine truths to which they pointed beyond themselves. Theirs was a theological interpretation of the Bible. When interpreted in this light, the Bible has much to say about marriage and not, as some today affirm, very little.

On theological grounds, in accordance with what they understood to be the whole thrust of the Scriptures and their message of divine redemption in Christ, the Word made flesh, the Reformers regarded marriage as both ordained and sanctified by Christ. Whereas there is a recognisable form of marriage that is created and ordained by God for everyone in the world, they held that in Christ God has sanctified and redeemed marriage from its state in the fallen world and restored it to its original character and purpose as taught by Jesus himself.[1] In its deepest sense true marriage, Christian marriage, is altogether different from an unchristian marriage. It is of a different order, for, it is "in Christ".

This was wonderfully summed up in a booklet on Marriage, published by the St Andrew Press, and long out of print, where in the opening sentences it said, of Christian marriage, it is "a union between man, God and woman, between three people, not two". (This is in contrast to a non-Christian marriage where there are only two participants). Marriage may not be broken. If sadly it is broken not only is the relationship of man and wife marred but the relationship of both with God is immediately affected and marred. It could not be otherwise. Adultery is an attack on God and his relationship with us and our partner in marriage, as David acknowledged in his prayer of confession.[2] This is something which all of us need to ponder especially when, today, the divorce rate is so high.

The Relationship within Christian marriage is patterned on God's covenant relationship with his people

Again and again, marriage in the Old Testament is likened to and is called to mirror the relationship of love and grace which God chose to enter into with his people Israel. In the New Testament it is likened to and is called to mirror the relationship of Jesus Christ with all his beloved followers. In the Old Testament Israel is called God's spouse.[3] In the New Testament the Church is called the bride of the Lamb the heavenly Bridegroom. This is the wonderful relationship into which we are called by God in Christ. Husband and wife in their relationship one with another in marriage are called to reflect the infinite patience, endurance, compassion, forgiveness and love which God continually manifests in his covenant relationship with us and his people. Jesus said, "As the Father has loved me, so have I loved you. Now remain in my love. ... Love each other as I have loved you".[4] We are called to behave in love toward God and equally toward our partner in marriage, in the way that the Father behaves in love toward his Son and in the way that the Father and the Son in love and grace behave toward us and all their covenant people. We are called in marriage to be patient one with one another, to be forgiving and loving even as Christ is patient, forgiving and loving toward us. This is an immense challenge which none of us can accomplish in our own strength. We need constantly day by day to receive through the Holy Spirit the gift to love as God loves.

Christian marriage takes place within God's covenant relationship with his people. Through the Spirit of God, it is grounded on and sealed by his covenant relationship

That is to say, Christian marriage is more than just patterned on God's covenant relationship with his people, just as the Christian life is more than being patterned on the life of Christ. We are weak, sinful and of ourselves are unable to relate to Christ and to imitate Christ and we are unable of ourselves to make our marriage partnerships reflect the holy, loving relationship of God with his people. What we cannot do, therefore, God in his creative, redeeming grace does for us when in repentance and faith we turn to him in

Christ. According to Scripture, God through his Holy Spirit unites us with the Person of Christ so that we actually share in the life of Christ, are clothed with Christ and made, however inadequately, to reflect him. He places our marriage within the covenant so that our marriage, in Christ, is made to share in and, in some way, to reflect Christ and the grace and beauty of his covenant relationship with his people. Through his Holy Spirit it is grounded on and sealed by and within his covenant. In this context, Paul writing to the Church in Ephesus says, "Submit to one another out of reverence for Christ. Wives, submit to your husbands as to the Lord.... Husbands, love your wives, just as Christ loved the church and gave himself for her."[5] For Paul, Christian marriage takes place only within the covenant. Within that context does he understand it and within that context must we seek to understand the many references and allusions to marriage in the prophets.

When sin entered the world with the Fall it infected the whole of human life in its personal and social structures. Men and women are no longer what they ought to be. Their relationships one with another, the relationships between men and women and not least between man and wife are all spoiled. The relation of men and women to creation also became infected. This is evident in the pain of child-bearing for women and in the struggle of man with thistles and thorns in the cultivation of the land. In Christ, however, that state of affairs has been put on a new basis. Through the atoning sacrifice of Christ, God reconciles us to himself. He reconciles people to one another and ultimately will renew all creation, cleansing away all the pain and imperfection. He forgives people and heals them in his grace and sanctifies and blesses the union of man and woman in marriage in a holy and unique way that is governed by the Gospel of God's saving, reconciling and sanctifying acts.

It may be noted that, in many respects, the Reformers viewed the event of marriage in a way not unlike that in which believing Jews continue, from Old Testament times, to understand it as involving a relationship with God within the sacred bond of the covenant. According to Old Testament Scripture, Jews may not marry someone outside the covenant, that is, someone who did not believe in the Living God and who had not identified himself or herself with the covenant people.[6] According to the Talmud, whereas there is a form of marriage for the Gentile world that is of God, marriage in its deepest sense before God only takes place within the covenant and "in the Name of Heaven". Therefore, to 'marry out', is for orthodox

Jews a very serious matter. It is held to involve a denial of one's faith. The one who does it cuts himself or herself off from the believing community, and from the parent family.

For devout Jews the words of Hosea 2:19,20 form an integral part of the marriage service. These are the words which God speaks in renewing his covenant with Israel. Standing with his bride within the canopy, or *chuppa*, the bridegroom affirms these words of God's covenant and affirms them with regard to his bride thereby affirming that his marriage is embraced or inter-locked within the covenant. "I will betroth you to me for ever; I will betroth you in righteousness and justice, in love and compassion. I will betroth you in faithfulness, and you will acknowledge the Lord". Thereupon the bride and bridegroom are handed a cup of wine, the wine being a sacrament or seal of their union. It is their belief, that without wine the marriage would not be sealed, that is, no wine no wedding, which helps us to understand the significance of the miracle in Cana of Galilee, when Jesus turned water into wine, presumably to allow the wedding to proceed. In the New Testament, Paul, deeply influenced by the Old Testament and by Rabbinic teaching, affirms that a Christian must always marry a Christian,[7] and marriage is "in the Lord". As stated earlier, Paul, by calling on husbands to love their wives, "just as Christ loved the Church",[8] is, with the Old Testament, and with Rabbinic teaching, placing marriage between one man and one woman within the covenant. There, by grace, it reflects God's relationship with his people, and is sealed by the body and blood of Christ.

The considerable loss of the Jewish roots of our faith and the failure to take the Old Testament seriously has prevented many Christians from understanding the significance and depth of the biblical teaching on marriage. In Christ God has set our life on the new basis of his grace in which he gives himself wholly, unreservedly, to us in redeeming love and calls forth from us a corresponding movement of love and self-giving in Christ. We are summoned through his love to give ourselves in love to one another in Christ.[9] We are to love one another in the same way and to the same extent in Christ as he loves us. Within that context, husband and wife are called in marriage to give themselves unreservedly, totally, one to the other in the Lord, such that they interlock and become one flesh, and in a sense one whole person. As one whole person they are called in their intimate personal relationships with one another to reflect God in his relationships with us. Marriage in Christ, Christian marriage, is drawn into the covenant relations of God with his people. It is grounded on it, and God's covenant becomes constitutive of it.

In the light of Scripture there are now a number of practical observations which we can make and which have deep significance for all Christians entering into marriage.

Marriage is God's gift

The Orders for Marriage in the Service Books of all denominations, Presbyterian, Anglican, Baptist, Methodist and Roman Catholic, make it clear that "marriage is provided by God as part of his loving purpose for humanity since the beginning of creation ..."[10] When we see and hold marriage as God's gift to us then our marriage becomes very precious, very sacred to us. It is something which in its character as God's gift, will constantly evoke a sense of wonder and thanks to God. It encourages each partner constantly to thank God for the other and for both to give thanks for their love. When each partner gives thanks to God for the other then each looks on the other with a new dimension, seeing the other as God's gift - and their children as God's gift. Seeing marriage as God's gift, gives to marriage a deep sense of sanctity and permanency. To opt out of it would be tantamount to turning one's back on God.

Marriage is a calling of God[11]

God calls a particular man and woman into a life partnership. His calling embraces the whole area of both their lives and lasts, not for a temporary period, but as long as they live. No third person can share that calling - not even their own child. They enter into it in their freedom and through their love for each other. Despite their freedom, however, in choosing to enter into marriage and their seeking under God to maintain their relationship, it is God's calling to them to be married to each other, just as it is God's calling for others who in their freedom have chosen to be unmarried. When we recognise marriage both as a calling of God and as God's gift, then the particular marriage of each of us, acquires its true dignity. Our marriage becomes special and distinct.

Sadly, the majority of people today, non-Christians and Christians, seem to think that the decision to marry is solely a matter of human choice, their choice. They believe that, as man and woman, they are free at any moment of their choice to opt into marriage and therefore free to opt out of marriage, if and when they grow tired of each other's company or cease to love one another. They feel that as free people their marriage is their responsibility. It is entirely their affair. Everything is up to them so they think that they can do as they like! They fail to realise that each marriage should be regarded as a gift of grace and should involve a special divine call which demands a special recognition which a man and woman require to seek and discover in prayer. They fail to realise that their union, if it is a union in Christ, involves three people, that is, themselves and God, not just themselves - and any separation between themselves as husband and wife will deeply affect their relationship with God. It is to God that a man and woman must give account for their marriage.

Marriage depends on faithfulness

In giving us marriage, God calls us into life-partnership. To this extent marriage is more than love and ordinary human endeavour. Marriage must spring from love if it is to take shape as a life partnership. It must continually be fed and sustained by love if it is to grow and blossom and bring joy to the participants. It must involve continuous endeavour under God to make the marriage a lasting joyous union. The essence of marriage, however, is deeper, more comprehensive and more lasting than is possible by what normally is understood as the love of husband and wife, and more than the couple's own will and endeavour. It consists in the call of God and depends on a couple's God-given faithfulness to that call. That which forms the basis of Christian marriage and that which deepens a couple's love the one for the other in all the changing circumstances of life together is God's continued call and a couple's recognition of that continuing call and their God-given faithfulness to it. It is this which enables them, "for better or for worse; for richer, for poorer; in sickness and in health; to love and to cherish" each other until death parts them.

Marriage is a calling of God, and its joyous fruition a goal which a man and a woman must strive after

A happy life partnership does not just come about once a man and a woman have been married. It does not automatically arise, even when a man and woman genuinely love one another. It is something which must be sought after and worked for and prayed for. Happy life partnership falls into nobody's lap. In this respect the relationship of two people in marriage is somewhat akin to Israel's relationship with God. God called Israel into lasting covenant relationship with himself. God remained faithful in his calling and in his love for his people. But through the long years of the Old Testament era, his people were frequently wayward, unfaithful, unloving and unhappy. It took long years of personal encounter and partnership with the Living God, years of hardship and suffering, years of striving after God in obedience and faith and love, before Israel, as represented by the Apostles and the believers, became the people who really rejoiced in their covenant partnership. In something of the same way, a man and a woman have to work at their marriage through the years in loving personal encounter and partnership. It is through long years of personal encounter and sometimes of hardship and suffering, when a couple have learned truly to depend on each other, that marriage and joyous love begin truly to develop and blossom. A couple have to work at their marriage with understanding, with a growing awareness of each other's needs, with continuing deeds of love and care for the other, with humour and, above all, with prayer, because ultimately such a loving, joyous marriage is God's gift to them.

The Church and her pastoral care for others

The Church must be very sensitive, compassionate and understanding of other people's problems, particularly when they are caught up in marital problems and sexual sins. The Church must avoid being judgmental. As God freely forgives all our sins in Christ, so God forgives our marital failures and sexual sins, however grievous. As the Church seeks to represent Christ to the world, she must seek to show the understanding, the compassion, and the love of Christ when encountering and seeking to help people in marital failure and break-down.

In regard to sexual sins, the Church, in order to be true to the Gospel and in order truly to help those who have erred, must stress that such sins are a breach of the covenant. They affect in the deepest and most personal way a person's relationship with God. They mar the image of God, they attack and mar our relationship with God in Christ. Therefore they must be faced, acknowledged and repented of. The Church must lovingly help a person to do this, if that person would enter fully into God's forgiveness and be restored to union with Christ.

The Reformers rightly noted that the Old Testament distinguishes between what is called in the King James Version "sins of a high hand" and all other sins, and that the New Testament accepted this distinction. In the Old Testament liturgy special ordinances and sacrifices were prescribed for the expiation of all other sins, but not for sins "with a high hand". For sins "with a high hand", such as idolatry, murder, adultery and homosexuality, no liturgical ordinances or expiatory offerings were prescribed. They were sins against the covenant, the penalty for which was death. In that event the guilty person could only cast himself on the mercy of God. That was what happened to king David when he committed adultery and, by the sword of Ammon, murder. He knew that in his case sacrifice was of no avail.[12] Hence he flung himself entirely on the mercy of God in contrite recognition that his sin was essentially against God. "Against thee", he cried, "thee only have I sinned". And God forgave him as he forgives every sinner, no matter who they are, when they fling themselves in utter contrition on his mercy. In Christ God has made full provision for forgiveness for every kind of sin including those of a "high hand"; guilt is dealt with through the atoning sacrifice of the incarnate Son of God which is offered once for all on the cross.

Marriage belongs to God's act of creation

This should be clear from what has been said. Marriage is part of creation. It is not just a human, social institution as so many humanists and secular thinkers wish to affirm today. It is affirmed as God's act in Genesis 2:18-25 and re-affirmed by Jesus in Matthew 19:4-6 and in Mark 10:6-9. All the Churches affirm this Scriptural position. In this secular age in which we live, when many couples choose to live together without wishing to get married, the Church must proclaim and insist that marriage is of God. It belongs to his act of creation and to his purpose for mankind and was taken up and affirmed in his act of redemption.

Marriage is a continuing act of creation

God did not simply create marriage, or the institution of marriage, away back in the beginning, and then, as it were, leave man and woman in their freedom to get on with their relationship with each other and to work out their marriage in their own way, as best they might. Thankfully he does not so leave any individual man or woman who trusts him and whom he has called into marriage. Left to themselves each partner in a marriage could and frequently would seek to struggle in their sin for a false individualism, to assert himself or herself and to dominate or tyrannise over the other. History surely bears testimony to that. All of us have witnessed it, if not in our own marriage then in the marriages of others whom we know.

The Gospel proclaims that God has not abandoned man and woman in their most intimate relationship. In Christ God goes with a Christian man and woman. He is present in Christian marriage continually creating and building it to his glory and to man's and woman's mutual comfort and happiness. By his Holy Spirit he brings us again and again to the cross in humility, repentance and renewal. For the cross is the place where we are made by the Holy Spirit to die to ourselves and to rise ever again as a new person, one new person, man and wife, in Christ Jesus. This is something which must and does happen again and again. Having committed ourselves, our love and our marriage to the Lord, the Lord presides over our marriage, he assumes the responsibility for deepening our love and building our marriage, seeking to perfect it through the years. In Christian marriage, God is always present in all his creative redeeming power and love.

Marriage is a total and all embracing fellowship of love, for life

In his covenant with us in Christ, God gave himself to us, and goes on giving himself to us, in all his wholeness and entirety. This is the incredible wonder and mystery of the incarnation. Something happened to God as it were in the incarnation. God has given himself and goes on giving himself in entirety to us in Christ. In Christ he has for ever united men and women to himself. As his giving to us is total, so his claim on us is total. He claims that we give our all to him, and in doing this, so also we give our all one to another. We may not give only part of ourselves to the other and be blessed by him. We cannot rightly be married to our partner and at the same time be married, for example, to our work or pleasure, far less to someone else. Marriage as a life partnership in love means that each is called to give himself or herself totally to the other, so that it becomes impossible to see, hear, think, speak or live apart from that other who is our partner in marriage. Of course, we are all sinful and sadly in our individualism and self-centredness, we do not give ourselves in loving mutual totality to one another. This, however, is what God calls us to do and what each couple must strive to do in Christ. It is what is involved in "becoming one flesh", that is "one whole person".

Christian marriage is essentially monogamous

The totality of that physical-spiritual loving and caring to which a man and woman are called in marriage is only possible in a monogamous relationship where all others are excluded. Marriage portrays God's covenant relationship with us. In Scripture God is portrayed as jealous of any other would-be lover to whom we might give our affection. He is single and wholehearted in his love for us and demands of us a single and wholehearted love for him. Our love for him must, as it were, be monogamous and in our oneness with him in the Spirit he demands that our love for one another as husband and wife be monogamous. As Barth says, it is God's election of us and his covenant with us which is renewed and sealed through the atoning sacrifice of Christ which gives unconditional and compelling character to the requirement of monogamy.

Clearly, God's people took a long time to understand and accept that monogamy is God's will. In the Old Testament, polygamy was widely practised even by the fathers in the faith quite unthinkingly - despite the fact that, in various decisive passages,[13] monogamy is clearly God's purpose. This slowness to understand and carry through God's will in marriage, we can only attribute to the blindness of sinful human nature.

When we turn to the New Testament and to the coming of Christ as the fulfilment of the covenant, polygamy immediately disappears. From the beginning, monogamy is accepted and recognised as God's will. Never did the Church doubt this or hesitate over it. All the passages which treat of marriage in the New Testament, clearly refer to the relation of one man and one woman, although it is not easy to point to particular texts which expressly forbid polygamy and universally decree monogamy. Certain passages[14] clearly imply it, and the Apostles and early Church clearly understood the covenant and its fulfilment in Christ Jesus as the true basis of monogamy. It is probable, as this writer believes, that their certainty about the rightness of monogamy follows on from the miracle at the marriage in Cana in Galilee. Following that marriage, which took place in a Jewish context, Jesus Christ was seen henceforth as the Lord over marriage, the One in and through whom alone the marriage between one man and woman takes place. The Apostle John said, "He revealed his glory",[15] referring not so much to the actual miracle as to the revelation of who Jesus is in the context of marriage.

This is all the more significant when we consider that the Jews who did not accept Jesus Christ continued to practice polygamy. Many of them continued to do so right up to the thirteenth and fourteenth centuries and only embraced monogamy when compelled to do so by the laws of the country in which they resided. Equally significant is the fact that no other religion in the world, other than the Christian religion, has of its own accord embraced monogamy or given to men and women that mutual dignity and status which is demanded in a true monogamous relationship. As Barth says, it is the free electing grace of God, manifested in the fulfilment of the covenant of Jesus Christ, which alone gives compelling and ultimate force to the requirement of monogamy.

Our physical sexuality is of God

Because questions of sexuality will be considered more fully in later chapters of this book, I mention them here, only briefly. Since God claims the whole person, and requires that in marriage man and woman give themselves totally to one another, so his claim and demand sanctifies our physical sexuality. God has created our physical as well as our spiritual being and so sanctifies both. Hence, the sexual desires of husband and wife for each other are in themselves good, holy and lovely. They are an integral part of their whole being in relationship to God and each other. God in creating and sanctifying man, male and female, includes their sexuality within their humanity, so that the physical love with which they love one another is important, being integral to their whole love for one another. Any feeling of guilt or shame in this sphere is misplaced. Instead there is great cause for joy and thanksgiving. As our physical nature is a vital part of our being, so our physical nature and sexuality are a vital, God-given part of our relationship in marriage. The words, "they will become one flesh",[16] undoubtedly refers to physical, sexual, as well as spiritual union. Sexual desires and true love are indissolubly united in marriage. Marriage is a question of the whole man and the whole woman and of the total union of both.

Trial marriages and pre-marital relations

Because God's claim on us is all embracing, in that he claims the whole of us and all that concerns us and because he demands in marriage that we each give our all without reserve to the other in a life partnership, there is no room in Christian thinking for trial marriages, where there is no total commitment to the other for life. Likewise, there can be no exploring or expressing our sexuality before entering total commitment in marriage, although some Church leaders today seem to approve of this!

Again, there must be no extra-marital sexual relationships. Various passages of Scripture expressly forbid each and all of these.

The whole thrust of Scripture, the placing of Christian marriage within the covenant which was renewed and sealed in Jesus Christ, through his atoning sacrifice, make these kind of sexual relationships incompatible with our union in Christ.

God calls man and woman into marriage in such a way that man becomes truly man and woman becomes truly woman only in relationship to each other

Man and woman are different and God calls them in marriage into relationship with each other. They are equal in dignity and status before God, they are equally loved by God and are called to share equally in his glory and divine inheritance. At the same time they are different, and are given a different responsibility and are called to a different service. They differ in function.

Because they are different in responsibility and service so, in marriage, they are able to help one another and each to complement the other's need in accord with the purpose of God.[17] In marriage, for their mutual happiness it is important that each acknowledges that the other is of equal importance to God and equally loved by God. At the same time, it is important that each acknowledges with joy that they are different and have a different responsibility and service to each other, to God and to society. The one must not seek to dominate the other or seek to deny to the other his or her rightful contribution and service. Neither must seek to usurp the place of the other or try to fulfil the other's function which is inevitably different. Equally, neither must reject or despise their own peculiar service and responsibility. Each must rejoice in his or her own manhood or womanhood and rejoice in the manhood or womanhood of the other without which we cannot have a happy marriage.

As Barth rightly says, God, in creating us either male or female, requires that we should be fully the one or the other, that we should acknowledge our sex and not deny it, that we should rejoice in it and not be ashamed of it, that we should fruitfully use all the potentialities of our sex rather than neglect them and at the same time, should stick to the limits of our sex rather than try to transcend them. Only so can we men and women live in obedience to God's will and as male and female complement one an other, to the other's and our own mutual joy and fulfilment. The man becomes truly man in relation to the woman and the woman becomes truly woman in relation to the man.

This in no way denies that a single man or woman cannot by the grace of God find complete fulfilment in Christ. We must affirm that they can and do. Only in the order of God's creation and in the creation of marriage, each finds his or her fulfilment in and through the other. If either, or both, endeavoured to deny their own or the other's different responsibility and contribution (and sadly this happens frequently today), then both would suffer and fall short of the kind of fulfilment which God purposes for us. In genuine love and care each must encourage the other to be what they are and without in the least feeling threatened by the other's sexuality encourage and assist the other to make their maximum contribution. In encouraging and enjoying the fulfilment of the other in their sexuality, each is fulfilled in their own sexuality.

The difference between men and women is not limited to the biological sphere in that women have children and men do not. This is a false argument which unhappily is stated by some feminists. The difference of men and women is comprehensive in that it affects their entire being. They think and feel differently so that their whole contribution is different but in a way that is entirely complementary to the other and such that, in marriage, they become "one flesh" or "one whole person". This is true, however, not only in marriage but also in society as a whole so that whether we are married or not we complement one another, we enrich and fulfil one another, we keep one another sane!

There can be no clear definition of the role of men and women in marriage or in society

Inevitably, in the light of what has been said, the question is asked, "What is the function of a man or of a woman, apart from child bearing?". There have been attempts at the systematisation or definition of the roles of men and women. Well known writers and theologians, such as Emil Brunner, have attempted it. All such are generally attacked, this time I believe rightly, by the feminist movement, although there is no doubt a good deal of truth in what these writers and theologians say, and in what Professor Brunner says. There can be no real, or clear, systematisation of roles.

Our covenant relationship with God is not controlled by systematisation and laws. We are called in covenant into a living, personal, encounter, called into a living relationship with the living God who continually calls, challenges, commands through his living Word and Spirit and through his own Person. Any regularity to which we are called in daily obedience is not due to an abstract order or system or law. It is due to God being faithful to himself in his holiness and love. We must reject, therefore, any and all attempts to systematise the sexual orders, or roles, in marriage and in society. We must simply affirm, in accord with Scripture, that men and women are different and have a different contribution to make and we affirm, in accord with Scripture, that we cannot define nor yet definitely describe this differentiation. To attempt to do so will always be unhelpful and will lead us into trouble. For we would be claiming for ourselves a knowledge of the will of God for a particular man and woman which we do not and could not have. God does and will lead men and women to serve in marriage and in society, in wonderful and unforeseen ways right outwith the defined systems that we have attempted to create for them.

Providing that men and women are obedient to God's Word and Spirit, God will lead them along the lines that he wants them to serve. They will remain the sexual beings that God wants them to be. Their roles will never be inter-changeable. God ordains men and women to be different and when they live in obedience to God they will always be true to their own sexual characteristics and will affirm and rejoice in those of the other. This is essential to a happy marriage.

Before leaving our consideration of marriage in the light of Scripture, let us look briefly at two further issues, which are important in that they can and do militate against a happy marriage. Both issues will be considered at greater length later in this book.

Homosexuality

Scripture expressly forbids homosexual relationships. They are contrary to the natural order created by God. They are contrary to the Biblical doctrine of man and woman. The God-created, God-given, sexual differences of men and women, as already stated, are complementary and vital for true human fellowship, wholeness and fulfilment in marriage as God intended. These differences cannot rightly be set aside as they are in homosexual relationships.

According to Scripture man and woman in marriage are called by God to give themselves totally to each other in love. It is utterly impossible for a man to give himself in the totality of his being to an other man and likewise for a woman to give herself in the totality of her being to an other woman. Yet some wish to argue that homosexuals can give themselves in "loving relationships (which) are non-exploitative, non-manipulative, equal".[18] That, however, falls far short of the totality of physical-spiritual self-giving of the one to the other in love which God demands in a Christ-centred marriage.

Some Christian leaders advocate a more liberal attitude to sexual relationships and want the Church to affirm "the Christian worth of homosexual unions" which are "reliable, ... permanent, honest, and exclusive, that is, non-promiscuous".[19] Their argument, so they say, is based on "love". If a homosexual relationship between two men or two women is loving, stable and non-promiscuous then "it may be regarded as legitimate and good".[20] Many in the Church of England and in the Churches in the United States are seeking to argue along these lines.

In claiming to base their argument on love, such people, are I believe, seeking to detach love from the Person and saving work of Christ. But the New Testament never speaks of love apart from the loving self-giving of God in Jesus Christ. Love was actualised in the atoning sacrifice of Christ through which he lovingly restores men and women into union with himself, heals the broken relationships between men and women and their fellows and lovingly heals and restores the marriages of men and women to that status in grace which he purposed from the beginning. When we are commanded to love, we are called through God's Spirit to share in his love for the world in Christ. We are called to share in his self-sacrificing love. But always it is his love, in which we are called to share. Those who argue in favour of recognising homosexual relationships as right, are as it were, endeavouring to detach love from the Person and saving work of Christ and seeking to give love a kind of independent status of its own, independent from Christ's atoning sacrifice! They then seek to use their idea of love to argue for the value and worth of some of the very relationships which Christ came to heal and restore! Through their interpretation they are actually critising the validity of God's Word and its relevance in the sphere of marriage for our day. Could anything be more contrary to God's will?

Feminism

There is a helpful and Christian feminism which rightly seeks the acknowledgment of women's contribution to Church and society and their equality with men in dignity and status. This is to be welcomed and encouraged. There is, however, an extreme, almost militant, form of feminism which does not recognise and affirm the complementary nature of men and women in their personhood and contribution. It is this form of feminism which is so detrimental to marriage.

In affirming with Scripture that God created us either male or female, we are affirming that there is no other creaturely being other than male or female. Man and woman cannot transcend their sexuality. They cannot be other than the man and woman that God created them to be. They are in the depths of their being different from each other although complementary for their own and each other's fulfilment. They must not therefore aspire beyond their own and opposite sex to a third and supposedly higher mode of being who is neither man nor woman.

Yet the temptation is present in some quarters to aspire to become a human being who is neither male nor female, except outwardly and externally as if his or her sexuality as male or female was only temporal and provisional. It is not true to say as one woman once said to the present writer that the only difference between men and women is that a woman bears children and a man does not, for their sexuality is only accidental and therefore external! This, in a spiritualised form, is a movement of escape from sexuality and escape from what is really human. It is an attempt to deny our God-given manhood and womanhood.

No doubt, there are understandable reasons, intellectual, economic, social and political, which motivate such a desire by some feminists. However, we must insist, Biblically, that we cannot hold up, or aspire to, an abstract masculinity or femininity. There is no such thing as a being, or person, who as it were, is neutral and not entirely either man or woman. This kind of view really denies that man and woman find their fulfilment in marriage only in and through each other and together become one whole person. It is destructive to the marriage relationship.

Sometimes in this connection and seeking to argue that sexuality is only temporary and provisional, people mistakenly quote what Jesus said, "At the resurrection people will neither marry nor be given in marriage; they will be like the angels in heaven".[21] Here, however, Jesus is speaking about marriage not about sexuality. He does not say that there will be no men and women in heaven. Nowhere does the Bible say that. It says that in the beginning God created man, male and female, and God does not reject what he has created. He affirms it, redeems it and exalts it. There will be men and women on this earth and in heaven for all eternity. Therefore, as Barth has said, each man and woman owes it, not only to himself or to herself but also to the other, always to be faithful to his or her own sexual characteristics and to those of the other, to affirm them and to rejoice in them. Fellowship and marriage is always threatened when there is a failure at this point either on the one side or the other.

Conclusion

True marriage is patterned on and reflects God's covenant relationship with us. It takes place within the covenant, is grounded in, conditioned and sealed by that covenant and demands that a man and a woman give themselves totally in love for life to God and to each other. Jesus Christ commands that we love and cherish one another as he loves and cherishes us even to the death. None of us in our sin and individualism is able fully to do that. Therefore all of us need, day by day, to kneel before the cross that we might continually share in Christ's death and resurrection. As we die with Christ to our sin and our sinful selves so we rise united with each other in Christ. For a happy, fulfilled marriage, we need to pray day by day that Jesus Christ will live in us that we might live in him, clothed together with his righteousness, purity and love.

[1] Matt.19:4-6; Mark 10:6-9

[2] see Psalm 51 and particularly verse 4

[3] consider the message of Hosea

[4] John 15:9,12

[5] Ephesians 5:21f.

[6] Deuteronomy 7:3,4; Joshua 23:12,13; Ezra 9 and 10; Nehemiah 13:23-27; Malachi 2:10-16

[7] 2 Corinthians 6:14

[8] Ephesians 5:21f.

[9] John 15:12

[10] quoted from *The Book of Common Order* of the Church of Scotland

[11] Several issues raised here have been raised by Karl Barth in his Church Dogmatics (cf III.1 pp 304ff, 311ff; III.4 pp 116-240)

[12] Psalm 51:16

[13] Genesis 2:18-25 (which speaks of man and woman as helpers to each other and becoming one flesh or one whole person); 1 Kings 11:3; The Song of Songs; Hosea 1:1-3; Malachi 2:13-16

[14] Matt.19:5; Mark 10:7-9; Ephesians 5:31; 1 Timothy 3:2; Titus 1:6

[15] John 2:11

[16] Genesis 2:24 (and see 1 Cor.6:16; Ephesians 5:31)

[17] Genesis 1:27f. and 2:18f.

[18] *The Scotsman*, 5th March, 1994

[19] *idem*

[20] *idem*

[21] Matt.22:30

Chapter 3 COHABITATION

William D. Brown

The Office of Population Censuses and Surveys for the U.K. reports that 1972 was the record year for marriages. In it the number of marriages was 426,000.

1993 was the lowest year in half a century. In it the number of new marriages fell below 300,000. That is a drop of about a third. Since 1979 the number of single, never married women cohabiting has trebled to a figure of one in four in 1993.

In the early 1970s, one in ten women in first marriages lived with their future husband before marrying; now seven out of ten do so. First time couples are living together for two years now, compared with one year twenty years ago. The minister of a well endowed middle class parish in Edinburgh reports that he has 84 marriages in his diary in forty of whom the couples are living together, one of them being one of his elders!

In 1993 among adults under 50 it was found that 56% men and 59% women were married - the lowest proportion since 1931.

One third of all marriages now end in divorce. Those taking place in Church are rather more successful, while a third of all of the babies born are being born out of wedlock.

1 A BRIEF GLANCE AT THE HISTORICAL BACKGROUND OF COHABITATION

The inheritance from Rome

Cohabitation as we understand it depends on mutual consent whereas in ancient times, as in many non-Christian cultures today, the woman was never asked for her consent.

The Roman Empire was declared Christian by Emperor Constantine in the fourth century. From the eleventh century the Church grew greatly in influence. The clergyman as a clerk in holy orders was centrally placed to draw up the marriage contract between the parties for the Church Court. The Church encouraged people to get married at the church, and produced a liturgy to accompany the legal transactions. It now had to clarify its position. It was effectively faced with three choices. They are reflected in our practice to this day.

(a) The Church could follow Roman Law with its concept of contract and the consent of both partners.

This is preserved in our insistence on a legally recognised ceremony taking place in a legally recognised place or by a legally recognised official, with a legally recognised Marriage Certificate, signed by both consenting parties before witnesses.

(b) The Church could follow the practice of arranged marriages which had taken place according to tribal customs, where the handing over of the bride by her father was the definitive act.

This is preserved right up to today by the question, "Who gives this woman to wed?" and the practice of the bride being given away by her father.

(c) The Church, facing many widespread and primitive practices where people lived communally, might accept that sexual intercourse was the beginning of marriage.

Lack of sexual intercourse is recognised in both Canon and Civil Law as a cause for annulment for a marriage that has been legally contracted. From this we can see that the recognition of cohabitation by the Church and the civil law goes back a very long way.

Before the Reformation the Church's liturgy was available for many, but in many remote places less so. Among the many poorer people where no property or cattle were involved law had little place. Sexual intercourse or conception provided the defining point. Because of this there was a great deal of irregular conducting of marriages from the local blacksmith upwards. Forced marriage, bigamy, handfasting, and marriage between inter-related people, were prevalent in small communities.

As in a great many other matters laxity was spread across Europe, and in the Church it reached such scandalous proportions as to help precipitate the Reformation. The Council of Trent by the Decree *Tametsi* in 1563, and partly no doubt also for denominational reasons, enacted that apart from exceptional cases, the presence of a priest and two witnesses was among conditions required for a marriage to be valid.

What is interesting for our subject of cohabitation is that again it is the presence of a priest, not the actions of a priest that were specified. As in the days when he only was there to draw up and witness the contract, so even here the emphasis was on the consent of the participating parties.

The inheritance from the reformation

Following the Reformation, in Scotland consent was given either by the word of parties, both being present, usually at a morning service; alternatively, by declaration of future intent, which was binding betrothal, sealed by later intercourse. Marriage by habit and repute continued to be upheld.

In England Lord Hardwicke's Act of 1753 was intended to put an end to irregular marriages by specifying that marriage had to be in the parish Church of one party, both being over twenty one and not related within the forbidden degrees. All this might have achieved the consent of the Crown, the government, the Church as well as the marrying parties in respect of their various interests, but such law rests for its implementation upon public consent at large. This is the factor that is so often forgotten and which has led to the present situation.

How is this public consent to be secured? By referendum? By Parliamentary Act? By Royal Decree? How will it be enforced? By what sanctions? Who will adjudge? Which Church's standards should be enforced? How would the marriages in neighbouring countries be treated? So we are now into the very problems that underlie our contemporary handling of issues like marriage, cohabitation, divorce, adoption, abortion, genetics, pornography and fertilisation. Dealing with these matters is not as simple as passing a law. Failure to carry the consent of the public at large meant that there followed a huge increase in irregular marriages, with cross-border flights to places with different laws, parties betaking themselves to lax clergy, legal fiddles, deposed or unregistered clergy, legal cases creating ingenious legal loopholes.

Concerning cohabitation, in evidence to the U.K. Royal Commission on Marriage in Scotland, 1865, each of the main churches in Britain took pretty much the same line. They upheld marriage by habit and repute. In Scotland they did so partly out of nationalistic loyalty to stop English interference, partly out of denominational loyalty to avoid acknowledging the Established Church, and partly for practical reasons. The Free Church of Scotland, among the strictest of the contributors said:

> In regard to marriage by habit and repute it affords the sanction of a virtuous connection to that which may have commenced in irregularity, while it is fitted to deter licentious men from indulging in concubinage under the veil of a pretended marriage. It gives effect to the mutual consent of the

parties evidenced by a course of conduct more publicly and unequivocally than any one formal act or declaration before a registrar or clergyman, while the doctrine of legitimation *per subsequent matrimonium* tends to convert a relationship which was injurious, into one which is beneficial to society, and give all the children of the same parents the benefit of the same status.

Some of the nineteenth century social background

Dr J.M. Strachan of Dollar, made a careful study of Parish Registers of five parishes in Stirlingshire, Scotland. These were varied in character including woollen manufacturing districts as well as agricultural. He himself had a large midwifery practice, and was in a unique position to bring two sources of knowledge together.

He reported that among agricultural labouring families nine out of ten women, at the time of marriage, either already had illegitimate children, or were pregnant. Among wool manufacturing families only a third of this rate was current. Among middle and upper classes he had never attended a single childbirth where the child was not born until after nine months into the marriage.

These facts must be compared to the current statistics which indicate that one in four unmarried women are cohabiting, and a third of all babies are born out of wedlock. The real motivator so far as the State was concerned appears in his words:

Parties go and live as man and wife without any ceremony... and there is no question about it until they become burdens on the poor funds; and then it becomes an important question whether they are married or not, because if they are not married, the burden of the woman and children falls on the woman's parish, the children being illegitimate, and in the other case upon the man's parish.

Legitimacy then had to be established by legal process before the Poor Law Guardians. Where the father did not acknowledge the children, the evidence was accepted either of promise having been made followed by subsequent *copula*, or of cohabitation by habit and repute.

Effective controls on cohabitation

God's will concerning marriage is clear. It is generally that men and women should get married and have children with his blessing. If however, society at large does not consent to follow God's will, then the restraints imposed by the enactments of Crown, or Parliament, the strictures of pulpit or parents, are not always effective.

Control by parents and family are implicit in what Dr Strachan says, "If pregnancy occurred... the family intervened and hurried marriage forward." Another driving force toward control was the finances of State social services, where we have shades of our present day Child Support Agency.

The sanctions which were most effective however were the strong social structures which could enforce the subsequent marriage. A minister colleague who had a parish near Inverness told me it was local tradition that with the occurrence of a pregnancy the fellow always married the girl. In Switzerland so strong was the local community that if the young man in these circumstances did not marry the girl, no one would employ him. The only thing he could do was emigrate.

The problem of cohabitation is growing extensively today in our society and even among Church members. We must press for legislative support for family values, but law can only go so far. The cultivation of a strong Christian social attitude is the only way forward. The question is how may this be done. We have much to learn from past mistakes.

2 THE WAY OF CENSORIOUSNESS

This associated the Church with judgment, not the Gospel

One solution, in the past, was for the Church to urge punitive measures upon extra-marital activities in society and upon its members. There are those who think along these lines today. The reformers repudiated the casuistry which permitted double standards; instead rich and poor, clergy and lay, became subject to discipline. The civil power and nobles were seen as rebukable, and even the King on his throne, as evidenced in the electrifying exchanges between the King in the gallery and the Minister in the pulpit across the Holy Rude Church in Stirling.

Discipline was considered to be necessary for the strengthening of the body of Christ and for the spiritual welfare of all. All had a part in it. Acts of profession of faith, marriage, baptism, communion, ordination, and also discipline had all to take place in face of the Congregation. As Ministers and Elders went about catechising and preparing the people for the sacrament, they encouraged church members to keep a watch on their neighbours as part of their caring Christian duty to them.

This however required penalties and this is the problem in this approach. The Privy Council Act of 1564 said that fornicators should be progressively fined, imprisoned, have their heads shaved and pilloried. If persisted in, both offenders would be "ducked in the foulest pool of water in the town or parish" and eventually banished. In Edinburgh the North Loch was used. Adultery had the penalty of being scourged at the cart's end while paraded through the streets or banished. It even had a technical death penalty, which seems never to have been enforced.

All this created a resentment against the Church and a mental association linking the Church with law and judgment, rather than with the proclamation of the gospel of the grace of God.

This made the Church seem preoccupied with sex

Because of the conception of two interwoven kingdoms, that of God and that of the State, the jurisdictions of ruling bodies were also blurred. In many towns the Kirk Session and Town Council often comprised the same men. Chris Vermouillen, in his Master's thesis, recalled that the first police post in Glasgow was in the Session House of the Tron Church. It was the Kirk Sessions which dealt with fighting, drunkenness, Sabbath breaking, swearing, dishonesty and also sins such as avarice and pride.

In his doctoral thesis Kenneth Boyd argues that it was not so much a matter of being preoccupied with sex, but rather that as the other jurisdictions were removed from the Kirk Sessions it left them mainly occupied with such matters. Certainly, looking back through my own Church's records I noticed that the Kirk Session over a five year sample had no other item of business than the sexual misdemeanours of members.

However the sermons of the day, the records of Church meetings, biographies, and the Reports of General Assemblies show that it is just not true to say the Church was obsessed with sex; nor that it was unconcerned with wider social issues beyond it. The major social issues which dominated the Church's attention were the spread of venereal disease, the curbing of prostitution, drunkenness, illegitimacy, infanticide, and the ills relating to bothies and housing. It happens that these were interlinked with sexuality, but the force that brought them to the fore was the energetic Temperance Movement which used the sex scandals to give force to their arguments.

These then received a severe impetus when the first figures for the Registration of Births, Deaths and Marriages (Scotland) Act 1854 became known. Other severe major social factors now bore upon our society and added to the trend. The Industrial Revolution filled towns with filthy slums whose packed verminous closes were crowded with shebeens (or drinking dens) and brothels. There was great need for social amelioration.

In the country the Agricultural Revolution created bigger farms and more social problems. Frequently men were separated from their wives and together with single men were herded into central bothies where the men slept upstairs and the women down. Often there was roystering long into the night and both sexes dressing or undressing in the same room. After each Agricultural Fair labourers were accustomed to move on to new places, with the result that they were not accountable to the discipline of a fixed society, which in other places ensured that the Romeo father faced his responsibilities. At the same time also many cottages were pulled down to avoid the poor being a financial drain on a particular Parish.

Against this accumulation of social factors the Churches did their best. The Revd James Begg, one of the radical Ministers, cried for houses for working people. "People were unable to get married", he contended, "because they had nowhere to live, and if houses were available more children would be born in wedlock". He spoke against the bothies and their night meetings, the expense of looking after unmarried mothers, and the way the illegitimate grew up as beggars and in crime. He called for "a property owning Christian democracy".

The very name of the Kirk's Committee is revealing of the attitude of censoriousness. It was called "The Church of Scotland Committee for the Suppression of Intemperance".

The Church of Scotland and the Free Church of Scotland dominated our national life. The Roman Catholic Church however, through its declared practices, was no less censorious.

The end result of going down this path of censoriousness was not that the Church achieved purity either in the Church or in society. The contemporary records we have referred to show that it did not. Robert Burns was not deterred in the slightest from his rompings in the haylofts and boudoirs of Ayr, Kilmarnock, Dumfries, Moffat, Glasgow, Edinburgh and elsewhere. His perception of the Church was not of the welcoming Gospel and its joys and inspiration to holy living, but only the censoriousness, however justified, of the Presbytery of Ayr.

Some dreadful consequences

The combination of these factors made the Church appear preoccupied with sex, and helped society to elevate the gravity of sins in this area to the highest status. As a result people found it harder to understand the Gospel of grace and forgiveness, joy and love.

All too often it was the poor serving girl who, having been taken advantage of, was put out of her job, with no hope of subsistence apart from begging or prostitution. It led to the desperate secret visit to an unhygienic abortionist, or the sad entry in the newspaper about the young woman's body found under the bridge, with a note that a post-mortem examination showed her to have been with child.

In his book *One Way Left*, George McLeod wrote of an ancient Govan Kirk Session record, where a young man was required to stand outside the Church gate in a white sheet as a sign of public repentance. The record tells that the Kirk Session discontinued the punishment with the terrible words, "Him having gone aff his heid".

Kenneth Boyd cites the report of Ayrshire lawyer William Aiton to the Board of Agriculture in 1811: "Too many of the clergymen of Ayrshire, still keep up the ridiculous farce of public repentance, for breaches of the seventh commandment; though that stool has been the cause of so many children being murdered".

The censorial attitude directs attention to an individual's personal sins. Its worst side effect is to deflect attention from collective and larger social issues. For most of the period covered here, slavery was the norm throughout the world. Working conditions in our land were often indistinguishable from slavery. Politics were frequently corrupt. Democracy as we know it did not exist. The Session Clerk of my first congregation was actually hanged for advocating the idea, which was thought to be socially dangerous, that everyone should have a vote. That was in the 1790's just after the French Revolution and it was called Jacobinism.

As we study the desperate efforts of our fathers in the faith who tried sincerely to face up to the evil that they saw around them, let us not make cheap accusations of hypocrisy. They were more kindly than we often allow. Rather, let us learn from their mistakes. They failed to retain the assent of the people while the identification of the Church with judgment, the tragedies, the social injustice, and the unbalanced thinking that accompanied the path of censoriousness, must make us all tremble.

3 THE PATH OF TOLERATION AND LAXITY

On the bridge of warships there used to be a lever. When the shells from enemy gunners got too close for comfort, a smoke-screen was laid to try and confuse the enemy. The arguments of those who wish to avoid God's wishes for mankind in marriage might be likened to smoke-screens and can be readily answered.

The smoke-screen of dismissing Scripture as "time bound"

Of course different parts of the Bible addressed different situations, and of course there is a need to discern what was the constant will of God in those past situations. God's will for marriage and condemnations regarding fornication were given by Christ and the Apostles not simply to the Jews, but to the Church; not simply for 'those' days, but for 'these' days, and his concept of marriage has an eternal dimension which will outlast heaven and earth.

The smoke-screen that says "We must not judge"

When a certain Cabinet Minister was caught in a scandal his reply was that it was the newspapers and the public who complained who were the hypocrites, as if it was they not he who had sinned! Others pointed to the treatment by Jesus of the woman taken in adultery as if to say, by their interpretation, that the scandal should simply be passed over and dismissed!

Certainly Jesus protected the woman taken in adultery from punishment, but he didn't tell everybody to accept her behaviour, and he told her to go and sin no more. Her behaviour had to be stopped forthwith. Condoning sin condones the evil being perpetrated by it on other people.

The smoke-screen of 'love'

Love is much used as a smoke-screen in theological debates. One speaker told the General Assembly of the Church of Scotland of conducting a funeral for someone in a homosexual relationship. He argued with some passion that he had no doubt there was true love there. No doubt there was. But this cannot make holy what God has explicitly forbidden, or change the pattern of marriage Christ set out. Love is the greatest motivator, but like all other gifts can be misused.

When a man runs off with a woman other than his wife the relationship is not sanctified because love is present. It is misdirected love. God calls it adultery and forbids it.

When someone is obsessed with money, there is no doubt that love exists. The Bible explicitly says it does, but it is misdirected love, and the love of money is rightly described as the root of all evil.

The love of power turns love from service into domination. It makes a potential saint into a vicious tyrant. In the Nazi era the most feared man in Europe was Heinrich Himmler. His Gestapo and S.S. men ran the concentration camps, the gas chambers, the hangings, the beheadings, the tortures and atrocities by which 10 million people were murdered under the Nazis. It was the worst mass crime in the history of the world. It was done out of love for power, love for Hitler, love for the Nazi cause.

In the film *The People's Century - 1993* (BBC 2, 31:8:96) a newsreel clip showed Himmler giving an account of the Final Solution to a huge crowd who thundered back their approbation. He said, "It was an unpleasant task. But we did it out of love for our people"! He claimed he did it out of love!

Love which violates a young boy or a little girl, is 'Paedophilia'. It leaves a terrible mark upon them for the rest of their life. It is such a total perversion of all that love is.

These are all examples of misdirected love and in no case does it make holy the forbidden practices to which the word is misapplied. The New Testament concept of love focuses on the word *agape*. This has virtually no classical usage, but is used in the N.T. about 250 times. It is richer than either the compulsive physical passion described by *eros*, or the intimate family affection described by the word *philia*. This is the basis of God's outreach to the world in John 3:16, when he so loved the world that he gave his only begotten Son to save us. It is beautifully detailed in 1 Cor 13 as outgoing rather than self-centred; as giving rather than possessive; as self-effacing rather than arrogant; as kindly rather than demanding and cruel.

Proper love includes telling someone when they are on the wrong path. It also involves caring for the wrongdoer, even while they may require chastening. As parents still love their child whom they chasten, so God still loves someone even though he or she requires correcting in prison.

Mankind has love, and mankind has devised its own ideas of marriage with varying success. Such love should never be confused with God's idea of love, nor mankind's ideas of marriage with God's idea of marriage. It should never be waved as a smoke-screen to justify cohabitation.

The smoke-screen that the marriage certificate is worth no more than a bit of paper

It is not the marriage certificate in itself, or the bit of paper, that is important. It is the Christian commitment to marriage certified by the certificate that is all important. To affirm this we cannot be concerned with this or that particular cohabiting couple and what they might or might not have in their relationship. Some achieve a great deal. We have to look at the principle as a whole.

(a) Christian marriage is a lifelong commitment. Replacing it with cohabitation conduces to shallowness of commitment and all too often impermanence of commitment.

Christian marriage starts from its roots in the eternal covenant given by God. Cohabitation by its very nature starts from the basis of a wilful rejection of God's will. A couple practising cohabitation may in their relationship manifest some elements of God's will. They themselves however have set their own terms of contract and restraints, and these, of necessity, fall far short of what God wants for them. So the canticle of consecration to God is replaced by the cry "I did it my way!"

Christian marriage demands a sincere commitment for life and that it be God's rich idea of love that is present, not man's.

People say, "What difference does a piece of paper make?" If a couple do have in mind that dimension of love and life-long commitment which God demands what is there about the marriage certificate, the bit of paper, that they cannot sign?

(b) Christian marriage involves total lifelong caring

Cohabitation falls far short of this.

A human being is a very sophisticated being. He or she takes nine months before birth to gestate, eighteen years or so to develop physically, and a quarter of a century for emotional, intellectual and spiritual capacities to mature. A human being has the deepest emotional, intellectual and spiritual personal needs of anything in the known Universe. These simply cannot be provided for in a series of one night stands, or serial short relationships of cohabitation. They are demanded for us by God and can only adequately be provided for in lifelong Christian marriage.

Murdering someone is a most serious crime indeed. Yet the suffering incurred by the victim may be small compared with the suffering through the entire lifetime of another human being, who is brought into the world without the provision of total, proper, physical, emotional nourishment, character training, spiritual teaching, and the means for personal fulfilment and the realising of his or her eternal destiny. Prison records say that 95% of persistent offenders come from such a background of suffering and deprivation.

God's idea of love demands the provision through lifelong mutual caring for that full range of human needs for ourselves, our partner and our children. Surely it can only be achieved by following him, not rejecting him.

(c) Christian marriage is intended to minimise financial insecurity. Cohabitation undermines security.

It is astonishing how on radio phone-in programmes it is so often women's voices that try to justify cohabitation. The arrangement is a terribly unwise one for a woman. All too often it offers her, perhaps more so than the man, little security.

A woman is not like a car. It is an abuse to treat her as a car, by living with her and using her body, but on the understanding that when she becomes older, or doesn't produce a child, or fails to please, or another more streamlined model becomes available, she may be replaced at a whim.

They say "What difference does a bit of paper make?" Try saying that when you go to buy a car and are asked to sign the hire purchase agreement!

When the woman has given years of her life to live jointly with a man and when she is left unemployable by age and reasonably wants a share of her partner's estate after his death, try saying to the judge, "I feel married"! In sheer financial terms, that document could be the most valuable piece of paper that may ever pass through her hands. It may be worth many tens of thousands of pounds.

A Marriage Certificate which locks into the law of the land is a well defined matter, giving both parties a clear position both in human law, and divine law. Overwhelmingly it is the woman who suffers most when she agrees to throw away the rights which we in the Church, and many outside it, have striven to give to her. These rights touch on such wide matters as the precise terms of the ownership of the home, the pension rights, savings, investments, tenancies, hire purchase agreements, the rights in connection with children, their education, moral and spiritual upbringing. All these and others are part of complex Acts of Parliament which have been developed over centuries. The lawyers are supposed to have a toast, "To the man who makes his own will". Many matters other than wills can become imprecise when people try a do-it-yourself approach to marriage law.

There may be some women who can ride the disaster of a break-up, but it is a grievous thing to be a young woman struggling to bring up a child, her education interrupted, unable to go out to earn, with a constricted social life, living in the squalid poverty of mean social security, dependent on the parents from whom she had hoped she was financially independent, the target of political nasties. "My false lover took my rose, but ah! he left the thorn with me", may be from a song by Burns, but it is also the oldest story in the book.

For a woman, that marriage certificate carries the legal right to be maintained and protected during any pregnancy that the man may incur, the right that children born of that relationship should be provided for by adequate maintenance for their first sixteen years. It embodies rights in inheritance, and rights in pension.

While many cohabiting relationships may be stable, surely true love for our partner demands that in this variable life we provide the maximum security that we possibly can for the most vulnerable member of the partnership. What difference does a piece of paper make? Let us turn the question round. "If that piece of paper doesn't mean a thing, why then doesn't the man put his signature on it"?

(d) Marriage was also given to us as a means of containing certain kinds of disease. "Pick and mix" cohabitation may not.

The marriage laws contain the degrees of relationship across which God forbade matrimonial union. A high rate of imbecility and other inbred diseases follow where this God-given defence is broken.

We are also told that by the end of the century 40 million people, 92% of whom it is expected will come from the third world, will be infected by the Aids virus. A friend back from working abroad said, "Everyone you met was either going to, or coming from, a funeral". Innocent people may and do contract Aids yet primarily the contracting of the Aids virus is the result of the rejection of God's laws.

Aids is only one of several deforming sexually transmitted diseases which all too often are the result of peoples' sin.

Of course many cohabiting people remain faithful to each other and there are some married people who do not. Yet in Christian marriage God gave society an arrangement which if we follow, enables partners to know that they are protected from many powerful infections, and that their body is not indirectly connected to a network of unknown sexual histories. Through the sacraments and Christian worship God also gives us much needed help to keep our vows to be faithful in marriage.

The difference between God's idea of marriage and that of sinful mankind is for millions of people today the difference between life and death through disease.

(e) Cohabitation deprives its followers of God's glorious vision.

In all this critique of cohabitation this is quite the most serious. When God made mankind he said, "Be fruitful and multiply and replenish the earth". That is a big enough remit. The Church doesn't believe that sex is sinful, but that it is holy.

To any who have read of God's hopes for us in marriage, of his standards of behaviour between husband and wife, of the wider nature of God's love of which their personal passion is a part, and the end product when we stand in glory before our Maker, what a come down, what a human tragedy, it is for two people to live in a tiny world of their own making. One thinks of the proud mouse with its crumb of cake under the table in the banqueting hall of the royal palace.

In all the stresses of life what a rich vision it is to know that in marital physical relations our hands and bodies are God's loving provision for our partner, that people can actually pray to the God who designed our bodies the way they are, to be helped to make a go of things. What an honour to be part of God's provision for drawing our partner along the path of a developing godly character and of eternal salvation.

What a joy, that pierces the pain of parting, to be able to write in Mary Livingstone's words to her husband. "If I should go before you to that palace in the sky, ten thousand, thousand welcomes will be waiting you on high".

"What difference does the possession of a marriage certificate make"? The statistics show that more cohabitations break up than do church marriages. This is so despite the fact that some are married with shallow spiritual dedication.

Cohabitation is not a matter of being carried away by an act of impulse or passion, into a sinful act. Cohabitation by its very nature is a persistent, deliberate rejection of God's provision for humankind of permanent commitment to one another, of spiritual nurture, of legal justice for the weaker partner, for the containment of disease, and for the bringing up of the next generation in godliness and worship.

Cohabitation may imitate various things God wants for us. It may manifest in its relationships a form of love. Essentially however it is the substitution of man-made standards for those of God. It does not accord with God's will and is not for the temporal or eternal welfare of mankind. Laxity concerning it cannot therefore be the appropriate way for Christians, or the Church to go.

4 CONCLUSION

William Temple, was a very clear thinker. In a study called *Why and How Should the Church Interfere in the Social Order?* he percipiently says: "The method of the Church's impact upon society at large should be twofold. The Church must announce Christian principles and point out where the existing social order at any time is in conflict with them. It must then pass on to Christian citizens, acting in their civic capacity, the task of reshaping the existing order in closer conformity to the principles".

John Calvin goes uncompromisingly right to the core of the matter:

As the law under which man was created was not to lead a life of solitude, but enjoy a help-meet for him ... the Lord made the requisite provision for us in marriage, which, entered into under his authority, he has also sanctified with his blessing. Hence it is evident that any mode of cohabitation different from marriage is cursed in his sight..... those who are assailed by incontinence, and unable successfully to war against it, should betake themselves to the remedy of marriage.... The Apostle shows this when he enjoins, *nevertheless, to avoid fornication, let every man have his own wife and let every woman have her own husband".* (1 Cor 7:34 - Calvin's *Institutes* 1:viii:41-44)

Our witness to society must start with the straight declaration of the centrality and rightness in God's sight of Christian marriage. It is not just that we have the right to make that witness in our society. It is our duty both to God and to humankind. We require to make it courageously but with deep understanding, tenderness, sensitivity and compassion toward our fellows, many of whom do not share the light and joy of Christ and with the continuing awareness that we are all sinners in continual need of God's sustaining and forgiving Grace.

Chapter 4   THE CHRISTIAN FAMILY

David C. Searle

Exodus 13: 1-16

The Lord said to Moses, "Consecrate to me every firstborn male. The first offspring of every womb among the Israelites belongs to me, whether man or animal."

Then Moses said to the people, "Commemorate this day, the day you came out of Egypt, out of the land of slavery, because the Lord brought you out of it with a mighty hand. Eat nothing containing yeast. Today, in the month of Abib, you are leaving. When the Lord brings you into the land of the Canaanites, Hittites, Amorites, Hivites and Jebusites - the land he swore to your forefathers to give you, a land flowing with milk and honey - you are to observe this ceremony in this month. For seven days eat bread made without yeast and on the seventh day hold a festival to the Lord. Eat unleavened bread during those seven days; nothing with yeast in it is to be seen among you, nor shall any yeast be seen anywhere within your borders.

"On that day tell your son, 'I do this because of what the Lord did for me when I came out of Egypt.'

"This observance will be for you like a sign on your hand and a reminder on your forehead that the law of the Lord is to be on your lips. For the Lord brought you out of Egypt with his mighty hand. You must keep this ordinance at the appointed time year after year.

"After the Lord brings you into the land of the Canaanites and gives it to you, as he promised on oath to you and your forefathers, you are to give over to the Lord the first offspring of every womb. All the firstborn males of your livestock belong to the Lord.

"Redeem with a lamb every firstborn donkey, but if you do not redeem it, break its neck. Redeem every firstborn among your sons. In days to come, when your son asks you, 'What does this mean?' say to him, 'With a mighty hand the Lord brought us out of Egypt, out of the land of slavery. When Pharaoh stubbornly refused to let us go, the Lord killed every firstborn in Egypt, both man and animal. This is why I sacrifice to the Lord the first male offspring of every womb and redeem each of my firstborn sons.' And it will be like a sign on your hand and a symbol on your forehead that the Lord brought us out of Egypt with his mighty hand."

My work involves travelling widely throughout Scotland and therefore I see a fair bit of the Christian Church of all denominations in our land. While it would be true to say that there are congregations which are growing, both in spiritual depth and numerically, the general picture is a very sombre one. I was recently in one church which twenty years ago was packed to capacity, but where today only a smattering of people gather on the Lord's Day. The elders told me that they didn't know what had gone wrong. Somewhere along the line, rot has set in and has eaten away at the vital foundations of the fellowship's life until today they are facing a crisis as to whether they can even continue to exist.

When I was a boy, my own home town on the east coast of Scotland had twelve parish churches. Though the population of the town has increased by about 40%, today there are only four congregations left of which two at least are struggling to survive.

Problems of affluence

What has gone wrong with the Church of our day? Why could congregations get along very well in days when people had linoleum on their floors at home, hardly anyone owned a car, and only the very wealthy could afford a holiday abroad. Today when most families have a car (many have two cars!), most have wall to wall fitted carpets, automatic washing machines, dishwashers, microwaves and foreign holidays, why is the church in such crisis?

We have at least part of the answer in the passage quoted above from Exodus 13. The key phrase on which the problem turns is in v.5 - *when the Lord brings you into a land flowing with milk and honey* - the point being that down the generations the great enemy of the Church of God is not persecution, or opposition, or lack of funds; the great enemy is prosperity. For it is when we have plenty, and life becomes easy, that God's people begin to turn away from Him.

I do not want to be misunderstood as advocating a doctrine of 'Christian prosperity'. However, it is a fact that when Christians live according to their faith and are hard-working, conscientious, reliable and honest, then they often prosper. I am not saying that is invariably the case. But often that is what happens because living by basic Christian ethics frequently brings its own success.

Now it is the very prosperity which comes as a result of Christian living that brings the believer into dangerous territory. *The land flowing with milk and honey*, a land which God gives, is the very source of the problems that can threaten the church's existence. Because along with prosperity can come spiritual lethargy, and the things of God can be neglected. If father and mother grow cool in their love for God, the chances are high that the children will show no interest at all. Indeed, over the years I have noted a depressingly regular pattern: a devout, spiritual couple honour God and are blessed with material prosperity; their children reap the benefits of a lifetime of hard work, but though professing Christians, do not show the same commitment to Christ as their parents showed; the grandchildren, brought up in a luke-warm Christian family, where there is plenty of money and this world's goods come in abundance, grow up without any spiritual interest whatsoever and rarely, if ever, enter a Christian place of worship.

Safeguards

God is fully aware of the weakness of human nature. Therefore built into Exodus 13 are three safeguards against this hazard that has faced every generation of God's people. Great dangers faced God's people when they leave Egypt and settled into the land of Canaan. So the Lord gave three instructions in order to guard their faith and to keep them from backsliding.

1 FAITH CELEBRATIONS

The first safeguard took the form of a festival called "The Feast of Unleavened Bread". It was very simple. For the Passover and the following seven days, the people were to have a holiday, and were to eat no bread made with yeast. Indeed, all yeast was to be entirely cleared out of their homes. These seven days of holiday at Passover were to be called The Feast of Unleavened Bread. What was the meaning of this festival?

It meant first of all that they had been delivered from slavery. The bread without yeast was to be called *the bread of affliction*. It was reminding them negatively of the bad old days when they were slaves in Egypt; but positively it was reminding them of their deliverance by God.

Second, it meant that for seven whole days they had to remember that. Not just the night of the Passover, but for a whole week. The change of diet was something no one could fail to notice. As all yeast was banned for a week, the pattern of eating in every home changed and the bread used was significantly different. Everyone in the home was obliged to take careful note.

It meant, third, a celebration. This week constituted a festival, a time of joy and family reunions. It was a time of coming together and relaxing. All ordinary work stopped and only essential work was done. It was a week everyone looked forward to. "Goody, goody, no school this week!" "Is Granny coming on Friday, and Uncle Tom and Aunt Elizabeth? Great!" Because Uncle Tom was a favourite with the children and Aunt Elizabeth always brought delicious home-made sweets and goodies. A celebration.

Strong families

For God's people living in the era of the New Testament and in these modern times, we can sum up the principles of the Old Testament Feast of Unleavened Bread in three words: Family, Assurance and Celebration. Family, because while the festival was nation-wide, its focus was on each family. Assurance, because it was reminding them of their remarkable redemption from slavery and deliverance into glorious freedom. Celebration, because the festival was a time of rejoicing and fun. This is God's first safeguard against a faltering, failing Church.

In other words, in the divine provision for the future of the Church is the intention that the centre of each congregation will be strong families: families that stick together and make time to be together; families that live in the firm conviction of God's redeeming love in the Lord Jesus; families able to celebrate and have happy times together. That is the kind of family this Feast of Unleavened Bread was seeking to create.

A top priority

The faith festival implies parents have real faith. It demands that in each home spending time with the children is a top priority. We are talking about marriages that are stable and loving. We are talking about families that worship together. Having fun, relaxation and laughter together is the most natural thing in all the world for them - all in a context of a living faith in God as Father, Saviour, Friend.

Now this might appear to be the most unlikely defence of the life of the Church of God. But let me assure you that it is absolutely fundamental to the life of a strong and healthy congregation. Because the problems for congregations really begin when parents are woolly about their faith, are not quite sure whether God really is God, and are uncertain as to whether Christ really is Saviour. Where there is that hesitation, when it comes to setting the course the family must steer through the hazardous seas of today's society, with treacherous moral currents and swirling waters over hidden rocks, there is no clear and safe way being charted, and soon the boat either begins to take in water, or runs aground and is wrecked.

We all know the problems: undesirable places to which our children's friends go; activities in which their friends are allowed to engage; seemingly endless money their friends have to spend. What pressures today on families through the teenagers! But God's provision in this faith festival is that the family that *prays* together and *plays* together also *stays* together. This is the family that will withstand the storm. And this is the family that is a pillar of the Church of God.

A museum of memories

Those of us who are parents ought to be working to create for their children what Edith Schaeffer has called *a museum of memories*. I know that already we have certain celebrations built into our culture - Christmas, Easter, summer holidays, birthdays and the like. But why not work at creating your own family culture of celebrations? By that I mean special things you do at certain times; favourite places you go to at other times; occasions when you deliberately take the family to entirely new places. So that you are building up for them a *museum of memories* to which they will look back with pleasure and affection.

I find as I study the Old Testament something that surprises me more and more. I find that the People of God were a people who knew how to celebrate. True, their festivals were religious festivals, 'faith festivals' we have called them. But they were holidays, times of fun and laughter and family reunions. They were creating memories of the pleasure and security of family love.

There is an increasing and urgent need for Christian parents consciously to work at this. Parents need deliberately to plan family life to build a *museum of memories*. It has to begin from the earliest days. Outings, little treats that have something of the ritual about them so that the children can look forward to them. Yet all this is impossible unless plenty of time is invested in the family.

I recall a little story a six year old wrote for her teacher, called "My Granny", with the rather touching sentence, "Grannies are people who have time for children". My teacher friend thought there were sad undertones - had mum and dad any time for their children? Indeed, knowing the child's family, the teacher told me they were caught up in a whirl of activity and used Granny quite shamelessly as a substitute parent. While Granny was willing to oblige, was it not tragic that the parents were neglecting their own responsibilities towards their daughter? She would only be six years old once in her life. Those years were slipping past and being almost entirely lost to her parents, to say nothing of lost opportunities to engage in the ongoing work of building a character of faith for the future.

That then was the Feast of Unleavened Bread. A family time of relaxation, all in the context of praise and worship as the unleavened bread, the 'bread of affliction', reminded them of God's mighty redemption and his ongoing loving care of them.

The call is for Christian parents today to make the microcosm of their families an essential part of the macrocosm of the Family of God. If mother and father are faithful in worship, and if they clearly enjoy and appreciate the fellowship of the wider church family to which they belong, then it will be so much easier for them to extrapolate these Old Testament principles and apply them to family life today. They will then be applied in the context of the spiritual Israel, the Church of Jesus Christ.

2 THE INSTRUCTION OF CHILDREN

The instruction of children has already been laid down in Exodus 12 where we are given an account of the Passover. *When your children ask you, "What does this ceremony mean to you?" then tell them, "It is the Passover sacrifice to the Lord...".*[1] We have it again here in ch.13, parents teaching their children the faith: *On that day tell your son, "I do this because of what the Lord did for me when I came out of Egypt".*[2]

Children in ancient times

Let me try and explain a little about family life in the early days of the people of God. There were no schools in early Old Testament days. The children stayed at home with mother, and in their early years she taught them all she knew. That was a most important time of learning. But at the age of eight, the boys went to work with their fathers. From his father each son learned three things: his trade, his nation's history and his faith.

Maybe father worked with leather; maybe he was a joiner and worked with wood; or a tailor and worked with cloth; or a farmer and worked the land. But whatever the family occupation might have been, the boy joined his father who taught him how to earn his living. Alongside that, he taught his son about God, and the story of God's people. That teaching was supplemented by the boy's attending the village council meetings and also attending public worship to hear the priest reading and explaining the Scriptures.

Here in Exodus 13 , as in the previous chapter, we have it laid down that each father must teach his own sons these things, and, by the same token, each mother must teach her daughters. Has this family order from so long ago anything to say to us today?

Upside-down Sunday Schools

The first point I have to make may come as a surprise. I want to ask the question whether the Sunday School *as we have it nowadays* was ever the intention of those who first started Sunday Schools. You see, the first Sabbath Schools were never intended for the children of Christian parents. They were for so-called 'ragged children', for boys and girls whose parents never went near a church. They were started as part of the church's outreach to the needs of the day.

But what has happened to that original purpose for the Sabbath Schools? They have become the place for children from Christian homes to go, often as an alternative to church. We have turned the original concept of Sunday Schools upside-down, making them into what they were never intended to be. Instead of being outreaches to the parish, they are now mostly congregational organisations for the baptised children of church members.

Negative lessons

The unintended and unfortunate result has been that many parents think that the Christian training of their children is being done *for them* at Sunday School. That, however, is a tragic fallacy. The Christian nurture of believers' children can never be done in the Sunday School alone. Consider this simple fact: at an over optimistic estimate, the teaching and learning time in any one year offered by an average Sunday School is less than forty hours. By contrast the time a child spends at home with its parents, deducting time for sleeping and school, is well over four thousand hours in a year. In other words, mother and father have over a hundred times more influence on their children than any Sunday School teacher can ever have!

Whether mother and father realise it or not, whether they like it or not, they *are* teaching their children all about the Christian faith every hour they spend with them. They may be teaching them to criticise the minister or poke fun at the singing in church. They may be teaching them to laugh at certain people who attend church, or to 'do down' the Kirk Session. They may be teaching them to lie in bed on a Sunday morning, and only bother with church occasionally, just to keep up appearances. It is quite astonishing how many disturbing lessons parents can be teaching their children about the Christian faith.

A miracle needed

I believe that if we could somehow gather together all the thoroughly negative lessons some parents have consistently been teaching their children about the faith, and weigh them against the teaching given faithfully in Sunday School for those few hours in any year, we would be driven to our knees to cry out to God for a miracle. Because God has to overturn a colossal weight of anti-Christian (however unintentional) parental teaching by the slenderest weight of the little we can do on a Sunday morning The odds are about the same as a mouse taking on a horse, for those in the Sunday School have less than forty hours against the parents' four thousand hours!

The implications of this are great. It means that however excellent a Sunday School, however well its work may be done, however committed its teaching staff, nothing can ever be an adequate substitute for the Christian teaching of the children by the parents at home. The Bible doesn't have it wrong telling *fathers* to teach their sons, and *mothers* their daughters. That is the proper and wise way of Christian nurture.

Strong families—strong fellowships

It is a massive error when parents think they can safely leave the godly nurture of their children entirely to the church. Yes, the church has its role. Of course it does. But the church's role was never intended to, and never can, replace the role of mother and father. Indeed, when the church is left to fulfil a role it was never intended to fulfil, then it gradually decreases in numbers and becomes more frail in its life, because at the heart of a strong fellowship will be strong families, and families are made strong when parents nurture their children in the faith.

I have watched this carefully for thirty five years. I have watched homes and families where parents give no clear Christian guidance, and I have seen whole congregations going down and falling apart like a slow motion film of Hiroshima being struck by the atomic bomb. For years, I have asked the churches' education departments to prepare materials to guide parents in training their children in the Christian faith - all to no avail.

Some parents are already taking the teaching of their children seriously. But for every couple who undertakes this responsibility, there must be a hundred who do little or nothing. Or worse, there are many who without realising what they are doing teach lessons that are entirely negative and can only have the effect of turning their children away from God.

Parents training their children in the faith was *the second safeguard* for the life of the Church of God.

Please do not think for one moment that I am suggesting Christian families should operate independently of the local congregation. "The Christian family is a microcosm of the macrocosm of the Church family". Parents must be encouraged and helped by the local fellowship to fulfil this difficult and important task God has given to them. Congregations ought to be doing far more to show the way. I will enlarge on ways in which this might be done later on in this chapter.

3 A MEMORIAL IN BREAD AND WINE

There was a third safeguard God gave against the eroding influence of this earthly life undermining His work of grace and goodness among His people. It was through the law about the redemption of the first-born son in every Hebrew family.

First-born sons

Each first-born boy had to be redeemed. That means, a price had to be paid as the cost of the child's life. The law extended to animals as well. First-born animals were to be sacrificed, or else redeemed, i.e., bought with a price. A donkey, being an unclean animal, could only be redeemed. I understand that still today in orthodox Jewish families a ransom is paid for the life of the first-born son.

It is easy to see why this practice was built into the warp and woof of Israelite life. It was to remind the people of their redemption from Egypt and of the Tenth Plague when their first-born sons were redeemed by the blood of the Passover Lamb. In dramatic, vivid terms that deliverance was to be etched upon their lives. Every first-born son must be redeemed, and the ransom paid to God. Every first-born lamb or goat or calf must be redeemed or else given to God in sacrifice. In an agricultural society, hardly a month would go past without each family and village being reminded of the night of their deliverance from slavery.

While the direct successor to the Jewish Passover is the memorial in bread and wine our Lord has given to his people, the redemption of the first-born also speaks eloquently to every believer of the price that was paid for our redemption from slavery. The memorial of the Passover was reinforced by the redemption of the first-born. Both pointed to the divine deliverance.

The cost of grace

If God decreed that his people should look back to the accomplishment of their salvation on a regular ongoing basis as well as at the annual Passover Feast, so we must also often look back and often be reminded of the cost of grace. I agree, we don't *need* to take the bread and wine of the sacrament to remember the cost to God of His love in forgiving us sinners. Whenever we who are God's people meet together, we do so in the Saviour's Name and he who bears the marks of the Cross is there among us. Nonetheless, the Lord's Supper is God's appointed way of reminding us of our redemption and bringing us to feed from Christ as we share in the communion of his body and his blood..

Most, if not all, parents know their faith often grows dim. Most honestly want to have a warm, burning faith and always be close to Christ. But that doesn't come naturally to any of us. That is why Christ himself has provided the way to feed the flame of living faith. We must often come to Calvary, often bow before the Redeemer, often remember it was our sins that drove the nails into His hands and feet, it was our pride that forced the thorny crown on to His brow. We must often remember the Lord and receive him by faith. We must build into our family lives that memory of Him.

It is at this point that the Christian family finds its centre and focus in the local congregation. Every child of God belongs to a wider family. Do you remember the very first words addressed to Saul of Tarsus by a fellow-Christian after the experience of the Risen Lord on the Damascus road? Ananias said to him, "Brother Saul..." One who had formerly been the most dreaded enemy and opponent of the Church had now become a *brother*. It is at the foot of the Cross and at the empty tomb that believers are joined together by the Spirit of Pentecost as members of one Family. God is Father, Christ Jesus is Elder Brother and the Holy Spirit makes him real to us and applies all the benefits of grace to our hearts.

No Christian family can really fulfil its God-appointed role apart from meaningful participation in the local church. Nevertheless, the movement is entirely two-way. The local fellowship needs strong family in order that it also may be strong and fulfil its role. The relationship between the two is entirely and essentially complementary.

Conclusion
What I have tried to show in this chapter is that the health of each Christian family is also bound up with the vitality of the local fellowship. But also that the health of each congregation of God's people is inextricably bound up with the spiritual health of each Christian family. Further, I have sought to emphasise that the

spiritual health of each family is the concern of God who has given us clear Scriptural guidelines to enable parents to bring up their children in the knowledge and love of God.

I conclude by offering first some simple suggestions on practical ways in which we can try to work out these timeless principles in our homes and families, and second, ways in which the local fellowship can play its part and help parents in their responsibilities. Most parents and Christian congregations will already have guidelines which they have worked out for themselves, but the following are offered from the present writer's own experience and in the hope that they may be of some small help to others.

4 PRACTICAL SUGGESTIONS FOR CHRISTIAN PARENTS

• Daily Bible reading and prayer with all the family. It is a good idea to ensure that children have at least fifteen to twenty minutes each evening before bed when mother or father (or both) spend time together in devotions. It can be deeply reassuring to children to have all of mother's or father's attention as a Bible story is read and prayers said night by night. As soon as children are old enough, it is wise to encourage them to take active part in this time together by sharing in the reading and praying. Parents should resolve to turn off the television and give quality time to their children on the most regular basis.

• Grace before or after each meal, perhaps a grace in which all the family take part.

• Honour the Lord's name in the home. The name of God and his Son are sacred, and children should learn by example that those who reverence and serve God also reverence his name.

• Make Sunday the happiest day of the week. You might adopt the practice of always leaving some small treat on your children's plate at Sunday breakfast—a bar of chocolate, for example. Use the day of rest as a family day when the children enjoy quality time with you. Make Sunday a day to which they look forward with great anticipation. Manse families have to work especially hard at this as where there is a minister in the family, Sunday can be a day of some stress and hard work. But though my own children were brought up in a manse, we still worked hard to make Sunday a very special day for them.

• Practise Christian forgiveness in the home. Children all firmly believe that their home is the best in the world. Parents should work to make that childlike belief a reality. When mother and father love each other, then sons and daughters experience the beauty of *shalom* - health, well-being, wholeness. Parents will often disagree and even have quite heated arguments. Best if such arguments are firmly under control in front of the children. But it is absolutely essential that when there have been tensions, parents forgive, make it up and express again their love for each other clearly and tenderly. At the heart of our faith is a cross. The cross speaks of forgiveness, mercy and love. Father and mother must every day exercise that forgiveness and mercy towards each other. The children are immensely reassured when they know their parents still dearly love each other when the argument is over.

• It is also important that parents learn, when appropriate, to say sorry to their children. This is one of the ways in which godly repentance can be taught by example. It does not demean a parent to admit a mistake or unintended injustice. Rather, it will help to strengthen the bond of love and trust between parent and child.

• Mean what you say and say what you mean. We believe that God keeps his word to us and that his promises are absolutely sure. We base our whole lives on the Word made flesh, that is, upon our Lord Jesus Christ. If a hallmark of the nature of God is his faithfulness to his word, then Christian parents should also be faithful to their word. That faithfulness must work its way into family life by the way we honour our promises to our children. We should not issue warnings against bad behaviour if we do not intend to carry out those warnings. We should not lightly make promises with no real intention of fulfilling those promises. Our children should grow up knowing they can depend upon us and that our word is absolutely trustworthy.

• Dare to discipline. Parents need fair sanctions which are both loving in their purpose and clear in their message. Unruly, disobedient children are not happy, secure children. It is essential that parents are fully agreed on disciplinary action. There is nothing more calculated to create insecurity and bad behaviour as children's realisation that they can play one parent off against another. Unless mother and father are clearly united in the sanctions they take, the result of any attempt to discipline will be entirely counter-productive.

• Have a family diary. As children grow into their teens, they naturally begin to develop a life of their own with special friends and a host of activities, many of which are helpful and positive. However, family life still needs to be preserved. A good idea, therefore, is to have a family diary which is regularly reviewed and in which family time is agreed. When the family are all together (say at the end of a meal), the diary can be discussed and the teenage children fill in their own activities, while parents ensure family time together is also built in.

• Have at least one daily sit-down meal together. In some homes, father leaves for work too early to share breakfast with the family. If mother is also working, the start of the day can be very pressurised. But an evening meal should be the general rule when all share and where the family bonds are preserved. Best to organise the sit-down meal when children are not going to be dragged away protesting from some favourite tv programme. In my own home we always found the early evening news time the most satisfactory tv break for our meal together.

• Be aware of all your children watch on television. Best not to allow personal tvs in the children's bedrooms. This practice is widespread today, but is fraught with serious problems as children often view late at night without any parental guidance or awareness of what they are watching.

• I personally have grave reservations about committing the care of one's children to 'child minders'. I know that there are exceptional cases. But I believe that to hand over the nurture of one's children to another is an abrogation of Christian responsibility. The argument is usually that both parents must work to pay the mortgage. Then I would ask which is the more important, to provide parental care and love in a humble home, or deprive the child of that parental care and love and substitute it with a more affluent home? My own home as a small child was a very poor home in terms of material standards. But it was one of the richest homes in the land in terms of my parents' godly love and teaching. Is it the 'cost of living' which drives so many parents today to use child minders? Or is it the 'cost of living it up'?

• Keep the lines of communication open. It is too easy for growing children to retreat into their own shell. They hear things from their friends at school which clearly contradict all they have been taught at home. The conflict between the home and the culture they encounter outside the home can bring depression and a withdrawal from parental confidence. Parents, therefore, must work at graciously and tenderly keeping open communication with growing teenagers. Be bold enough to talk explicitly about the moral standards portrayed in tv programmes. Explain patiently why Christians have different standards. Be a real friend to your adolescent family. Be a friend they love and trust and with whom they can share their fears and uncertainties.

• Accept your children. However much they may hurt and grieve you, never give them the impression you have rejected them. Certainly you may well have to convey clearly to them on occasion that you disapprove strongly of certain actions they have taken. But that disapproval must never lead them to a sense of personal rejection. They must always know you love them, whatever they do.

• Welcome your children's friends into your home. Make your home one to which your children are not ashamed to bring their friends. That does not necessarily mean that a Christian home will have all the modern gadgetry of the 1990s. It simply means that your home will be clean, cared for, orderly and with space where friends can relax and chat.

• Pray for your children. You have given them to God. Daily commit them in faith to his loving care. One mother whose son became a notorious black sheep of the family and brought much shame on the family name made a practice of daily thanking God for her boy's salvation. She constantly committed him to God and held on to God's covenant in childlike, clinging faith. At the age of forty-seven, her son was amazingly converted from the life of a professional gambler and is today a minister of the Gospel leading many to living faith in Christ. So pray in faith for your children.

When a member of the family may be going through some particular crisis such as illness, difficulties at school or problems at work, then join together as a family to commit that situation to the Lord. A family united in prayer for one its members is a family whose ties of love are holding firm and are even being strengthened as God enables them to work together through the crisis.

5   THE ROLE OF THE CHURCH

• The congregation's role must begin, if possible, at the marriage of a man and woman. There ought to be pre-marital classes to prepare the couple for the enormous changes which married life will bring.

In a generation when so many marriages fail within the first few years, it is a matter of the utmost urgency that each fellowship develops or adopts some programme of instruction to point the way forward before ever the wedding takes place.

• A baby's baptism (or dedication, if infant baptism is not practised) is an important event for every family. The meaning of Christian parenthood needs to be spelled out clearly, and its responsibilities taught. As the congregation share in the joy and celebration of the miracle of a new life, the relationship between family and fellowship will be developed further, and firm foundation provided on which to build for the future.

• Follow-up after baptism is crucial. If baptismal instruction has included (as it ought) pointing out to parents their task of teaching their children the truths and duties of the Christian faith, then help should be given from the child's earliest years. All my former congregations provided baptised children with suitable material which mother and father could use to give the Christian teaching to their little children. We found that having established that principle at the baby's birth and in the pre-school years, parents were more likely to continue in that way as the children grew older. It is sad that too many congregations receive children as babies, but then abandon them in the (forlorn) hope that one day they will turn up at church some Sunday.

• Single parents need very particular support and help. Too often, it works the other way, and they receive less support than married couples. The minister and elders should appoint a group to work out ways in which those struggling alone to bring up children can both be helped in their task at home and also made doubly welcome in the fellowship. How this is done will depend on the resources of each congregation, particularly their resources in terms of people. In various ways, what is lacking through a missing parent (for whatever reason) needs to be more than made up for through members of the church family.

• The local church also needs to be acutely aware of the heritage of societal problems which every community in our land today shares. The church's teaching and preaching needs to be explicit and relevant. Issues of morality and ethics need to be spelled out without any possibility of misunderstanding.

I am referring to the teaching and learning process that ought to be going on at many levels within a congregation, from the pulpit right through to the Sunday School and certainly in any Bible Studies or house groups which are functioning. The day of hiding one's head in the sands and hoping issues of morality will look after themselves has long since gone. If the churches do not provide instruction in these matters, then be certain that society will. Also be sure that what society and the media will teach will be directly opposed to the teaching of the Christian faith.

• Some congregations have found it helpful to provide support groups for parents. There might be a group for parents with pre-school children, another for parents with children of primary school age, and yet another for parents with teenagers. Such groups might meet on a monthly basis and engage in studies prepared or suggested by the minister or some other competent person who is in touch with the problems being faced. There can be enormous encouragement derived from such groups. Single parents should be encouraged to join, as often friendships between families can develop in this context which can offer much needed support for those struggling alone.

• Finally, every congregation should guard against the tendency which has become so pronounced during the second half of our twentieth century to divide up the congregation into little groups on the basis of gender and sex. I am not discounting support groups just referred to. Rather I am referring to the paramount importance for the congregation to engage in worship *together* on the Lord's Day. The idea that little children (and that is soon extended to children who are not so little!) should not be present when the Body of Christ is met together, not least, around the Lord's Table, goes directly against the whole teaching of the Bible. When it is understood that children are welcome and ought to share in the congregation's worship, then the whole character of that worship must reflect the togetherness and unity of the family of God. What could be more relevant or attractive than that in today's society?

[1] vs.26f.

[2] v.8; see also vs 14,15 where the exhortation to parents regarding their children is repeated.

Chapter 5 CHILDLESSNESS

Graham and Alison Dickson

Couples who have been able to have children of their own relatively easily will never be able to understand fully the depth of feeling that childless couples experience. The longing to hold your own baby in your arms, to wipe away the tears from the face of your own upset child, to be able to comfort and encourage, to tuck your own child into bed at night, to see a child - a part of yourself - growing up. To stop being just a couple and be a 'family'.......[1]

In those few words Dr Ray Mealyea captures the reality of childlessness.

So much has been written in the last few years about the subject that it is difficult to know what can be added. Yet the present authors have been asked to contribute and do so in the hope that what they have to say might be of help to even one person who reads.

Some biographical detail might be useful at this point. We married in 1983 and hoped, as many couples do, to begin our family after about two years of marriage. By late 1985 nothing had happened and we began to get concerned. We spoke to our local GP. who was extremely helpful and sympathetic and we embarked on medical investigations which to date have found no reason for our infertility. We pursued the medical line as far as two attempts at G.I.F.T.[2] treatment, both unsuccessful. We then switched tack and applied for assessment as prospective adoptive parents. This took some months but in September 1991 we were approved. We had a four year wait until the local Social Work Department contacted us in June 1995 to say they had a little boy called Lee, who was two and a half years old. They felt he was right for us and we for him. Lee came to live with us in July 1995. We hope he will soon be our adopted son.

What follows now is an attempt to understand our experience during the last twelve years from a theological point of view. To do this a number of different approaches have suggested themselves as possible. It would be an option simply to go through our experience chronologically. Or, since the experience of childlessness is very similar to that of bereavement, it would be plausible to look at a scriptural understanding of grief and use the recognised stages of grief as a framework for discussion. However, a third approach commends itself above both of these.

In the Bible there are at least seven women, and by implication seven couples, who are mentioned in connection with their infertility; Sarah (Genesis 16, 18, 25), Rebekah (Genesis 25), Rachel (Genesis 30), Manoah's wife (Judges 13), Hannah (1 Samuel 1), the Shunamite (2 Kings 4) and Elizabeth (Luke 1). During the last few years we both have often gone to these characters and read in their experience our own. The approach here is therefore to take three biblical characters as paradigms and to analyse the experience of and issues raised by infertility with their help. If theological reflection is sought then this seems the most appropriate approach.

To this end we have selected one childless man, Abraham; one childless woman, Hannah and one man who was not childless but whose experience is nonetheless helpful and relevant - Job.

ABRAHAM AND THE PAIN OF CHILDLESSNESS

We begin with Abraham. Abraham obviously suffered from social pressures and his distress that Sarah could not give him a child is shown in Genesis 15:1-3.

After this, the word of the LORD came to Abram in a vision: "Do not be afraid, Abram. I am your shield, your very great reward." But Abram said, "O Sovereign LORD, what can you give me since I remain childless and the one who will inherit my estate is Eliezer of Damascus?" And Abram said, "You have given me no children; so a servant in my household will be my heir."

This is a very honest statement of Abraham's feelings. He obviously felt that all God's blessings were useless, they meant nothing because he was deprived of children. Here was one of the most godly of men and this is how he felt. Many would argue of course that children were more important to a man then than now. It is often said that children, particularly sons, were essential because the Jews believed they lived on in their sons after death. Therefore, if they were childless there would be no afterlife. Some say it is the same in the East today, but not in the West, that there is no social stigma about not having children. Don't you believe it!

A couple associated with our parish recently benefited from successful fertility treatment after many years of infertility. Their story appeared in a feature in the Daily Mirror[3] about Male Infertility. The husband confessed he had never been able to talk to anyone about how he felt. Every month when his wife failed to become pregnant he felt he would "be better out of it". He is a farmer and he cited what happened to bulls who failed to produce offspring. He rather felt the same should happen to him.

Children are very important. If you want a child, then the inability to have one is heartbreaking and the lack of a family seems to put you in a different social stratum. In Christian circles the stigma seems to be emphasised even more, as stress is laid on the God created *family* structure.

In *Choices in Childlessness*[4] the authors state that, "In much of our society it is socially unacceptable for a couple to be childless. Expectations about infertility are widespread.... Such expectations are very strong and can have powerful effects on those who fail to fulfil them." They acknowledge the pressures of society and, later, they emphasise the Christian point of view:

> Procreation of children.... may seem as a special expression of the faith that the future is not to be determined by the powers of this world, but by the power of the crucified and risen Son of God. Children are a symbol of hope. They may appear to be hostages to fortune, but Christians see them as in fact pledges of the love and fidelity of God.

This significance of children for the Christian community has been expressed as follows:

> There is much that could be done that might be considered more important than having children. Children take time and energy, psychologically and physically, that prevents us from being better scholars, important businessmen, serving the poor or attacking the structures of injustice. But it is the Christian's claim that God's kingdom is not to be built by us, that gives us the patience, in a world of injustice to insist that nothing is more important than having and rearing children. We do this not because we hope our children will choose to be the next generation of those who carry the story of God in the world. We must remember that our hope is not in our children but in the God who gives us and them grounds of hope.

For Christians, children are one of the highest vocational callings and as such, childlessness within the Christian community is even harder to accept. The desire for children is natural and deep and one might say God given.

ARE CHILDREN A RIGHT?

This raised the question for us "Are children then a right that we can demand of God?" Many today feel this is the case and that all means possible must be used to achieve it.

The conclusion we came to was no. The whole tenor of scripture seems to go against such an attitude. When we searched the scriptures we were faced with passages like Psalm 127, which says ,"Sons are a heritage from the LORD, children a reward from him." The message there seems to be that children are a blessing and a gift from God, but not a right. Abraham was given a promise. He did not claim a right.

The language of rights is foreign to the Bible. The scriptures deal much more with the language of responsibility. Ephesians Chapters five and six are a case in point. These passages deal with relationships in marriage, the family and the workplace. Today, in every one of these spheres, we hear of the language of rights - women's rights, workers' rights and children's rights. But the scripture text never mentions rights. It deals not with what we may demand but with what we may give. Insofar as rights are mentioned at all they are God's rights - his right to demand of us whatever he may ask.

This brings us back to Abraham. Later in his spiritual pilgrimage God asked Abraham for the son he had given. Then God said, "*Take your son, your only son, Isaac, whom you love, and go to the region of Moriah. Sacrifice him there as a burnt offering on one of the mountains I will tell you about.*" (Genesis 22:2). God asked Abraham to show his love by sacrificing his only son. Were we willing to sacrifice our desire for children if that was what God asked of us? Were we willing to say with Jesus "Not my will but yours, however hard that is?" To be honest the answer was often "no" on our part.

Yet we could recognise that God had the right to ask anything of us. It is not only Abraham that God has dealt with this way. God has done the same throughout the ages. He did it with Job. He did it with Jonah. He did it with Joni Eareckson. If our faith meant anything we had to be willing to be wholehearted - no exclusion clauses.

We wrestled often with this over the years, acknowledging the truth in our heads but with our hearts slow to follow. We suppose we did come to the point of surrender in the sense that we could admit children were not our right and were determined that childlessness and the desire for children would not become an obsession. Obsessions are really idols and that, clearly, could not be compatible with Christian faith.

DRAWING THE ETHICAL LINE

Determining this helped us begin to draw lines as to how far we would pursue our desire. We looked again at Abraham. Abraham had the promise of children and future generations but he then grew impatient and decided to help God out. This raised the question of how far we should 'help God out'. Should we, for example, seek medical help? If we did how far down that road should we travel?

We decided without too much difficulty that there was no theological problem about seeking medical help. After all we do not hesitate to do that for a malfunction of the vascular, the digestive or any other main system of the human body. Why should the reproductive system be any different? We see infertility as a medical problem and one that can have serious physical and psychological effects because of the stress and anxiety it creates. It needs to be treated. We would argue because of that it also needs to be adequately resourced within the NHS and available equally throughout the country. This is not the case at present. The treatment infertile couples may receive is something of a lottery depending on which Health Board they come under. Some Health Authorities offer treatment and others do not.

Having decided that medical treatment was permissible for the Christian we then had to face the second question of how far we should go with it. Here, Abraham's experience stood as a warning to us. Abraham decided to help God out but his actions led to very sad consequences. *He slept with Hagar, and she conceived. When she knew she was pregnant, she began to despise her mistress.* (Genesis 16:4) Ishmael was born and centuries of conflict between Arab and Jew have followed.

This early form of surrogacy was all that was available to Abraham and Sarah. Today there is a bewildering array of possibilities facing the infertile couple beginning with straightforward treatment with fertility drugs and going on to G.I.F.T., I.V.F., A.I.D., A.I.H., and surrogacy.

The attitude of many in contemporary society is that either each couple must 'do what is right for them' or 'go to any lengths'. Our post modern, relativistic society will always say the end justifies the means. This is an attitude with which we could not agree .

We felt that we could accept everything up to and including GIFT. but we could not accept IVF or any of the forms of treatment that introduced a third party into our relationship. The difference between GIFT and IVF is this. With GIFT the woman's ovaries are artificially stimulated to produce more eggs than usual in a cycle. They are removed and mixed with the husband's sperm outside the body and then re-introduced into the fallopian tube. If fertilisation occurs it will occur naturally after this.

With IVF fertilisation occurs outside the body in a test tube. The best embryos are selected and implanted again in the woman. Spare embryos are left over either to be frozen, destroyed or used for some other purpose. The problem for us was the creation of spare embryos. We believe that life begins at conception and we could not countenance the destruction of an embryo. The doctors of course argued with us that the body destroys spare embryos all the time. Our reply was that children die naturally too but that doesn't mean that we deliberately kill them. It was after the failure of GIFT that we felt our point of surrender to God must come. To go any further we felt would be wrong. Verses such as Psalm 20:7 seemed to feature in our reading at the time. *Some trust in chariots and some in horses, but we trust in the name of the LORD our God.* To go any further we felt would be to trust in modern day medical "chariots and horses" and not in the Lord. It would be idolatry in fact which, as we have said, was something we were determined to avoid.

THE DANGERS OF IDOLATRY

The track record of idols is that ultimately they destroy those who worship them (Romans 1:18ff). We could see that infertility could do that if it became our idol. Infertility does destroy some marriages. It can have a devastating emotional impact on a relationship as is shown by Elkanah who said to Hannah 1 Samuel 1:8 *"Hannah, why are you weeping? Why don't you eat? Why are you downhearted? Don't I mean more to you than ten sons?"* Hannah was so taken up with her childlessness and grief that Elkanah felt excluded altogether. She was giving so much emotional energy to her problem that there was little left for her marriage.

Sexually too, childlessness can be destructive when it becomes an idol. When undergoing treatment the woman's monthly cycle has to be followed religiously and every detail noted down. Joy Cooke describes it this way:

> We were ruled by temperature charts. My first thought in the morning was inevitably related to this subject, as I would roll over to turn the alarm clock off and pick up the thermometer in one movement. My turn to fall asleep again, until Ian removed the thermometer and nudged me awake to take a mug

of tea, record the reading on the graph and glance to see whether it was the right time of month.

As we approached the 'fertile period' we had been told to abstain from love-making for three days prior to the expected temperature rise. Then we were to have intercourse on the day of the temperature rise, not on the next day, but the one after that. Wedlock had become wedclock and it didn't make for a relaxed approach.[5]

Obviously if this kind of thing continues over many months, or even years, the effects are going to be destructive in a marriage.

Infertility creates financial pressures too. Where NHS treatment is not available couples must seek private clinics. Even where NHS treatment is available it will only be for a limited number of attempts and if these fail the only further recourse is the private sector. With each course of treatment costing something like £2000 some couples will easily spend £20000 and maybe take out a second mortgage to finance it. This creates its own pressures especially if the treatment is successful and one partner (or maybe both in the case of multiple births) has to give up work to look after the baby.

We wonder too if there is an ethical issue for Christians in the area of multiple births. Where these occur a great deal of state help is required in terms of income supplements and practical support. Is this ethical in a world where many other children, already born, are in need of the security of a good home? Could the pursuit of the idol of natural children actually lead to the failure to help the most needy children who are already part of our society?

Such questions caused us to turn from seeking medical help to pursue the different option of adoption which, we believe can be given theological justification since God himself adopts us into his family as his children through grace in the Lord Jesus Christ. All these issues arose for us through meditating on Abraham's experience. So let us move on now to a second character, Job.

JOB

Job was a man with everything. He was "blameless" (Job 1:1). He was a God fearing man and his faith led him to shun evil. He had integrity, maturity and reverence. He was well off too as Job 1:2-4 reveals, yet obviously did not covet prosperity. He was the kind of person God could trust with riches, possessions, social standing and family. Job 1:4 suggests a close family who delighted in visiting each other. All in all Job was a man for whom things usually seemed to go well. Success had come to him rather easily. Failure was alien to his experience.

Up until we faced the prospect of childlessness we have to say this had been our experience too. We came from comfortable backgrounds and had received good education doing well at school and university. We rejoiced to be married to each other soon afterwards. Graham was called as minister by the second vacancy committee that heard him on the first meeting with them. Our faith had never really been tested. Childlessness began to do that as nothing else had.

THE TESTING OF FAITH

Failure was new to us and failure in this most intimate area of life struck at the very heart of our identity and our faith. Why should God deny us this blessing? Was it because of some sin in either or both our lives? Was it punishment for something? Did God love us at all? Was it really worthwhile being 'righteous'? How could God give children to those who were patently unsuitable for the task of parenting and yet deny us the chance to give security and love? Was God really there at all? There were all these questions of a negative nature arising out of feelings of failure and guilt. No matter how much we prayed they never seemed to be given an answer. This experience seems to us very like that of Job reflected in many passages e.g. 19:7-20:

7 Though I cry, 'I've been wronged!' I get no response; though I call for help, there is no justice.

8 He has blocked my way so that I cannot pass; he has shrouded my paths in darkness.

9 He has stripped me of my honour and removed the crown from my head.

10 He tears me down on every side till I am gone; he uproots my hope like a tree.

11 His anger burns against me; he counts me among his enemies.

12 His troops advance in force; they build a siege ramp against me and encamp around my tent.

13 He has alienated my brothers from me; my acquaintances are completely estranged from me.

14 My kinsmen have gone away; my friends have forgotten me.

15 My guests and my maidservants count me a stranger; they look upon me as an alien.

16 I summon my servant, but he does not answer, though I beg him with my own mouth.

17 My breath is offensive to my wife; I am loathsome to my own brothers.

18 Even the little boys scorn me; when I appear, they ridicule me.

19 All my intimate friends detest me; those I love have turned against me.

20 I am nothing but skin and bones; I have escaped by only the skin of my teeth.

There were some more positive questions too. Was childlessness a blessing in disguise? Did God know that despite our instincts we would somehow be hopeless parents? Was God doing this to save us from the pain of a miscarriage or a handicapped child? These questions received no more answer than did the negative ones.

What if God never gave us answers? Would we still trust him? Like Job we began to sense that despite the pain of it all there must be a purpose. God must be in it somewhere. After pouring out his feelings in Chapter 19 Job goes on to say in the same Chapter,

25 I know that my Redeemer lives, and that in the end he will stand upon the earth.

26 And after my skin has been destroyed, yet in my flesh I will see God;

27 I myself will see him with my own eyes - I, and not another. How my heart yearns within me!

We struggled a great deal but basically our struggles were struggles of faith. From Job's experience we saw it was because we had faith that we struggled at all.

We saw that we had to accept that we might never have answers but that God had answers just the same. We had to trust him. What other option was there?

JOB'S COMFORTERS

Yet our friends, like Job's did not always see things that way. We were actually sent a book once by Derek Prince entitled *Blessing or Curse: You can Choose*. It was about the curses and blessings of Deuteronomy and the message clearly was that our childlessness was due to some unconfessed sin in our lives - just the approach Job's friends took with him. We found this extremely hurtful and it only served to create further gloomy introspection.

Most of our friends, thankfully were not like that. We found that real friends were those who didn't try to give answers when there were none. They simply listened to us, suffered with us and affirmed us as individuals and as a couple. They loved us, which is what any suffering person most needs. Those who suffer do not need sermons of pat doctrine preached at them; they need true humanity from their friends. Job's friends patently lacked that. They knew much about truth but little about grace. We are thankful for our friends who knew both and who waited with us to discover whether God would reveal his purpose in our suffering. This brings us to our third biblical character - Hannah.

HANNAH - PURPOSE IN SUFFERING

In reading of Hannah's experience we again found many echoes of our own. For example she was extremely sensitive to the comments of Penninah, her rival in love. We found we were often over-sensitive to the comments of other people. Parishioners would say to Graham, "Is your wife still working then?" in a kind of questioning voice that, rightly or wrongly, made us feel guilty about not having children. Eventually Graham gained enough courage to say something like, "Things in life don't always work out the way you plan them". Without saying too much this gave the hint something was wrong and those kind of comments soon stopped.

But there was also the sensitivity to other people always talking about their children and there was the pain which inevitably accompanied the happy news of another pregnancy among our family, circle of friends or even the parish. That pain never lessened with the years although it was always easier once the pregnancy produced an actual baby who naturally drew love and affection.

But it is not that aspect of Hannah's experience which was most important for us. It was rather the fact that through her own grief and sorrow she began to understand something of God's agony over his people and his purposes for them. Hannah's prayer in chapter two of 1 Samuel surely shows that as Hannah struggled with her own grief she grew in her knowledge of God.

Hannah lived in times when the people of God were in spiritual and moral decline. There was plenty of religion still. People still went to worship but there was no real heart devotion or holy living. Everyone, as the Book of Judges says, "did what was right in their own eyes". Everyone had their own ideas about God, religion and morals. There were no objective standards because the Word of God was scarce. An unfaithful priesthood had failed to teach it. Where there is no vision the people perish and with no spiritual vision the nation was politically unstable, under threat from the neighbouring Philistines and ripe for invasion. From this prayer of Hannah in chapter two of 1 Samuel we see Hannah was convinced God was about to begin a work of renewal through her son. The focus of that prayer is God and His Character, His Word to her, his purposes; it is not on herself or even her precious child which she is about to part with, but God whom she praises.

But how and where does such a work of God begin? In this case it began in the suffering soul of Hannah. The bitterness of her childlessness made her pour out her heart to God. There she found release for her tension. No doubt her prayers at first, like her sorrow, were intensely personal. Childlessness, as we have indicated already, is not an easy thing for anyone, man or woman to speak about; it is too painful and personal. Hannah's prayers would have been like that at first, maybe in danger of being self-pitying and self-centred. She was probably very confused at times not knowing what to pray. She would, like Job, protest her innocence and ask why God was punishing her. Yet at the same time she would be asking him to show her where she had displeased him. That is all in 1 Samuel chapter 1.

Hannah's prayer in chapter two shows us how her praying changed as time passed. Her world grew bigger and the issues she confronted grew far larger than just her own sorrow and disgrace. The writer of 1 Samuel, whoever he was, tries to show us that. He tells us in chapter one that it was whenever Hannah went to the Temple that she became more unsatisfied and miserable and the tension between her rival and herself grew worse. We might have expected the opposite surely? Surely going to Church ought to have helped her and brought her peace and contentment. Why was it then that these visits made things worse?

It was because on those visits she was confronted with problems far more serious than those of her own home circle and a sorrow far more acute than her own. When she got there she saw so much that was wrong - the degrading practices that went on, the evidences of pagan superstition, the temple prostitutes, the drunkenness, the blatant greed of the priests stealing the sacrifices of the people. She began to think how God must feel. She thought of the love he had lavished on them in the past and all he meant them to be and she felt shame, concern, anger - a burden. She felt a burden and calling to his service in this crisis, especially in the service of prayer. She saw what was needed was a Saviour, a new leader, a man called and gifted to change all this and so, gradually, her sorrow became re-oriented. She was no longer concerned for herself so much as for God's glory and the blessing of His people. Her prayer in effect became, "Thy Kingdom come, thy will be done".

Is this not where God points all of us whenever we suffer in any kind of way? Was this what God was trying to teach us? For ourselves, we began to believe it was. At the risk of being misunderstood we would say that, for us, the pain of childlessness revealed to us something of the pain of God himself as he looks upon a fallen, Christless world.

The grief of childlessness is acute. But it has no focus and no object. It just seems to stretch forever into the future, even to the loneliness of old age. But God's grief must be even more acute because his grief *has* a focus. He grieves over a humanity made up of individuals who are walking the face of the earth yet who are spiritually dead and seem intent on remaining like that for all eternity.

In Hannah's story God was working Hannah's grief into his good purposes. In some senses we are now beginning to see how God has been working all things together for good for us too. We would never have had Lee come to live with us if we had children of our own and we feel sure we could never have produced a child who gives us as much pleasure as he does.

Yet we are very aware that for many who read this there will still be no resolution of any of the questions childlessness raises. Papers like this are always written by those whose story has a happy ending. But there is something else we need to bear in mind and it is this. At the beginning of this paper we cited Dr Ray Mealyea speaking of the pain of childlessness which those who have never experienced it cannot understand.

She also goes on to say this:

> On the other hand childless couples will never be able to understand the frustration of parents who just want a moment to themselves, parents who are exhausted by the constant demands of small children, who really don't want to hear the word 'Mummy' again for at least 20 minutes, parents who long to have a week-end away from their kids, who think that their childless friends should be glad of their freedom.[6]

The author recognises there that parenthood is not, and never has been, a bed of roses. We now realise that as we hurt in our childlessness and complained of the insensitivity of others to our pain, maybe we were insufficiently sensitive to others who carried the burdens of child-bearing. With good cause the proverb says that "the grass is always greener on the other side of the fence".

From all this we draw the conclusion that for childless couples parenthood will not solve deeper problems, real spiritual problems. The gift of children will not teach what the Bible calls purity of heart, defined in a prize winning sermon by the Rev Barry Overend as "the secret of how to wear your successes without arrogance and to bear your failures without resentment; the secret of how to admire without envy, reproach without malice, care without condescending and love without lusting"[7]. Nor will the advent of children in and of itself create the contentment which Paul indicates is something the Christian ought to have regardless of whether he or she is in need or has plenty (Philippians 4:12).

Is not producing these qualities of character what God's work in the human soul is all about? The work of the Spirit is to create the character of Christ in us. It is to cause us to live like Christ for the glory of God. That is what Hannah learned through her childlessness. Our childlessness may have been one of God's ways of teaching us the same. Was our childlessness therefore really the answer to our own prayer to be like Christ? Was the answer we demanded of God actually staring us in the face all the time? We rather believe it was. Prayer is a dangerous thing! Contentment in the Christian life does not find its source in receiving God's gifts but in knowing and loving the Giver Himself.

CONCLUSION

The grief of childldessness has been God's way with us. Through it he has been opening us up to a deeper appreciation of his majesty and grace and with it, we hope, a deeper compassion for others. He has a great deal more to teach us yet. With others he may have to use something entirely different, yet equally painful. God is the Surgeon of the human soul, the Great Physician and when he wounds it is only and always to heal. He always makes the right kind of incision in the right place at the right time.

Many years ago we read these words of Edith Schaeffer, written in connection with marriage but with a wisdom that would apply to much of life. She wrote:

The solution to a fight, argument, difference of opinion or unthoughtfulness on the part of another person is not splitting up and finding other human beings to live with, but learning to understand the other person and seeking to find solutions which are not perfect but which are *possible*. When people insist on perfection or nothing they get nothing. When people insist on having what they daydream of as the perfect relationship they will end up having no relationship at all. (*The waste of what could be by demanding what cannot be is something we all do at different times in our lives and it is tragic*).[8]

We believe that as we went through the agony of childlessness we were, many times, in danger of doing just that. We were in danger of wasting what could be by demanding what could not be. Yet God allowed the childlessness to make us aware of that and to reveal his heart to us.

Joy Cooke relates the experience of one woman she knew, called Marilyn:

Marilyn told me how she fought long and hard to come to terms with God's harsh ruling and to accept the knowledge that she would never have her own genetic children.

'It took me a long time to accept that God really didn't want us to have children of our own. I was very rebellious and I had to pray daily about this, until finally God gave me the strength to accept it. When this happened I knew that it was a big step forward'.

What had Marilyn learnt that she would like to pass on to others who had no hope of ever having a family? I think the most important thing you have to learn is to live with yourself and accept the situation as it is. You have to find out what God actually wants for you. You see, it is so easy to get caught up in the norm; marriage, a house, a mortgage, a car, a colour television, a video, a holiday abroad and a family. But is this actually God's norm, is this what he wants for you?[9]

What God wants must be best, because God is God, even when we cannot understand his reasons. This is the place God has brought us to through our pain. He will use the pain for good purposes according to His Word. He will use whatever we suffer to discover more of his will and to make us more like the Christ we claim to follow.

One bible passage that Alison found helpful throughout our experience was Psalm 119, verses 105-112:

105 Your word is a lamp to my feet and a light to my path.

106 I have taken an oath and confirmed it, that I will follow your righteous laws.

107 I have suffered much; preserve my life, O Lord, according to your word.

108 Accept, O Lord, the willing praise of my mouth, and teach me your laws.

109 Though I constantly take my life in my hands, I will not forget your law.

110 The wicked have set a snare for me, but I have not strayed from your precepts.

111 Your statutes are my heritage for ever; they are the joy of my heart.

112 My heart is set on keeping your decrees to the very end.

After meditating on these words she wrote:

I could recognise that I had suffered but that was not the end of the story. God, through his word was going to renew me. In spite of all my struggles, God had some purpose in it all. Having a child was not the most important thing - having a heart set on keeping God's laws to the end was what God really wanted.

These words place the issue of Childlessness where it surely belongs for the Christian - where every issue belongs for the Christian - firmly under the Sovereignty of God.

A PRAYER FOR THE CHILDLESS FAMILY

"O Lord, our Lord, how majestic is your name in all the earth. You have set your glory above the heavens. From the lips of children and infants you have ordained praise."

We thank you for all the joys and blessings of family life and for your faithful love and help when things are difficult and fraught. But today we want to pray especially for those who long to have children and cannot. May you be present to comfort in the midst of that strange grief which has no focus for its tears and no object for its love.

Help them to cope with and conquer feelings of failure and low self-esteem. Help husbands and wives to be able to be honest about their feelings with each other that you may pour out your Spirit to cleanse and to heal. Give them wisdom to know the avenues to explore in terms of medical intervention or adoption that all may remain within your will.

Help them to make the most of all the opportunities that their added freedom gives albeit unsought and unwanted. May they not waste what is possible by dreaming about what is impossible. Bring them to the point where they can say with Job: 'He knows the way that I take; when he has tested me I shall come forth as gold'.

Help us all, whatever our situation in life, married or single, childless or blessed with family, to be sensitive to one another's needs and to carry one another's burdens, for the sake of Jesus' Name. Amen.''

[1] *Childlessness* - p 3, a paper given by Dr Ray Mealyea to a Study Group of the Church of Scotland Board of Social Responsibility on Human Fertilisation and Embryology.

[2] GIFT stands for Gamete Intra-Fallopian Transfer.

[3] November 29th 1995.

[4] The Free Church Federal Council and the British Council of Churches 1982 cited by Joy Cooke, *Why Us Lord?* (Marshall Pickering 1985) pp 42-43.

[5] Joy Cooke, *op.cit.* p 55.

[6] Mealyea, *op.cit.* p. 3.

[7] *The Times* 4th November 1995. This sermon won the Newspaper's 'Preacher of the Year' competition.

[8] Edith Schaeffer, *What is a Family?*, p. 70.

[9] Joy Cooke, *Why Us Lord?* (Marshall Pickering 1985) p.144.

Chapter 6 SINGLENESS

David C. Searle

Introduction

The question of singleness is one that requires to be addressed urgently by the Church today for a number of reasons. First, about one third of members of churches in the United Kingdom are single. While the churches are attempting to offer pre- and post-marriage counselling, little is being done at present to offer help to those who are single.

Second, while singleness was for generations regarded as an honourable state, there is a modern insistence, fostered by the media and accepted by society, that all should seek personal satisfaction in sexual intercourse. This trend is unquestionably bringing great pressure on many single people who are being persuaded that they are not really experiencing life in its fullness unless and until they have a sexual partner. Further, there very often can be an unspoken depreciation of singleness even within the churches with the result that many single people can be made to feel that they are second class citizens. Compare, for example, the way in which unemployed persons feel when in company they are asked the typical introductory question, "What do you do in life?" It can often be the same for singles some of whom find it hard to answer that they are unmarried.

Third, the whole basis of the decision to marry actually depends upon a high view of singleness. Unless singleness is accepted by society as good and fulfilling, too many young people will decide to marry, at times unwisely and without careful thought, simply to escape from the 'trap' of singleness. That certainly is the case for an increasing number today, both within and outside the churches. I know of young women especially who were resolved to marry at all costs because they were afraid of being 'left on the shelf', and so they consequently married without due thought and soon regretted their choice of marriage partner. Had the single state been more honourable in society's thinking, those young women might have been less hasty.

For these three reasons (among many others), singleness is an issue of some urgency for the churches to examine. It is important that, as in all areas of daily living, Christian thinking should not be dictated to by secular society, but should be based upon the mind and will of God revealed to us in Scripture and through our Lord's teaching and example.

Biblical Base

There can be no doubt that in the Old Testament era, singleness was most uncommon. It was understood from Genesis 1:28 (*God blessed them and said to them, "Be fruitful and increase in number; fill the earth and subdue it"*) that men and women were to marry since procreation was a divine command. However, certain significant people in the Old Testament were unmarried. Apart from Nehemiah and Daniel, whom many presume to have been eunuchs by virtue of their appointment to the civil service of Persian emperors, we know that Jeremiah was unmarried,[1] and suspect that Elijah may also have been unmarried.

When we come to the New Testament, it is clear that John the Baptist was unmarried, and that Paul (whatever his marital status might have been in earlier life) saw singleness as ideal for his calling to be a missionary and church planter. We could also include the four daughters of Philip the Evangelist in the unmarried category,[2] though the argument from silence may be erroneous; we cannot know whether they remained unmarried all their lives.

Consider the Lord's own saying about singleness in Matt. 19:8-12:

8: *Jesus replied, "Moses permitted you to divorce your wives because your hearts were hard. But it was not this way from the beginning.*

9: *I tell you that anyone who divorces his wife, except for marital unfaithfulness, and marries another woman commits adultery."*

10: *The disciples said to him, "If this is the situation between a husband and wife, it is better not to marry."*

11: *Jesus replied, "Not everyone can accept this word, but only those to whom it has been given.*

12: *For some are eunuchs because they were born that way; others were made that way by men; and others have renounced marriage because of the kingdom of heaven. The one who can accept this should accept it".*

The context is a discussion about divorce. When the Lord states that ideally in God's purpose for men and women divorce and remarriage should be restricted to cases of marital infidelity, the disciples apparently find such a standard so unattainable that they ask whether celibacy is therefore to be commended. The Lord's answer requires careful study.

First, *"Not everyone can accept this word, but only those to whom it is given."* This may be taken as intended to refer to the Lord's statement on marriage and divorce. Understanding it in this way, he is saying that not everyone can accept so high a standard. Some will accept it and live by it. Many cannot.

The question is whether Matthew intends us to understand these words not only as a comment on what the Lord has just said, but also as applying to what he is about to say about celibacy. Calvin certainly understood them as introducing the saying on singleness:

> If anyone imagines that it is to his advantage to be without a wife and so without further consideration decides to be celibate, he is very much in error. For God who declared that it was good that the woman should be the helpmeet for the man, will exact punishment for contempt for his ordinance. Men arrogate too much to themselves when they try to exempt themselves from their heavenly calling [sc. marriage]. That it is not open to all to choose which state they please, Christ proves from the fact that continence is a special gift. For when he says that only those are capable of it to whom it is given, he plainly means that it is not given to all. This convicts the arrogance of those who do not hesitate to claim for themselves what Christ so clearly refuses them.

While we suspect that Calvin is here tilting at the Roman Church's insistence that its priests be celibate, for our purpose in thinking about singleness it is interesting to note that he sees the gift as referring not only to the highest standard of marriage, but also to singleness in certain cases - for *those to whom it has been given*. (Other commentators also regard verse 11 as referring back to the divorce saying.[3])

It is nonetheless surprising that, after pointing out that marriage is a creation ordinance and therefore a divine gift which ought not to be dissolved, the Lord should then go on to say that for some singleness can also be a gift of God. Other commentators resolve the problem by suggesting that verses 10-12 did not originally belong to the divorce discussion but have been slotted in here by Matthew as a suitable place for them.[4] This would mean, of course, that the reference of verse 11 is to singleness and not to the earlier discussion on divorce.

Second, the saying about singleness:

12: *"For some are eunuchs because they were born that way; others were made that way by men; and others have renounced marriage because of the kingdom of heaven. The one who can accept this should accept it"*.

- **Some are eunuchs because they were born that way**

Of the three categories of those who are unmarried, it is the second and third which mostly concern us. I am taking this first category the Lord speaks of as referring to those who do not marry because they are physically incapable of consummating a sexual union: *some were born that way.* I am not for one moment suggesting that single people in this first group should not be part of our concern, but rather that this first group are perhaps few and far between compared to the second two groups. However, what we say about the other two categories will equally apply to the first category.

* **Others were made that way by men**

In her excellent little book on singleness, Heather Wraight calls those in this second category *single by circumstance*:

> For most people who are single, it is through no fault of their own, and they often feel they have been 'made that way by men', through the circumstances of their lives. I would put myself in this category, as would most of the single people I know.[5]

She goes on to speak of two generations of women this century who were unable to marry because the available men had been killed in the two world wars which claimed millions of lives.

There are also those who find marriage too forbidding because they experienced sexual abuse as children, or because they suffered greatly through the break-up of their parents' marriage. Every pastor is all too familiar with these pieces of human 'shrapnel' who are casualties of the shell-shock caused by the sins of others.

Included here also will be those who have longed to be married but 'have never been asked'. The prominent Anglican preacher and writer, J.W.R.Stott, was recently asked at a public meeting in Edinburgh if he was single because of a homosexual orientation. While those in the audience held their breath at the audacity of the questioner, Stott answered very calmly that he was grateful for the opportunity to assure those listening that his sexual orientation was thoroughly heterosexual, but that he was unmarried because he had never met the right person for him.

His answer leads us on to the third category the Lord spoke of:

* **Others have renounced marriage because of the kingdom of heaven**

This category would include those whose orientation is not heterosexual but who choose celibacy in order to be obedient to the laws of God which clearly forbid homosexual practice. It would also include missionaries who realise that they can only serve in certain inhospitable places if they remain single and therefore renounce marriage to fulfil their calling to evangelise. We should perhaps include certain ministers (and priests) who prefer singleness in order that they can wholly give themselves to the work of God.[6] (But we should note Calvin's strictures against those who insist on celibacy for religious reasons.) The publicity given recently to sexual aberrations by Roman Catholic priests confirms the Lord's words that only those to whom singleness has been given can accept it. Yet the gift may well be offered by Christ who enables singles to lead fulfilled and happy lives.

Paul's statements on the flexibility singleness gave him to engage in the Lord's work are often misunderstood. He was writing to Christians who were divided between the pull of a promiscuous society on the one hand and strict ascetic abstinence from all sexual relations on the other hand. He states that the Christian ethic has no room for sex outside marriage, but he also makes it clear that sexual relations within marriage are normal and God-given. What his discussion does teach us has been expressed well by Stanley Grenz:

> In the New Testament, then, single persons are welcomed as full participants in the work of the Lord. Their single status even offers pragmatic advantages for such service. But neither the single option nor a commitment to lifelong celibacy are ever set forth as the higher road to spirituality for believers.[7]

Coping with Singleness

If the apostle Paul could live life to the full as the Lord enabled him without a marriage partner, then ought it not to be possible for others to do the same? And ought not the Church to restore to a single life-style the honour and dignity which it deserves?

A choice of attitude

It has been suggested that in order to live a fulfilled single life, one has to be something of a radical in one's attitude.[8] This thinking posits the hypothesis that there are two different kinds of response to Christ's call to discipleship, that of the *steward* and that of the *radical*. The steward takes the gift of marriage and invests in it carefully, building a home and rearing a family for the sake of the kingdom. The radical, on the other hand, recklessly gives his or her life away for the sake of the kingdom. So the radical embraces singleness (as Paul did) in order to gain an independence through which to further the cause of the Gospel.

The radical is not terribly interested in preserving and hallowing the world as it exists. He is focused on the coming kingdom. He sees the practical demands of ordinary life as an interference: he would rather serve God only. Paul is his model. In him he sees an active, dedicated life in which no practical matter - finances, family needs, political realism - is allowed to interfere with the cause of God's kingdom.[9]

While this may be true of those in the Lord's third category, that is, those who renounce marriage for the sake of the kingdom, not all can be expected to have such a crusading spirit. There are many who come under Stafford's description of *steward* who have to face a life of singleness. They have passions that long to be fulfilled in intimate sexual experience; they have the deepest longing to have children; perhaps, most of all, they long to belong and to be loved. They have neither the inclination or disposition to be radical nor to choose singleness for the sake of the kingdom. Singleness has been thrust upon them.

But believers should bear in mind that Christ calls all his followers to reject the attitudes and standards of a world which does not care for God and to adopt a lifestyle which is marked by *renewal* and *transformation*.[10] If Christians are to embrace Christ's 'counter-culture' which demands we think and behave differently from others, then should our 'counter-culture' not also include our understanding of marriage and singleness? Unmarried Christians can choose to have a different attitude to singleness.

There are certain areas of living where the churches can be of enormous help to those who struggle with singleness. The first is by giving singles a clear sense of identity and helping them to make a clear choice. Not that they have chosen singleness, but rather that they can most certainly *choose to have a positive attitude* towards it. Such an attitude will be facilitated when a framework for living is provided by the church fellowship.

Belonging to a family

First, singles must know that they *belong to a family*. While many who are single already have a strong family structure of which they are part, many do not. Divorcees, those with a homosexual orientation, many widow(er)s are often more lonely than is realised.

The Old Testament makes it clear that God has a special concern for those who do not have the protection and comfort of an earthly family.[11] The New Testament describes the Christian Church in terms of a family in which God is Father, Christ is the Elder Brother, the Church is mother and the members are all brothers and sisters.[12] The Church therefore should fulfil its theology in practical daily outworking and provide a warm, strong family structure which embraces people living alone and makes them really part of its life.

This includes hospitality, perhaps particularly on a Sunday. It includes provision for holidays. Each summer, congregations of which I have been minister have organised holidays for members of the fellowship for whom holidays may be a problem. I think of single-parent families, divorcees, widows and those whose own families were not sympathetic to the Christian faith. My wife and I have personally included in our own holidays for many years single people and those with a homosexual orientation. Many who are single do not find holidays with other singles at all helpful; they appreciate the opportunity to share with a family. So we have arranged simple house parties and have booked either river cruisers which accommodate parties of eight, or accommodation in, say, a castle where a group of eight can be thoroughly at home and have a real sense of togetherness.

I am aware that Christian holidays are organised by various non-denominational bodies. However, I believe that there is a real need for each local fellowship to offer its members, both married and single, the opportunity to share a holiday on the basis of the wider family of the church.

Children

Second, single persons do need to be able to *care for children*. While some who are single find close contact with children too painful because of the deep emotional feelings that are aroused, most find regular contact with children helpful. I am not talking about consigning single people simply to work in the Sunday School or to act as unpaid baby-sitters. Rather I am suggesting that many single people would value a special relationship with a specific family with children so that a single man or woman could become a regular visitor to that family, and even be regarded as a member of the family. In today's society with high mobility, many children rarely see their natural aunts, uncles and grandparents. There is a real place for a Christian family adopting an "aunt" or "uncle" or "grandmother". Occasionally that does happen. But more often than not, the single Christian is expected to befriend another single Christian rather than to be included within a Christian family.

If a single person's home is suitable, occasional children's parties could be appropriate, or outings could be arranged for the children by the adopted 'aunt' to places of interest. It is significant that many men and women who have been mightily used in the work of the kingdom were actually nurtured in their childhood and youth by dedicated Christians who were unmarried, but who realised that the independence singleness gave could be used for the Christian nurture of children and young people. I myself thank God for certain dedicated Christians who were single and who gave time and love to me in order to keep me within a fellowship and to assist in my Christian upbringing.

Sexuality not sex

Third, single persons need to be able to *express and enjoy their sexuality.* It is a great mistake to confuse sexual activity and sexuality. Our sexuality is our essential masculinity or femininity. When God created man and woman, he created them a perfect pair. They were exactly complementary. While this complementarity is symbolised and expressed within marriage by sexual union, it does not need to be so. Men and women can work together and appreciate and benefit from the sexuality of the other in a purely business or professional relationship. For example, those working in a pastoral team, or as missionaries, will usually involve married people of both sexes working together with colleagues to whom they are not married. In their working relationship, unless the sexuality of each one finds full expression, and unless that expression is appreciated and valued by the others, there will be both tension and frustration. As a result of a such an unsatisfactory relationship the work will suffer.

On the other hand, where colleagues appreciate the sexuality of each other, and that sexuality is encouraged to make its full contribution to the working relationship, the work will flourish. I suspect it is true to say that men are more guilty than women in failing to encourage their working partners' sexuality to have its fullest expression in work. Men's besetting sin is that they either dominate their women colleagues and act as archetypal chauvinists or else they exploit their femininity and are guilty of sexual harassment (implied if not practised).

Both men and women have to learn to respect the other's sexuality and to discover the enormous rewards of working together as partners, allowing each other's sexuality to have expression within the working relationship. Often, women are far more 'people-oriented' than their male partners; consequently they have a particular understanding of many problems which will be complementary to a man's understanding. Fostering this male-female partnership is something in which the churches must give the lead. Single people can find great fulfilment in being accepted with a genuineness and reality which does not in any way stifle their sexuality. (I am not here referring to the place of women in the ministry. That is quite a separate issue for it may be as unbalanced in the male-female partnership as a male dominated ministry).

The meaning of sex

The traditional Christian ethic prohibits sexual intercourse outside marriage. In recent times, this prohibition has been misrepresented as narrow-mindedness and caricatured as the deliberate attempt to repress perfectly natural sexual desires. It needs hardly be said that the Christian moral stance which forbids sex outside of marriage has the highest and noblest reasons, namely, to guard the sanctity of sexual union and to safeguard the community of male and female. What then is the meaning of sexual intercourse? Stanley Grenz offers a threefold explanation of sexual union within marriage.[13]

First, the sex act recalls the commitment of husband and wife to each other. It is a kind of re-enactment of their marriage vows and thus is designed by God to represent and effect the marriage bonding.

Second, sexual intercourse also is an act of mutual submission.[14] In this way, husband and wife express to each other their desire to please each other. Sex outside a stable relationship of full commitment cannot communicate this vital element of marriage. Indeed, outwith such a stable relationship, sex will either have self-gratification as its goal or else will be a means of manipulating the partner.

Third, sexual intercourse implicitly declares that this relationship is open to another in that procreation is effected through sex. Although family may be carefully planned through birth control, basic to sexual union is this vital possibility of bringing another living person into the world, but not merely into the world, also into the union of husband and wife so that it develops into a family. Sexual union outside marriage will invariably fear such an openness, and do all possible to prevent a child invading the relationship. Hence, marriage is the only proper context for sexual union.

It is clear therefore that singleness precludes the sexual act. Nevertheless, these three meanings of physical union have their analogues within the life of the Christian community in that the bonding of men and women in Christ within the church must be allowed constantly to re-enact their mutual commitment in love, must be characterised by mutual submission, and must give birth to new life in those being added to the kingdom of God through the fellowship's evangelism.

Bonding

The subject of sexuality leads on, fourth, to the subject of 'bonding' in that the two are inextricably related to each other. We first read of bonding in Genesis 2:24: *For this reason a man will leave his father and mother and be united to his wife, and they will become one flesh.* While the bonding of a man and wife includes the 'sacrament' of physical union, it involves far more than that. The sexuality of the man and woman is expressed, as we have just noted, in their complementarity as male and female.

The single man and woman have the strong compulsion towards bonding even though they are not married. And that bonding can be achieved outside of marriage, for physical union is not necessary for it. In my view, the church's theology has failed to recognise that bonding is provided for within the theology of the New Testament. Believers are bonded to the community of faith. Baptism and the Lord's Supper are both characterised by pledges of spiritual bonding of believers together in Christ. *Because there is one loaf, we who are many are one body, for we all partake of the one loaf*[15].

Without this bonding, we are incomplete as persons. The male is incomplete without the female, and vice versa. We need other humans in order to find fulfilment and to be complete persons. Our churches tend to be far too individualistic and too few Christians are aware of the theology of bonding within the Christian community. Our togetherness in Christ demands a commitment to one another which is unfortunately rare in our society. Bonding is expressed in love and intimacy as well as in a deep spirit of commitment to one another.

Love

Fifth, singles must experience *love*. It is significant to note that the Bible never actually uses the Greek word *eros*. Yet the fellowship of believers is to be characterised by love, whether *agape, storge* or *philia*. Our reluctance in many churches to encourage deeper relationships (perhaps based on home groups) unquestionably denies many people the opportunity both to love and to be loved as they ought as followers of Christ. Some fellowships are fairly small and the group dynamics make it easy for those in the 'body' to care for each other in a compassionate, deep way. But in larger fellowships, the likelihood is that the dynamic natural to a larger group will cause people unconsciously to form unofficial associations within their church, and that is where single people can often be neglected. For example, the young people meet after evening service in someone's home; those with teenagers at University invite each other round to chat about their siblings' progress; those who have been on summer mission together go out for a coffee. But so many lonely people, on the perimeter of the fellowship, feel left out.

The problem arises most acutely when a single person moves home and is faced with (what can be) the daunting task of finding a new church to join. Small closer fellowships can be hard to break into. The unofficial groups are already established, and their configuration is a tight circle into which it can be almost impossible to find access. Singles in the fellowship have already paired off with other singles. And so the vicious circle continues its downward spiral.

Every Christian fellowship should consciously work at being in the form of an open horse-shoe configuration (as distinct from a closed circle) so that strangers are always welcome and find it easy to join the group. Those who are sensitive to the needs of other people should be ever alert to the stranger or lonely visitor and be ready with gentleness and loving care to invite him or her to join a group where bonding is in evidence, but where fresh bonding can take place. It demands sacrificial love for such an ethos to be prevalent within a congregation. Most people tend to be unconsciously exclusive in their friendship and enjoy having a few friends specially for themselves. If we are to keep our circle of friends wide open to others, our friendship love must be selfless and self-giving, not selfish and self-seeking.

Perhaps single people can have an invaluable role in a congregation by recognising the need for this openness and by offering loving concern and care to strangers who may come to church, searching for that indefinable 'something' that will meet their deepest needs. Too often such seekers enter and leave a church with little more than a nod and a handshake - sometimes they don't even get that!

I know well a single woman who has transformed an entire congregation through her selfless love. Every meeting of the church has been influenced by her unobtrusive work of quietly moving round from one group to another, welcoming newcomers and introducing them to established members of the fellowship. She is known and loved in her congregation and is recognised as having a ministry that has turned a very reserved group of people into an open, loving church which not only welcomes the lonely and the stranger, but also shares with them the love of Christ.

Intimacy

Arising from the need for love is the need also, sixth, for *intimacy*. Again, we must not confuse intimacy with sexual intercourse. It is only too possible to engage in the latter without the former. Conversely, it is certainly possible to have the former without the latter. I suspect that in facing the problem of aloneness, the single person actually craves more for intimacy than for a sexual relationship. David and Jonathan enjoyed true intimacy, but I do not for one moment regard their intimate love for each other as having been sexual.[16]

What do we mean by intimacy? Art Carey has attempted a definition:

- believing in someone and something above and beyond yourself
- developing a private vocabulary and communicating without words
- having someone who truly cares, someone who will stand by you when you get sick, or falter and fail
- having someone you believe in, and who believes in you, tells you at times that you're the best, and at other times that you can do better
- having a common history and mutual memories and a sense of having travelled together[17]

While many singles do have friends with whom they have developed a pure and enriching intimacy, there are others who are afraid of allowing another to become as close to them as that. They long for something, and in a society which deifies sex can mistake their desire for intimacy as the longing for the sexual act. The reality is that a chaste intimacy would answer deep longings within them.

Such a relationship is not easy. Society's lie is that intimacy will come by sharing someone's sheets for a few nights. But true intimacy needs much hard work. It needs commitment, communication, the willingness to run the risk of being hurt and, above all, time. No relationship of any value is instant, whatever the *Mills & Boon* stories might say. To become truly intimate with a friend, one must "go deeper and deeper into each other until there are no secrets left, no illusions, nothing but respect for each other's frailty and dignity".[18.]

A final issue that perhaps needs to be touched on is the matter of sexual tension and frustration which some single people unquestionably experience. We have tried to suggest that involvement with a family, care of children, expression of one's sexuality, love and intimacy will enable the single person to practise sublimation of sexual desires. But for some there will be a raging battle which has to be fought, and in which the heat of desire ebbs and flows quite unpredictably. Harold Smith makes the following comment:

> Single adults must learn to channel their sex drives in a way that will not offend. Thus, what one finds sublimating will be questionable to another. Many single adults find masturbation

a subtle sublimation of the sex drives. It rechannels the drive from illicit sexual intercourse. Many singles regard masturbation as the lesser of two evils.[19]

On the other hand, Heather Wraight reminds her readers that Jesus taught the lustful look and thought were in essence as wrong as the actual deed.[20] In today's society, it is vital that the single person works hard at maintaining purity of mind. Every thought must be brought into captivity and be obedient to Christ. Every one of us fails many times in this way, but we must remember that there is grace to cleanse and forgive each moment of each day, and we must never abandon the fight to keep our hearts pure, as Christ is pure.

This brief paper leaves many issues of singleness untouched. The final word must be to remind us all of Christ. He took children in his arms and blessed them. He shared a home and was welcomed into the bosom of many families such as that of Lazarus, Martha and Mary. He was particularly intimate with John, the disciple he specially loved. Let Christ be the pattern for those who for whatever reason find themselves living as singles. May we all live more and more to God's glory, and for the fulfilment of his kingdom.

[1] Jer. 16:2 "You must not marry and have sons or daughters in this place."

[2] Acts 21:8f.

[3] sic. Hendriksen, NTC Matthew, Banner of Truth, Edinburgh, 1973, p.718; Michael Green, Matthew for Today, Hodder & Stoughton, London, 1988, p.182.

[4] A H McNeile, The Gospel According to Matthew, MacMillan, New York, 1955, p.275.

[5] Heather Wraight, Single the Jesus Model, Crossway Books, Leicester, 1995, p.18f.

[6] See Paul in I Corinthians 7: esp. vs. 29-35.

[7] Stanley Grenz, Sexual Ethics, Word Publishing, Dallas, 1990, p.167.

[8] Tim Stafford, Sexual Chaos, IVP, Leicester, 1993, p.141ff.

[9] Idem. p.143.

[10] Romans 12:1-2.

[11] Exodus 22:22-24; Ps68:5f; Isaiah 10:2, etc.

[12] Romans 8:14-16, 29; Gal.4:26; 6:10; Eph.2:19, etc.

[13] Stanley Grenz, ibid., p.181-2.

[14] Eph. 5:21.

[15] 1 Cor.10:17

[16] 1 Samuel 18:1ff; 20:41f; 23:16ff; 2 Samuel 1:26.

[17] Art Carey, In Defense of Marriage, Walker, New York, 1984, p.89.

[18] Idem., p.123.

[19] Harold Ivan Smith, Single and Feeling Good, Abingdon Press, Nashville, 1987, p.54.

[20] Op.cit., p.83.

Chapter 7 DIVORCE: THEOLOGICAL AND PASTORAL CONSIDERATIONS

David W. Torrance

Marriage is one of God's greatest and most joyful gifts. It is always a privilege to be present at a wedding and to share in the happiness and joy of two people when together in love they take their vows in the presence of God and promise to be loving faithful and loyal to each other until death shall separate them. Life together is for them full of happy, joyous, expectation.

It is therefore very disappointing and utterly tragic for the couple and for their friends and well-wishers, when some years (or even months) later, the happiness and the joyous expectations are gone. The love which the couple had for each other and which they declared openly before others has apparently vanished (or vanished on the part of one of the partners) and the marriage which augured so well, ends in divorce. Tragically, in this country today, and in the countries of the Western world, this has become all too common. Recent figures indicate that at least 40 per cent of marriages in the UK will end in divorce. This is the highest figure for any European country.

It is God's will that marriage should be permanent, a lasting partnership for life. This is clear from the very way in which God created marriage. "For this reason a man will leave his father and mother and be united to his wife, and they will become one flesh".[1] That is, they will become one whole person, reflecting in their relationship with each other God's relationship with his people. In their togetherness they reflect the image of God. Jesus in quoting from this passage in Genesis put his seal on this interpretation and reinforced the permanence of marriage as belonging to the Divine command and added, "Therefore, what God has joined together, let not man separate".[2]

Although a matter of grave concern to the Church, it is not our concern in this chapter to ask, why God's will is not carried through and why so many marriages end in divorce. It is our concern here simply to accept that divorce is a frequent event and to consider what the Church's attitude should be, theologically and pastorally, when confronted with the reality and tragedy of divorce.

THEOLOGICAL CONSIDERATIONS

In this sinful world in which we live, despite God's desire for the permanence of marriage, is divorce in so far as it happens theologically acceptable? - and should the Church re-marry those who are divorced? These are questions with which the churches still wrestle and to-date different branches of the Church have given different answers. We need to look at various passages both in the Old and New Testaments in considering this problem.

IS DIVORCE THEOLOGICALLY ACCEPTABLE?

A passage in the Old Testament sometimes quoted in an attempt to try to justify divorce is Deuteronomy chapter 24 verses 1-4. "If a man marries a woman who becomes displeasing to him because he finds something indecent about her, and he writes her a certificate of divorce, gives it to her and sends her from his house, and if after she leaves his house she becomes the wife of another man, and her second husband dislikes her and writes her a certificate of divorce, gives it to her and sends her from his house, or if he dies, then her first husband who divorced her, is not allowed to marry her again after she has been defiled. That would be detestable in the eyes of the Lord". This passage became the subject of strong debate in Rabbinic circles and has been much debated in Gentile and Christian circles.

Ideally the Jew hated divorce. God had said, "I hate divorce".[3] The Rabbis had some important sayings. "God is long-suffering to every sin except the sin of unchastity". "Unchastity causes the glory of God to depart". "Every Jew must surrender his life rather than commit idolatry, murder or adultery". "The very altar sheds tears when a man divorces the wife of his youth".[4] In the light of this what does Deuteronomy 24:1-4, mean?

What is primarily at issue in this passage is the forbidding of the remarriage of a divorced woman to her first husband if she has subsequently married and been divorced or widowed. Moses says that if a woman has been divorced from a first and then second husband, or that second husband dies, she may not return and be re-married to her first husband. "That would be detestable in the eyes of the Lord". That is to say, this passage does not specifically authorise divorce and neither does any other passage in the Old Testament. Nonetheless by implication divorce is not ruled out. It is presupposed and accepted.

What is meant by "something indecent about her"? Some, like the school of Shammai understood it as meaning unchastity and nothing more. Others like the school of Hillel took a more open, permissive, view. It was their opinion that a woman could be divorced for many and even quite frivolous reasons, such as serving up to her husband a badly cooked or over salted meal! Sinful human nature being what it is, the majority of men in Jesus' day (a woman in Judaic law could not divorce) seemed to favour the more liberal, permissive, approach of Hillel to divorce. As a result despite the high ideals of Jewish teaching about marriage, in Jesus' day as in our day, marriage and the home were in danger of collapse.

Jesus in the Sermon on the Mount made clear how the Deuteronomic passage should be interpreted. Jesus said, "It has been said, Anyone who divorces his wife must give her a certificate of divorce. But I tell you that anyone who divorces his wife, except for marital unfaithfulness, causes her to become an adulteress, and anyone who marries the divorced woman commits adultery".[5]

In Mark 10:1-12, we have another, fuller statement where Jesus clearly condemns divorce. The Pharisees asked, "Is it lawful for a man to divorce his wife?" Jesus replied, "It was because your hearts were hard that Moses wrote you this law. But at the beginning of creation God made them male and female. For this reason a man will leave his father and mother and be united to his wife, and the two will become one flesh. So they are no longer two, but one. Therefore what God has joined together, let man not separate". From this passage we can say two things.

First, it is God's will that the marriage covenant should be permanent. The break down of marriage together with divorce have no part in God's plan for the world. Jesus' words make that abundantly clear. "What God has joined together, let man not separate". Marriage break down and divorce are grievous to God.

In his reply to the question of the Pharisees and the subsequent question of his disciples suggesting that it may be better not to marry, Jesus affirmed that marriage is a call from God to life-long, indissoluble partnership. Marriage and its continuance is not just a matter of human desire and volition. Jesus affirmed its permanency as a matter of God's call and command.

Second, because of sin and the inability of men and women to live perfect lives in this world, the Bible in its teaching accepts divorce in certain circumstances such as unchastity.

The Bible sets forth the claims of the Gospel. It declares its high ideals in regard to marriage and in regard to the whole area of Christian life and conduct on this earth. We are called to accept these ideals. We are continually challenged by them and called to endeavour by the grace of God to live up to them. Any falling short of these high ideals is sin and for that we need constantly to be cleansed, forgiven and renewed by His Holy Spirit. Try as we might however no one can live up perfectly to these high ideals. All of us constantly fall short. Furthermore in this sinful disordered world where nothing is perfect we are frequently faced with a conflict of duties and responsibilities. In these situations we need to seek to carry through those responsibilities which we feel to be the greater. We need to choose to do what we feel to be the lesser evil, accepting that for us it is practically right in the situation in which we find ourselves. Yet in so doing we need to ask for God's forgiveness in our falling short and for his renewal of us. We are men and women living in a sinful world, who are saved only by God's grace, not by our living righteous lives. We are men and women who are utterly dependent on God's grace and need constantly through prayer to receive His grace, His guidance and renewal.

Because of our inability always to maintain the sanctity and permanence of the marriage bond, the Bible in its teaching accepts divorce, when we are faced with an irretrievable breakdown in marriage. In these circumstances divorce may be the lesser evil. At times it may be desirable and right, even necessary, for a couple to divorce. This does not mean the hallowing of divorce. For even in these circumstances divorce together with all that has led to it is still wrong. It is wrong even although in these circumstances divorce may be the lesser evil and necessary. In divorce, however right and necessary, both parties need the cleansing and forgiveness of God.

Certain other passages in the Old as well as the New Testament also need to be considered.

In the Old Testament such passages as Ezra 9 and 10 and Nehemiah 13:23f are important. In them divorce is not simply accepted but encouraged and commanded when it is a matter of the Gentile and pagan partner leading the believing Jewish partner into evil practices and apostasy. Even so, this encouragement or command to divorce in these circumstances cannot be interpreted as denying or lessening the sanctity and permanency of marriage between two believing partners who belong to God's covenant people. These passages need to be interpreted in the light of the teaching of Deuteronomy chapter 7.

In Deuteronomy 7:1-4, the People of Israel are told that they must not inter-marry with any of the pagan peoples who formerly occupied the Land of Canaan, and they must not allow their sons and daughters to inter-marry. The reason for this Divine prohibition is clearly stated. "For they will turn your sons away from following me to serve other gods, and the Lord's anger will burn against you and will quickly destroy you". At Peor, the people of Israel sinned in this way. In accord with the evil advice that the prophet Balaam gave to Midian,[6] the Midianites and Israelites inter-married and, as a direct result, turned from following the Lord. "The men began to indulge in sexual immorality with Moabite women, who invited them to the sacrifices to their gods. The people ate and bowed down before these gods. So Israel joined in worshipping the Baal of Peor. And the Lord's anger burned against them".[7] There followed the swift judgment of God when many Israelites perished. God, through his prophets, continually reminded the people of their sin at Peor and its consequences,[8] for Israel continued to be tempted to inter-marry with other peoples and to turn from God. The same sin was a temptation to the early Church, as is clear from 2 Peter 2:15; Jude 11 and the letter to the Church in Pergamum.[9]

In Ezra chapters 9 and 10 and Nehemiah 13:23-27, it is this sin which is highlighted, and it is in that context that we must understand the recommendation to divorce. "The people of Israel, including the priests and Levites have not kept themselves separate from the neighbouring peoples with their detestable practices, like those of the Canaanites, Hittites, Perizzites, Jebusites, Ammonites and Amorites. They have taken some of their daughters as wives for themselves ...". Ezra and Nehemiah were deeply concerned that Israel might be cleansed from the sin of idolatry and all its evil consequences. Therefore Ezra said, "Let us make a covenant before our God to send away all these women and their children " ... "Make confession to the Lord, the God of your fathers, and do his will. Separate yourselves from the peoples around you and from your foreign wives".[10] Only in this way by separating themselves from pagan partners in marriage who would lead them spiritually astray, would Israel remain faithful and loyal to the Living God.

Because of the constant danger through inter-marriage, of turning away from the Lord and worshipping false gods, the command to separate themselves from their "foreign wives" should not be understood as denying nor lessening the sanctity and permanency of marriage between two believers or between two people who belong to God's covenant People.

In Malachi 2, we read, "Why do we profane the covenant of our fathers by breaking faith with one another? ...The Lord is acting as the witness between you and the wife of your youth, because you have broken faith with her, though she is your partner, the wife of your marriage covenant. ... I hate divorce, says the Lord God of

Israel".[11] In Malachi's day many Israelites had divorced their Israelite wives in order to marry pagan women from Ammon, Moab and Philistia whom they found more attractive. These pagan women inevitably led them spiritually astray and tempted them to idolatry. When God says, "I hate divorce", he is expressing his divine disapproval for their divorcing of their believing Jewish wives and as such is affirming that marriage to a believer is a call of God to life-partnership.

The paramount call was for Israel to be faithful to the Living and True God. What follows in Malachi 2:11f. is in keeping with the teaching of Deuteronomy, Ezra and Nehemiah. "Judah has broken faith. A detestable thing has been committed in Israel and in Jerusalem: Judah has desecrated the sanctuary the Lord loves, by marrying the daughter of a foreign god." The pagan wives with their pagan worship were polluting the Temple and causing their Jewish husbands to do the same and that was detestable in God's eyes.

Although the New Testament affirms yet goes beyond the teaching of the Old Testament our understanding of the Old is very important if we would understand the teaching of the New Testament and its application for our day. Paul gathers up the teaching of the Old Testament when he says in 2 Corinthians 6:14-16, "Do not be yoked together with unbelievers. For what do righteousness and wickedness have in common? Or what fellowship can light have with darkness? What harmony is there between Christ and Belial? What does a believer have in common with an unbeliever? What agreement is there between the temple of God and idols? For we are the temple of the living God. As God has said: I will live with them and walk among them, and I will be their God, and they will be my people". A Christian is commanded to marry only a Christian. Only so can he or she be a "temple of the living God". Only so can the Lord dwell with them and within them by his Holy Spirit and they together live in him and serve him. In the marriage of two believers the Lord is the foundation and cementing bond of their union. As such it is called to be permanent.

Our relationship with our marriage partner is called to reflect God's relationship with us. God does not reject Israel because she is unfaithful. He does not divorce her. His fidelity in Christ is our security. It is the ground and guarantee of permanence for all creation. As God is unendingly and unconditionally forgiving and loving toward us despite all our unfaithfulness toward him so we are called to be unending and unconditional in our forgiveness and love one toward another and toward the partner in marriage who may have been unfaithful. It is on the basis of God's faithfulness and unending love to us as well as the act of creation whereby man and woman in marriage "become one flesh", that marriage is a call to life-partnership.

In this the New Testament is even more explicit than the Old Testament. "Anyone who divorces his wife, except for marital unfaithfulness, and marries another woman commits adultery".[12] He "causes her to become an adulteress, and anyone who marries the divorced woman commits adultery".[13] "Anyone who divorces his wife and marries another woman commits adultery against her. And if she divorces her husband and marries another man, she commits adultery."[14] "Therefore, what God has joined together, let not man separate."[15]

In regard to adultery, it is important to consider what Jesus says in Matthew 5:27,28. "You have heard that it was said, Do not commit adultery. But I tell you that anyone who looks at a woman lustfully has already committed adultery with her in his heart". Jesus is going beyond the outward act of adultery. He is saying that we can also commit adultery when we cherish adulterous sin in our minds and hearts. Then we are just as guilty even although we do not actually commit the outward act. Jesus reveals the nature of sin in a much more radical way than does the Old Testament. When we apply Jesus' interpretation of adultery to what he says about marriage and divorce, then the sin of an unchaste heart and mind can cause an irretrievable break-down in marriage and lead to divorce, just as much as the outward act of adultery. The sins of the heart and mind are the main cause of marriage break-down. The New Testament in its teaching goes beyond that of the Old Testament. It affirms but makes explicit what is implicit in the Old Testament.

In this light it is helpful to compare what Paul says in 1 Corinthians 7:12-13, with what the Old Testament says in Ezra 9 and 10 and Nehemiah 13:23f and Malachi 2:10f. Paul says that a Christian husband or wife must not divorce their unbeliever partner if that partner is willing to live with them, although he does say, "But if the unbeliever leaves, let him do so. A believing man or woman is not bound in such circumstances". Paul is here speaking about a man or woman who has come to faith in Christ and been baptised after they have married. This is a different situation from a believer deliberately marrying an unbeliever which as we have already noted the New Testament forbids.

If we ask why New Testament teaching goes beyond that of the Old Testament we can only say that it is due to the Incarnation, death and resurrection of Jesus Christ. God has come. He has entered into this world in a new and fuller way in Jesus Christ and made his will more fully known and in Christ he gives us power more fully to obey him. At the same time the Church which was the believing community within Israel from Abraham's day and even in the Old Testament embraced Gentiles like Rahab of Jericho and Ruth the Moabitess as well as Jews, has been launched into the world and become quite clearly an inter-national community. The success and fruitfulness of the Church would inevitably produce a situation where one partner in marriage would be converted to Christ while the other remained in darkness. In this situation the unbelieving partner if he or she chose to continue in the marriage presented an evangelistic opportunity and the Lord would give the believing partner the grace and power both to remain faithful to Christ and to witness to the unbelieving partner in order to seek to win him or her for the Lord.

When Paul says in 1 Cor. 7:15, "But if the unbeliever leaves, let him do so", Paul is speaking of the unbelieving partner who remains obdurate in sin and who wants nothing to do with the Gospel and therefore does not wish to continue in marriage with a believer. Such an unbeliever could become a hindrance to the believing partner and might tempt the believer to depart from the Lord. Paul's recommendation here seems to harmonise with the concerns expressed in the Old Testament about an unbelieving or pagan partner turning the believing partner away from the Lord although in Ezra and Nehemiah believers were commanded to divorce their pagan partners.

The decision to divorce whatever the reason must always be for the people concerned an agonising and sad one. For a Christian it should only be taken after much prayer, thought and counselling.

To sum up then, the Bible affirms that marriage is a call of God to life-partnership. Marriage is not simply dependent on human desire and volition. Its permanency is a matter of God's call and command. A Christian may not marry a non-Christian but only a Christian. In a marriage of unbelievers, when one partner is converted to Christ, the believing partner must not divorce the unbelieving partner if the unbelieving partner chooses to remain. The unbelieving partner presents an evangelistic opportunity and as Paul says "is sanctified" by the believing partner.[16]

At the same time, the Bible accepts that because of human frailty and sin divorce may take place because of unchastity whether that unchastity is an outward act or of the mind and heart and when that unchastity leads to an irretrievable marriage break-down. The Bible also accepts divorce where an unbelieving partner can lead the believing partner into sin and apostasy. At times divorce is theologically acceptable. At times it is even desirable and necessary.

PASTORAL CONSIDERATIONS

What should the Church do when someone who has been divorced asks to be remarried in Church?

Many ministers feel troubled when they receive this request and have spoken of their concern wondering what it is right to do in the circumstances. One minister in conversation with me recently summed up his and their concern by saying that he always feels uncomfortable when asked to re-marry a divorced person and yet feels uncomfortable if he does not re-marry! I share his feelings. With over forty years in the parish ministry I have wrestled with the problem endeavouring as far as possible in each situation to discover with the people concerned and in the light of Scripture the mind of the Lord. I have each time found the issue challenging and often spiritually rewarding.

We cannot approach any pastoral situation in a legalistic way. Equally in a particular situation we cannot expect to have a proof text set of guide lines. Frequently there are none. Our endeavour must always be to try and understand the teaching of Scripture as a whole and let that be our light and guide. We must be continually guided by Scripture's teaching on Grace and salvation and be dependent on the Holy Spirit to apply the Word of God in a particular situation. In the remaining part of this chapter I will simply share with the reader what I have learned and endeavoured to practise.

Jesus said, "What God has joined together, let man not separate."[17] As a Christian Church we cannot rightly say these words at a marriage service and then allow man in the form of the State to put them apart! This though is what some Churches or Christians seem to accept. In so far as God and God alone can join a man and woman in marriage so God and God alone can put them apart. This fact must control our understanding and all that we seek to do in marrying and re-marrying persons who come to us for help. We must endeavour to help a person or persons who have been divorced through the State to understand this and help them to come to God in prayer with the request that God will put them apart from their previous partner, that he will forgive and heal and enable them to start life again.

It is always helpful to try in a loving compassionate way to know whatever is relevant and possible of the parties seeking to marry or re-marry. Only so can we in a loving way help the couple concerned. Many from their previous marriage have been carrying past hurts, feelings of rejection and guilt for which they need God's cleansing and deliverance before they can attempt to go forward into a new marriage. Both ministers and friends need to exercise great sympathy and understanding and be able to feel for them in their previous pain and rejoice with them in their hopes for the future.

I have never agreed automatically to re-marry a divorced person or persons. I have wanted first to try and explore with them something of what God is presently seeking to say to them. I have pointed out that as a minister I can marry them in the eyes of the State but I cannot marry them in the eyes of God. That is something which only God can do. A Christian marriage is not simply a union between two people, a man and a woman. It is a union between three, between man, God and woman or woman, God and man. If they want God to marry them and presumably this is why they want a minister to marry them in Church, then they must be willing to allow God to do for them and with them what only God can do. For that they must be willing in prayer to commit themselves and all that concerns them to God.

I have said to them that as a person or persons who have been married before, only God can put them apart from their previous marriage partner. They need God to set them free from their past and make them inwardly free to marry again, so that there are no hindrances or obstacles for their new marriage, nothing from their past to mar their future happiness. This of course is true of all of us no matter who we are or what our previous state. For all of us have sinned and until we have been cleansed forgiven and delivered by Christ we carry the burden of our own sinful past. Only God in Christ can and does set us inwardly free. Marriage affects and changes our entire being. We become what we were not before. We become a different person. Each partner in marriage is instrumental in changing the other. We cannot of ourselves therefore separate from our partner in marriage without losing part of ourselves. If we would seek divorce, then only God can put us apart. If we would re-marry we need God as it were actually to re-make us and set us inwardly free and free from our previous marriage partner so that we are free to re-marry. Even the party who in law is the innocent party, carries a responsibility for the previous marriage break-down.

Therefore each person before entering into a new marriage needs to pray and receive God's cleansing and forgiveness for anything and everything in the past which they regret and which is wrong in the eyes of God. Unless and until people have so prayed and received God's forgiveness and transforming grace they are not free to re-marry. God has not set them free. The failure of so many to do this and to commit their past to God and to receive his forgiveness and renewal is a prime reason why the majority of divorces occur among those who have re-married, or re-married after an earlier divorce.

I always ask a couple who have asked me to marry them, and where one or both have previously been divorced, to have a time alone with God in prayer. I ask them to do this as soon as convenient after leaving me. I ask them, if they have not already done so, to commit to God the whole of their past and to ask and receive God's forgiveness for all that needs to be forgiven and to set them free. I ask each of them to do this but equally I ask them to do this aloud when they are alone and together. I ask them to commit their lives to God and then having done that to commit their present love and one another to God in Christ. I tell them that only if they can assure me that they have done this will I marry (or re-marry) them. Here I simply accept their assurance about prayer, about their asking and receiving God's forgiveness and about their commitment to him, in something of the same way that as a minister I would receive and accept a person's confession of faith when they take their vows in being admitted to communicant membership. God alone knows where they stand before God and how sincere they are. It is not for me or any minister to judge them. I simply accept their word and confession. I also like to pray with them along these lines.

A few couples after reflection have told me that they were not prepared to go further. They were not now prepared to be married in Church and would instead go to the registrar to be married. The great majority however have gone forward along the lines suggested and have expressed appreciation for the help given.

From the time that I was first requested to marry a divorced person or persons until I actually agreed to marry them has generally been not less than three months.

I have never married a person who confessed to being the guilty party in the break-down of their previous marriage. To my knowledge, such a person has not approached me. If however a person was manifestly repentant before God I do not think my approach would be different from my approach toward any other divorced person. King David in the Old Testament was certainly guilty of adultery and murder through the sword of Ammon. He repented and God forgave him and must we not acknowledge that God may do so here? Any other approach would surely be legalistic and contrary to God's grace.

In agreeing to marry them I remind the couple of those two verses from two different Psalms in the Bible which are frequently, and in my own denomination regularly, quoted in the marriage service. "Unless the Lord builds the house, its builders labour in vain."[18] "Our help is in the name of the Lord, the Maker of heaven and earth."[19]

These verses make clear that if a house or home would be built secure then it must be built by the Lord. Without the Lord and his building there is no security. This is one common reason why so many marriages do not succeed. If the couple want the Lord to be the Builder and Maker of their marriage and home, then they must in prayer commit or re-commit themselves and their love to the Lord, ask him to put his seal and blessing upon them and on their love and their coming marriage. I always ask the couple to set aside time every day throughout the whole of the rest of their lives to pray to God, to read his Word and to endeavour to worship God as faithfully as they can together in Church and together seek to serve him so that they allow God to preside over their marriage. I point out to them that in the marriage service in the Church prior to their making their vows to God, we pray together. In that prayer we give thanks to God for his grace enabling us to draw near and share in all his love and salvation. We give thanks to God for them both and for their love to each other. Then in prayer we commit them both to the Lord. We commit to him their love for each other and ask that as they take their vows to God, God himself will join them together as man and wife in the Lord. In so far as this is what we do in Church, then if the couple have already prayed together in this way prior to their wedding they can enter more fully and meaningfully into the service when we pray this way in Church. We then affirm that God has so joined them and affirm the words of Jesus, "What God has joined, let man not separate".[20]

From time to time I have had some quite touching letters of appreciation in the months or years that have followed. I have seen a couple who were living together, after one had earlier been divorced because of a previous partner's unfaithfulness, come to faith in Christ. More than one couple after re-marriage have become very active and committed within the life and work of the Church.

[1] Genesis 2:24
[2] Matt.19:6; Mark 10:9
[3] Malachi 2:16
[4] William Barclay. *Daily Bible Readings*. Comm. on Matthew 5:31,32.
[5] Matthew 5:31,32
[6] Numbers 31:16
[7] Numbers 25:1-3
[8] Deut. 23:3-6; Joshua 22:17; 24:9-10; Micah 6:5
[9] Revelation 2:12-17
[10] Ezra 10:3 and 11
[11] Malachi 2:10,14,16
[12] Matt. 19:9
[13] Matt. 5:32
[14] Mark 10:11,12
[15] Matt. 19:6; Mark 10:9
[16] 1 Cor. 7:14
[17] Mark 10:9
[18] Psalm 127:1
[19] Psalm 124:8
[20] Mark 10:9

Chapter 8   FERTILITY, CONTRACEPTION AND THE FAMILY

Brigid McEwen

Irenaeus said in the 2nd century, "God's greatest glory is man fully alive",and as he, being a pupil of Polycarp who was himself a pupil of John the Evangelist, was only a few steps from the Lord, I like to think he knew what he was talking about. As John Paul II says in *Familiaris Consortio,*

> God created man in his own image and likeness, calling him to existence through love, he called him at the same time for love. God is love and in himself lives a mystery of personal loving communion. Creating the human race in his own image and continually keeping it in being, God inscribed in the humanity of man and woman the vocation, and thus the capacity and responsibility, of love and communion. Love is therefore the fundamental and innate vocation of every human being.[1]

Made in the image of our Creator we are all made out of love and for love and the more fully we resemble him who is love, who is indeed a dynamic community of love, the more fully we are ourselves, what he wants us to be, and the more fully alive we become. One of the ways in which we resemble our Creator is in the power of procreation, our fertility, our ability to become a parent. Through us, he peoples the world, and through our mortal actions he fills the immortal city. It is an astonishing thought that we share in his creative power. Such a power, the gift of fertility, requires our responsibility in its regard, our respect, indeed our reverence.

FERTILITY

Our knowledge of human fertility has increased dramatically in the past decades. It was only in 1924 that Ogino, in Japan, and then Knaus in Austria, became the first to realise that ovulation, the emergence of the female egg, was linked to the subsequent, not the preceding, menstruation. On this was based the Rhythm Method which served many women very well but, which being only a well-informed guessing game, ('Vatican Roulette') has long been superseded: first of all by the Temperature Method which makes use of the woman's bi-phasic temperature pattern to pinpoint when ovulation has taken place; and secondly by the Ovulation or Billings Method, based on the observation of cervical secretions, which indicates when she is about to ovulate, when she is ovulating and when she has ovulated. The information provided by these two methods is the basis of the combined or sympto-thermal method of Natural Family Planning. There is no question about the efficacy of NFP based on fertility awareness, witness Dr Ryder's article in the British Medical Journal. This is one way of controlling fertility - respecting nature's pattern, and acting accordingly. It requires mastery of the method (good teaching) and mastery of self.[2] Incidentally the Calcutta women in this study were taught NFP by Mother Teresa's Sisters of Charity who learn it during their novitiate and teach it as part of their apostolate in caring. This is one way of controlling fertility - respecting nature's pattern, and acting accordingly. It requires mastery of the method and mastery of self.

CONTRACEPTION

Contraception has the same purpose, controlling fertility, but a different approach. Strictly, literally, speaking, 'contraception' (against conception) only refers to barrier methods which act by preventing the encounter of the sperm and the ovum, namely, the cap, the condom, the diaphragm, the femidom, sponges, spermicides etc etc.

Some pills do have a contraceptive element in that they alter the characteristics of the cervical mucus and prevent the sperm entering the uterus, but their chief mode of operation is in the suppression of ovulation (ie sterilization) and in making the endometrium, the lining of the womb, unreceptive to the fertilised egg (ie abortion). The coil, or IUD of whatever form, and of course the RU 486, and the morning after pill, operate in this latter way; they are abortifacients. Injectable hormones such as Depo-Provera are not strictly speaking contraceptives either, but are sterilizing agents.

It is true that a certain impetus behind the movement for contraception came from a post-Malthusian standpoint. It was Sir Francis Galton, cousin of Charles Darwin (who had been much influenced by Malthus in his idea of the 'survival of the fittest') who was the pioneer of eugenics - a term he coined in 1883, an idea shared by Marie Stopes in this country and later by Margaret Sanger in the United States. But both they, and many others were genuinely concerned about over-burdened mothers, over populated countries and back-street abortions, and felt sympathy, and worked, towards, the dissemination of contraceptive information and supplies. Over the years the Lambeth Conference had spoken of contraception as "dangerous, demoralising and sinful" but in 1930 a resolution was passed permitting methods other than continence "where moral obligation to limit parenthood is felt".

The avowed aims for advocating contraception were and are:
- that families woud be happy because planned
- that every child would be a wanted child
- that abortions would decrease
- that sexually transmitted diseases would be greatly reduced

It only needs the (sad) recital of the present figures to show that none of these aims has been realised. (See Appendix)

BODY LANGUAGE

I think we have forgotten how important we are. Made in God's image of love and life, we also, like him, should be the embodiment of truth. Not only our words but our actions should say what we mean. Cuddling a baby, hugging our children and our friends, shaking hands, are all forms of body-language saying - "I love/ protect/trust you". The act of intercourse says the same and much more. It is a profound and powerful and sacred statement: "I love you, only you, totally, exclusively till death. I accept you in your totality. I give myself to you in my totality. I trust you totally. You are the person I would accept as the parent of my child". Again to quote from *Familiaris Consortio*:

As an incarnate spirit, that is a soul which expresses itself in a body, and a body informed by an immortal spirit, man is called to love in his unified totality. Love includes the body and the body is made a sharer in spiritual love.... Consequently, sexuality, by means of which man and woman give themselves to one another through the acts which are proper and exclusive to spouses, is by no means something purely biological but concerns the innermost being of the human person as such. It is realized in a truly human way only if it is an integral part of the love by which a man and a woman commit themselves totally to one another till death. The total physical self-giving would be a lie if it were not the sign and fruit of a total personal self-giving, in which the whole person, including the temporal dimension, is present: if the person were to withhold something, or reserve the possibility of deciding otherwise in the future, by this very fact he or she would not be giving totally. The totality required by conjugal love also corresponds to the demands of responsible fertility. This fertility is directed to the generation of a human being and so by its nature it surpasses the purely biological order and involves a whole series of personal values.[3]

In the ordinary way of things intercourse is devised for the fertilization of the female by the male and in the animal kingdom exclusively so. But in human beings it contains the unitive as well as the procreative element. Not only life but love are involved - "leaving father and mother, the man must cleave to his wife and become one flesh".[4] And they are still one flesh if by reason of her age or the time of the cycle the woman is not in fact fertile. The couple accept one another as they are.

But if procreation is separated artificially from intercourse by contraception, something very different is being said: "I accept you, but not your fertility. I give myself to you, but not totally." It may look the same (with barrier methods perhaps it does not feel the same) but the body is not saying what it means, or rather, is not meaning what it says. It is speaking an untruth. The unitive element is under threat. The couple are not at one.

Of course countless good people, loving couples put up with this state of affairs from the highest, most responsible motives and accept contraception with profound relief and thankfulness as perhaps a cross they have to bear, and one can only commend their seriousness of purpose and their self-denying ordinance. For many though it is a licence for self-indulgence. After initial caveats and limiting provisos (rather like those surrounding the Abortion Act) contraception has now been almost totally accepted in this country as a 'good thing'. It might be worth recalling what Gandhi said in this regard: "It has been left for our generation to glorify vice by calling it virtue".[5] Have we in fact been sowing thorns and thistles and expecting to get figs and grapes?

SOME EFFECTS OF CONTRACEPTION

By separating coitus from procreation, that is intercourse from the possibility of pregnancy, to many minds the field is wide open. It's fun, it's expected, there are few risks. Without elaborating the point it is not hard to see how this attitude leads to adultery and then to divorce, to promiscuity and sexually transmitted diseases and (especially when contraceptives were made available to the young unmarried and then to teenagers without parental consent) - to teenage pregnancies with abortion as the back-up when contraception fails.

It is the pleasure principle when people are used, not loved, when they are seen as things, not individuals, and from this stems the destructive force of contraception: it attacks the value of the human being and militates against feelings of self-worth. Without the possible procreative element, the person is not accepted in his/her totality which means that there is a break-down in the unitive element. The couple are not at one. They are keeping something back. They are not in total communion with one another. They are isolated individuals.

Curiously, sadly, this isolation, this loneliness, is now mirrored by the next generation, so that families are divided horizontally as well as vertically. It is not just the fact that couples have fewer children, that the microwave and the television (especially the one in the child's bedroom) do away with the family meal and with conversation, the whole attitude towards confidentiality in regard to adolescents' contraception, cuts the young off from their parents, that is if they are not already cut off by a broken home. No communion, no communication; the family fragments. It is not only the family that fragments: the cracks run through society, of which the family is the basis building block. (Incidentally just as there can be intercourse without procreation, so now also we can have procreation without intercourse. Witness not just test-tube babies and surrogate mothers but the syringe in the ice-box ready for the fertile time: using the man but not loving him or being united with him: having a child as a right or as the experience of mother-hood not as a gift, a gift of love.)

There is a significant effect on the individual which can be brought about by contraception - even or perhaps especially when urged on the young as the 'responsible' mode of action: "Do whatever you like, feel free to express yourself - just don't get (her) pregnant". Unless we are Michelangelo or Scott or Shakespeare it might be said that the most important and valuable thing we will ever do in our lives is to bring another human being into the world. Sexual intercourse is an action of great import and power with immortal implications. If those implications are constantly thwarted and there are no consequences to our actions in this important area (and should there be, abortion will deal with them) our actions are devalued and trivialized, we ourselves are diminished, and our masculinity and femininity lose their relevance. It does not matter *what* we do in the sense of 'what's the point? nothing's worth it'; and it does not matter *what* we do in the sense of there being no right and wrong. The first is the path to depression and suicide (which is on the increase particularly among young men) and the second, the path to violence which is compounded especially by the accepted idea of abortion. (It is lawful, ie 'good' to destroy helpless unborn children, therefore it is all right to bash your granny. The human mind, even if unschooled, can be pretty logical).

Our sense of our own worth has declined. We have forgotten how valuable and extra-ordinary we are. We have forgotten that the Almighty made us because he loved us and wanted us to share in his creative power and creative delight. It is not for nothing that the Song of Songs is used as an image of Christ's love for his church, nor that Christ's love for his church is used to illustrate married love. [6]

EFFECTS OF NFP ON THE COUPLE

As a teacher of Natural Family Planning & Fertility Awareness, I find that over and over again (after the initial question, "Why has no one ever told us about this before?") couples say that though they may have come to learn about family planning they are glad they came because they have learnt so much about marriage - NFP can be a school of love: it requires communication, consideration and self control. It is also the acid-test of a mature relationship. It is not just that there are no side-effects as with the pill (obesity, depression, headaches, loss of libido or possible health risks) nor aesthetic considerations as with condoms and caps etc, and intercourse is complete, normal and natural, this is an enterprise where responsibility is shared, and the lessons of consideration, loving kindness and self control are learned together. The couple have to communicate. They make love as and when they wish. If they want to avoid or postpone a pregnancy then they abstain from intercourse at the woman's fertile time; and this abstinence, far from being an insurmountable obstacle, becomes in fact a space where their relationship is rejuvenated. If on the other hand they would like to conceive a child they can tell the optimum moment and prepare themselves physically, psychologically, spiritually - lovingly - for such a great event, the start of a new life.

Fertility is regarded as a gift not a disease. The woman is not a patient under a doctor (and incidentally the pill is the only medication specifically designed to make a healthy system not work); she is an autonomous individual empowered by her own self-awareness (which as likely as not she learnt from another woman). She empowers him, her husband, who is fertile all the time, with knowledge of her own (lesser) fertility and they rely on each other for self restraint. "Chastity and discipline are the manly virtues which enable man to make the forces of nature the instrument of his freedom".[7]

The couple do not cost the state anything for free contraception (nor of course do the medical profession or the drug companies receive anything from them). They do not contribute to the pollution of the planet: the condoms on the beaches, the oestrogenic compounds in the water system. They do not suffer the iatrogenic effects of contraception which together with various abortion procedures contribute to much infertility. As has been said, "For the Best Results Follow The Maker's Instructions."

But passing on the Maker's Instructions and teaching NFP to married and engaged couples, only to adults in fact, is not enough. The knowledge of fertility awareness needs to be imparted much earlier to the young. Some of the current sex education material is so degrading that we should act swiftly to provide accurate decent information. Ignorance is no defence to the young under constant pressure from society, the media and their peers, who mature physically much earlier nowadays and who anyway have the right to understand their own bodies. In the early 80s the Drs Billings initiated a schools programme in Australia[8] to teach the pupils about their fertility and they found that the knowledge imparted a sense of self-respect and self-worth which is almost infectious. It is much more effective than 'assertiveness-training' which has rather un-Christian connotations. The girls realize that they have a complicated, delicately balanced, fluctuating fertility which is precious, special, and amazing. The boys realise this too in regard to the girls and in regard to their own constant fertility which in its particular way is no less extraordinary. The Billings find that the sexual behaviour of the pupils is far more respectful and responsible towards each other and the teenage pregnancies have significantly decreased. The different attitudes, the contraceptive and the fertility attitude to youngsters at school could be illustrated by what two doctors said to me. One, a doctor in a large manufacturing Border town said he wished he could put all the VIth form in the local school on the Pill. All sexually active? all medically fit? all mature enough for their fertility not to be permanently switched off? no contra-indicated medication? I am sure it was said half in jest, but I felt it was also wholly in earnest and I felt he was regarding the girls as cattle. The other doctor had a practice in a poor part of Glasgow (the practice itself is pretty poor as the doctor does not send women for abortion nor prescribe contraception which means considerable financial loss).[9]

He got a female NFP teacher to go into the local school and tell the girls about their fertility. They were deprived, 'hodden doun wee lassies' from tenements (and broken families), not very bright, under privileged. They heard all about their fertility and came out from the school 'walking ten feet tall'.

It was you who created my being,
knit me together in my mother's womb.
Thank you for the wonder of my being,
the wonders of all your creation.

Psalm 139

[1] *Familiaris Consortio; The Christian Family in the Modern World*. John Paul II, 1981. Part 2.II.

[2] *The British Medical Journal*, Sept. 1993, No. 307, pp. 723-6.

[3] *Familiaris Consortio*, Part 2:11.

[4] Cf. Genesis 1:27, Genesis 2: 23-4; Matthew 19:4-6; Mark 10:6-9; Ephesians 5:25, 28-31

[5] *'Must births be limited?' What Gandhi Thought*, by Krishnaswamy in *Way Forum*, 1957, pp. 19 and 51.

[6] Cf. again Ephesians 5.

[7] *Family Planning and Modern Problems*, Stanislas De Lestapis SJ, Burns & Oates, 1961.

[8] Creative love and Christian Sexuality Programmes run by the Billings Family Life Centre, 27 Alexandra Parade, North Fitzroy 3068, Victoria, Australia.

[9] For example, NHS: fees and allowances 1995/96. Contraceptive service fees: Ordinary Contraceptive fee per year £13.70 - IUD fee £45.90.

APPENDIX TO CHAPTER 8

The divorce rate is now more than one in three in the UK
1993 Fewer marriages: 299,000
More divorces: 165,000 (highest ever)
Couples Divorcing with children up to 16: 95,000
Children up to 16 with parents divorcing: 176,000
(OPCS Scotsman 23 August 1995)

1991 Brit. Med. Journal published survey based on women who had given birth 6 months previously showing proportion of unwanted pregnancies
1984 27% unwanted pregnancies, 70% using contraception
1989 31% unwanted pregnancies, 69% using contraception
(BMJ Vol 302 p147 1991)

According to the NSPCC, cases of physical abuse of children more than doubled from 1977 to 1989. In the same period abortions rose from 102,677 to 170,463 in England and Wales and from 8,174 to 10,997 in Scotland.
(NSPCC Publications: Trends in Child Abuse etc etc)

Since April 1968 4 million abortions have been performed in UK.
In 1993 168,711 abortions (462 per day) have been performed in England and Wales, 11,069 abortions (30 a day) in Scotland.

Only a tiny fraction of one percent of abortions have been performed in emergency for the stated reason of saving the mother's life or preventing grave permanent injury to her physical or mental health, or because of substantial risk of serious physical or mental handicap in the child. (In 1993 three such abortions were performed in England and Wales, one such in Scotland: SPUC June 1995 Update). Over 90% are for 'social' reasons.

Back in 1966, the British Medical Journal considered that accounts of back street abortion was vastly exaggerated. (*Legalised Abortion*: Report by the Council of the Royal College of Obstetricians and Gynaecologists, BMJ 2 April 1966 1 850-854.)

Live Births outside marriage   as % of all births
  1971 65,678   8.4%
  1991 211,294   30.2%   (OPCS)
In 1991, some 373,500 conceptions occurred outside marriage, i.e. 44% of all conceptions compared with 43% in 1990 - thus continuing the upwards trend.   (Population Trends No 73, Autumn 1993)

At the beginning of the century the illegitimate birth rate was 3% and pregnancy rare in girls under 16.
1945-56: under 16 conceptions rose to 200: 0.8 per thousand.
End of Sixties: conceptions 6.8 per thousand.
1991: girls aged 13-15, conceptions 9.3 per thousand.
(Dr Margaret White, *Children & Contraception*, Order of Christian Unity)

The BMJ in Feb 1992 Feb BMJ reported 8,000 girls under 16 attending family planning clinics. The abortion rate for teenagers aged 15-19 was 20.9 per thousand women (BMJ 1992 304: 275.1)

Pre 1950, Cervical Cancer was unusual in women under 40. From 1971-3 to 1986-8 percentage increase in women aged 25-34 was 154%. The risk of carcinoma of the cervix doubled in women who began their sexual activity before the age of 17 (Barron, *Sexual Activity In Girls Under 16* (British Journal Obs and Gyne, Aug Vol 3 1986)

Nursing Standard gives incidence of chlamydia infection in UK as between 3 and 4 million cases each year (Nursing Standard Oct 20 Vol 8 No 5 1993)

Part 3   SEXUALITY

Chapter 9   SEXUALITY - CREATED, CORRUPTED AND REDEEMED

Howard Taylor

Introduction

Our sexual instincts are God given and yet have so obviously corrupted many societies in the history of the world. In our own Western Society there is an increasing cruel sexual exploitation of children. Furthermore even the film industry is pushing the boundaries of what is acceptable by using ever younger teenagers in its portrayal of sex. Just as drug addiction requires more and more hard drugs to keep it satisfied so the sex instinct when given free rein generates more and more depravity - so that not even the elderly are safe from sex attacks. We are entering the night. Since God gave us our sexual instincts and made them pleasurable for our good, why has this happened?

In this paper I explore what lies behind the terms 'flesh' and 'spirit' as they are used in the Bible and especially in Paul to describe the contrast between the life of fallen humankind and the life to which the gospel calls us. I will relate this discussion particularly to our human sexuality.

The Bible speaks of the 'weakness of the flesh',[1] the 'sins of the flesh', and the 'body of death.' The statement "in my flesh there is no good thing",[2] does not mean that the physical body is inherently evil, but it does mean that it does not have the source of goodness in itself. *Cut off from God it can only degenerate.* This is especially true when one considers its sexual instincts - albeit God given.

The "works of the flesh" as outlined by Paul do not just describe sexual sin but nevertheless sexual offences do constitute a major part in the list of sins that Paul mentions as these "works of the flesh". Perhaps this is because the sexual urge is - commonly - the strongest of all the desires of the human body. The physical instincts and feelings of the body are God given. However they are not meant to be autonomous, but rather to come under the authority of the human will, which itself should be subject to the revealed righteousness of God. If our God given instincts begin to *rule* our behaviour then they are easily deformed and perverted and begin to mar our whole humanity.

Why are sexual sins so serious?

In the short term they may not seem so serious. There have been many 'good' men and women who have worked courageously and generously for the welfare of their fellows and yet have not been averse to having the odd affair on the side. We might remember - for example - Wallenburg and Schindler who both did so much to save Jews from the Nazi holocaust. We would probably judge them to be far more righteous than a mean spirited individual who - although faithful to his wife - cared nothing for the welfare of other human beings.

However sexual sin is very serious. It attacks the heart of marriage and family life and therefore the foundation of civilised society. In the long term - when widespread in society - it has devastating consequences for the future of the community. As family life breaks down, many different kinds of hideous evils begin to appear in society.

The flesh and the spirit in Creation

The creation of humankind is the climax of the creation of the animal kingdom, all of which is declared by God to be "very good".[3] Adam is made from the "dust of the ground"[4] and therefore belongs to the physical world of nature. Like the animals humans are commanded to be fruitful and multiply, and therefore with the animals humans share a God given sexual instinct. *One woman is given to Adam and so sexual relations are seen to be monogamous and heterosexual and for life.*[5]

We are given a form of companionship with the animals.[6] However the really fulfilling companionship is only realised in the man - woman relationship, because she is "one flesh" with the man. The term "one flesh" did not originally refer to sexual intercourse but rather to a creative act of God[7]. Nevertheless it is - from then on - expressed in sexual intercourse *and the birth of children.* Sexual intercourse is an intimate and pleasurable acceptance in our flesh of God's will that we hold all things in common with our spouses and we desire that this oneness *reach out beyond us in the birth of the children who will come from our flesh.* (Homosexual sexual behaviour can never, of course, have this further non-selfish dimension.)

However humans are more than mere physical creatures governed by instincts and feelings. We are made in the image of God and therefore share in something that reflects the freedom, authority and responsibility of God Himself. This means that our physical existence (flesh) must be open to that which is beyond mere physical being.

(We can see this if we think about our thinking and knowing processes. Clearly if we are to be able to think about the physical universe - including our own bodies brains and their instincts - our reasoning must not be controlled by the very laws of nature it wishes to understand. If our reasoning is simply the result of the laws of nature working on the "atoms" that make up our brains then it cannot be real reasoning at all, and it would not lead us to any real knowledge. This means that if materialism is true we cannot know that it is true and we could never say it was true! Our deepest personality cannot, then, be contained and enclosed within our flesh.)

Our personal life, free will, and self-consciousness must come from beyond our physical existence and ultimately be found in our relationship with God Himself. The decisions we make for the behaviour of our bodies (our actions) must not be controlled by our physical feelings - albeit God given - but by our knowledge of the Word and Spirit of God. Our physical feelings are to be the servants of our openness to the Divine. In that relationship our flesh lives in re-creative and healing harmony with our whole being and with God. Since our freedom of will cannot be contained and enclosed by the mere physical laws that govern our flesh, any attempt to look to our physical feelings alone for our decisions must lead only to the pretence of freedom. Such freedom would only be illusory.

From now on let us refer to this 'openness' as the human spirit or soul.

Our spirit our soul is to be open to the 'God of the spirits of all flesh'[8]. By His ever present Word and Spirit we are to live a truly free and fulfilling human life that is expressed in our flesh that is joyfully subject to our wills. This means that our decisions are not to be governed by our 'feelings' but our feelings are to be subject to our will that receives its knowledge of the difference between good and evil from God Himself. This does not mean we are to be mere slaves of the Lord for there are many good trees in the garden from which we can make choices[9]. We are free to choose between one good and another good. We can have this freedom because the Word and Spirit of God let us know what the difference is between good and evil.

1 Corinthians 2.11-12, 15-16 (NIV):

11-12 For who among men knows the thoughts of a man except the man's spirit within him? In the same way no one knows the thoughts of God except the Spirit of God. We have not received the spirit of the world but the Spirit who is from God, that we may understand what God has freely given us.

*15-16 The spiritual man makes judgements about all things, but he
himself is not subject to any man's judgement: "For who has known the
mind of the Lord that he may instruct him?" But we have the mind of
Christ.*

If we don't have this knowledge from God then our freedom to
choose between one good and another good is inevitably impaired,
and our humanity diminished.

So 1 Cor 2:14 (NIV):

*The man without the Spirit does not accept the things that come from the
Spirit of God, for they are foolishness to him, and he cannot understand
them, because they are spiritually discerned.*

The relationship: 'God - soul - flesh', enables the Word and Spirit
of God to constantly renew our flesh and keep us in that Eternal Life
which God intended from the beginning. To know God is indeed
Eternal Life.[10] Physical existence - left to itself - is bound to decay and
move from order to disorder. The laws of physics themselves tell us
that entropy - the measure of disorder in physical existence - always
increases unless the physical system is open to a greater order beyond
it. If an open system later becomes closed in on itself it can do nothing
but decay into disorder. If it is a living system this disorder means
mortality.

The flesh corrupted

The temptation to Adam and Eve in the Garden was to make
themselves as 'god', by eating of the Tree of the Knowledge of Good
and Evil. In other words they decided they were not going to get their
understanding of good and evil from the Word and Spirit of God but
from themselves.

This is very much the prevailing philosophy of modern Western
Society where it is believed that morality should be a private matter
- each individual making up his or her own mind as to the difference
between good and evil for him or herself.

This turning of the soul away from God means that it can only
be directed to the flesh with its instincts. This means that the physical
laws of the flesh are left to themselves and inevitably lead to the
degeneration of the flesh. The human will becomes more and more
subject to the feelings of the flesh and we find ourselves ruled by the
"fleshly mind".[11] It is not that there is anything inherently sinful in
the fleshly instincts -they were given by God Himself. It is these
fleshly instincts cut off from the Word and Spirit of God that
inevitably corrupt themselves and wreak havoc in our human being.

Gal 5:17: For the flesh desires what is contrary to the Spirit, and the Spirit what is contrary to the flesh. They are in conflict with each other, so that you do not do what you want.

Eph 2:3... gratifying the cravings of our flesh and following its desires and thoughts. Like the rest, we were by nature objects of wrath.

Our fleshly instincts are most obvious in our sexual urge because in normal circumstances this is the strongest of our physical impulses. Because it is so strong it is our sexual instinct that is most open to corruption and distortion. This means that the sexual instinct in us has the potential to do the most damage to our humanity and this leads us to feel ashamed of our sexual feelings. Before the Fall the man and the woman were naked and not ashamed. It is after the fall that they try to cover up their nakedness with fig leaves. It is our sexual instincts that make us most vulnerable to dehumanising forces.

In recognition of this, a great deal of the Mosaic law as well as the customs of Pagan nations, put such strong emphasis on rules and taboos to do with sex. In most societies sexual matters are kept private and are only talked about with euphemisms. Even in our sexually 'liberated' western culture, men will not normally discuss intimate sexual matters with one another but resort instead to coarse humour and crude remarks. However once our sexuality is really brought out into the open - through pornography and an unnecessarily explicit sex education for children - its capacity to corrupt itself is greatly increased.

The True Circumcision

The knowledge that my "flesh" has been corrupted leads me to want to be "delivered from the body of death"[12]. (Romans 7:24). *However to cut off my flesh in its entirety would be to commit suicide.* In the Hebrew Scriptures God gives the Israelites the sign of circumcision to demonstrate the need to cut out sin from our human life. The institution of circumcision in Genesis 17 is preceded in Genesis 15 by God taking an oath in which He passes between the two halves of an animal sacrifice. This self- maledictory oath in which the one taking the oath says: 'May this be done to me if I fail to keep the oath', is the greatest sign of God's covenant to work out His purposes in the history of Abraham's descendants. Circumcision is man's response to this in which the cutting of his foreskin is a sign of his acceptance of the covenant and means that he is saying 'May I be cut off from God's people if I deny the covenant.'

Gen 17:14 (NIV): Any uncircumcised male, who has not been circumcised in the flesh, will be cut off from his people; he has broken my covenant.

In the cross of Jesus God takes our flesh and suffers the consequences of this self-maledictory oath on our behalf.

The Hebrew word *basar* (flesh) is used in the Bible as a euphemism for the male sexual organ.[13] It is significant that the cutting of circumcision is done in this instrument of sexuality where our most powerful fleshly desire is to be found. Of course it is not just this organ that is the problem - the corruption involves the whole human body.

The real circumcision that 'condemns sin in the flesh'[14] is - as we have seen - the death of Christ when the whole of His frail human flesh is 'cut off from the land of the living'. *From then on the Christian initiation ceremony touches the whole of our human body.*

Col 2:11-12 In Christ you were also circumcised, in the putting off of the flesh, not with a circumcision done by the hands of men but with the circumcision done by Christ, having been buried with him in baptism and raised with him through your faith in the power of God, who raised him from the dead.

The gospel tells us that the Last Adam took to Himself our fallen flesh and in the struggles of His human life turned our flesh back to God.

Heb 5:7-9 During the days of Jesus' flesh, he offered up prayers and petitions with loud cries and tears to the one who could save him from death, and he was heard because of his reverent submission. Although he was a Son, he learned obedience from what he suffered and, once made perfect, he became the source of eternal salvation for all who obey him.

After the cry, "My God, my God why have you forsaken me?", he is able to commit his human spirit to God in the words: "Into your hands I commit my spirit". The great confirmation of the re-union of the human spirit with God is his resurrection in a "spiritual body".

The Incarnation

Before His death and resurrection is the Incarnation itself. Just as for Adam and Eve being "one flesh" is far more than their sexual relations - being founded, rather, on a creative act of God -so too the incarnation is far more than Christ's conception by the Holy Spirit and birth of the Virgin Mary. Nevertheless sexual relations are an integral part of the "one flesh" relationship of Adam and Eve, and so the conception of Jesus by the Holy Spirit in the womb of Mary is an integral part of the Incarnation. That, of course, is not to say that there is anything "sexual" in the conception of Jesus. But perhaps Mary's experience does point to something that takes up and transcends human sexuality in God's relationship with His people.

Luke 1:35 The angel answered, "The Holy Spirit will come upon you, and the power of the Most High will overshadow you. So the holy one to be born will be called the Son of God."

Our Lord tells us that there will be no marrying and giving in marriage in heaven[15]. This does not necessarily mean that the special love between man and woman will be gone but rather that - perhaps - our human sexuality will be transcended and taken up into that to which the best of this world can only be a shadow and pointer.

The Christian Life and Hope

The apostle Paul continues to exhort his readers to walk by the Spirit and not by the flesh. Because we still live in our earthly bodies we constantly have to face the battle between the flesh and the Spirit. For the deeds of the flesh to be put to death we need always - in the presence of Christ - to turn to God in worship and prayer so that our whole being is turned outwards and upwards to the Lord. Without worship and prayer our flesh will naturally turn in on itself and its corrupted desires will struggle to dominate our living.

However the full re-union of body - soul - Spirit cannot take place until we have followed the way of the Lord in the death and resurrection of the body.

---

[1] The NIV translates *sarx* as "sinful nature" but it would have been better to leave it as in most other translations as "flesh".

[2] Romans 7:18

[3] Gen.1

[4] Gen.2

[5] The Old Testament did allow divorce in certain circumstances. But this had never been the will of God. It had only been tolerated because of our hardness of heart. (Matt.19:13ff)

[6] Gen.2:18ff.

[7] Gen.2:22,23

[8] Num. 16:22

[9] Gen.2:16

[10] John 17:3

[11] Col.2:18

[12] Romans 7:24

[13] Lev.15:2

[14] Romans 8:3

[15] Matt.22:30

Chapter 10 SPIRITUALITY AND SEXUALITY

Elaine Storkey

In our current society exist two phenomena in curious juxtaposition. One of the phenomena is the sexualisation of our culture. Relationships, communication and explanations of our humanness have become charged with sexual meanings. And it is *sex*, not marriage or romance or courtship which draws up the secular discourse about the way people relate. Sex is also high on the agenda in the way people theorise as well as in the images they produce. Sex as biology, sex as a social construct, sex as autonomous choice all enter the debate, and fill the pages of textbooks in social science.

Most significant of all, however is the commodification of sex. Sex becomes that which we buy and sell in hundreds of different items, whether pornography, video nasties, teenage magazines or coffee. The problem is that the commercial exploitation of sex has ridden along with a genuine hunger for intimacy, and the two together have produced a neurotic obsession with sexual stimulation and fulfilment. So in capital cities like London it is impossible to move more than fifty yards without being confronted with issues of sexuality, whether of our own or that of someone else. It has become very much a part of our prevailing culture.

Alongside this cultural phenomenon is a second. I would describe it as a new search for spiritual meaning. The materialism and scientism of the twentieth century has left many people stranded in terms of fundamental human values. But rather than a return to orthodox Christianity the result has been a restlessness and a fascination with new models of spiritual meaning and experience. Western appropriations of Eastern mysticism, New Age thinking and feminist spirituality are all part of the contemporary exploration of our inner depth. Many of these new forms come together in an 'ecological spirituality', the pursuit for development of spiritual connectedness with the rest of the planet.

The fact that these two phenomena occur at the same period in time is not (I think) coincidental. I believe it is because they are closely interwoven as contemporary expressions of post-modernity. The revival of paganism with its linking of the sexual and the spiritual, a long-standing feature of some Eastern religions, has become one of the options available to post-modern people. Those for whom the modernity of a post-enlightenment culture was too sterile, too rational, too cerebral, too materialistic are now looking for a new fusion of the things of the spirit and the things of the body. The fact that they are not turning to the Christian church in their search for a connection between the two is significant. It denotes a rejection of Christian tradition in its understanding both of spirituality or sexuality.

This post-modern development rejects tradition *per se*. Yet there are two particular movements which stand high on the rejection list. First is the old Christian dualism, especially that of the medieval church where sexuality and bodiliness were despised and feared and where rationality and spirituality were seen as both distinctly human and closer to God. The gap between the two became a chasm which many fell into. Second is a later movement, the Enlightenment, where once again the rational and the cerebral were elevated, this time without any reference to God. Instead it was held that human rationality alone was capable of truthful enquiry and the scientific endeavour became the route to knowledge, truth, wisdom and insight. To the thinkers of the Enlightenment, religious belief and biblical revelation were mere superstitious dogma. Yet many post-moderns harbour a suspicion that the Church's dualistic thinking proved a greater ally of the Enlightenment than many Christians would care to admit.

Post-modernity discards each of these ways of seeing reality. It has, in Lyotard's words "an incredulity towards metanarratives",[1] towards, in fact, any cohesive framework of explanation. Post-modernity has come to represent the fragment rather than the whole, the surface rather than depth, the image rather than word. The search for any overarching meaning is regarded as futile, for meaning is that which we create for ourselves. We can now put together those things which were once regarded as incompatible for there is no need for old-fashioned coherence. It is experience and style rather than congruity or integrity which directs what we do.

Yet within postmodern culture there is a search of a kind. The concern that some have for *integration* is itself a hint that fragmentation cannot have the last word. Although it is not acknowledged as a 'metanarrative', the search for connections, for something more than random sets of experiences is a marked aspect of contemporary life. Included in this search for integration is a pursuit for the integration of the spiritual and the sexual. In this area at least, the dualisms and dichotomies of the past are seen to be over.

The problem is that this pursuit takes place in the context of a disengagement from a Christian understanding of human personhood. Because the person is no longer seen as creaturely, dependent, and made in the image of God another view of the person has to take its place. Although the rhetoric is of the end of 'metanarratives' there is in fact no real departure from the Enlightenment view that the human personhood is non-creaturely and thus subject to no higher authority. The difference is that individual style, self-creation or 'connectedness' replace rational autonomy as the location of personal identity. Yet if Christianity is true there is a great danger here. Without any acknowledgement or understanding of created humanness at the centre of the search for integration, the end result of even that search might yield something which does not encounter the reality of who we really are. Connectedness may be better than individualist rationality as a description of what identifies us, but even this can be idolatrous if it is not grounded in the truth that we are creatures of God.

The challenge to the Christian faith is to address and engage with these issues in a way which is both faithful to scripture and coherent and relevant to our present age. It also involves listening to the allegations against us and considering whether they have weight. For if we are to address the post-modern consciousness and contemporary ways of seeing spirituality and sexuality we must be prepared to confront those areas of our own thinking which have been less than biblical. Only then will we be in a position to offer hope to an age which knows deep spiritual hunger and restlessness of heart.

Three areas of concern will therefore shape the rest of this chapter. First of all I want to look at the way in which Christianity has been assessed in terms of its attitudes towards sexuality and spirituality, especially by its feminist critics. In this context I shall focus on the early Church Fathers and on the mediaeval witch-hunts. Second, I want to look at new, contemporary developments and here the focus will be on the revival of the Eastern religious ideas of sexuality and spirituality and the way these have been incorporated into the New Age. Contemporary feminist spirituality will also briefly be appraised. Finally, I want to ask how we respond to all this as Christians who believe that God has created our sexuality and that the biblical revelation speaks relevantly and coherently today.

1 Polarisation: Early mediaeval views of sexuality and spirituality

Church Fathers

It is by now almost customary to begin with the Church Fathers, and their legacy on both Catholicism and the Protestant tradition. The current attack on the Church Fathers has been related not only to their alleged misogyny, but also to their asceticism. Many of the early Christian writers, developed a kind of antipathy toward the body and all things that were sexual, and this revulsion reached a zenith in the writings of St Jerome (c342-c420). Asceticism itself might well be seen as the logical consequence of the uneasy marriage between pagan Greek dualism and a biblical concern about sin. For the understanding of sin was channelled through the 'Form-Matter' distinction of the Greek philosophers. 'Form' was the structure of reality, whereas 'matter' was merely that which came into being and decayed. The Greek tension between the materialistic philosophers and the Platonic idealists was never resolved, but it was certainly the idealists who left their mark on early Christian thinking.

In 'Christianising' the form/matter dichotomy a new tension between nature and grace was to become dominant in philosophic and theological thought. The division of reality into areas were related to the 'natural' and areas connected to the realm of grace produced a split which was to have significant long-term repercussions. Only one of them will be discussed in this chapter, namely the way in which the Matter-Form distinction took on a *gendered* nature. Medieval writers described the relationship between the sexes by a curious theoretical analogy: "Male is to female as Form is to Matter". In other words, the male appropriates something of the formal, rational, spiritual, logical element of reality whereas the female incorporates the earthy, bodily, transient, sexual, and fleshly. This meant that for many writers in the medieval period women were, not to put too fine a point on it, an insoluble problem! Because they were bodily, earthy, sexual and alluring they offered a perpetual temptation to men, and thus prevented many men's spirituality from being fully developed. Even a superficial glance at the writings of the Church Fathers yields some uncompromising statements about women, and some strange advice given to men and women about marriage.

Jerome was such an ascetic. He consistently presented marriage itself as harmful for all of us. Indeed, anything to do with sexual relationships should rightly be shunned by the church, by Christians and by the population as a whole. Even in his own day St. Jerome's teachings and lifestyle had influential appeal. For example, he is known to have been followed by a retinue of 'virgins' who accompanied him publicly. Many of them were now elderly matrons whose husbands had died and they along with their children and grandchildren tendered to his ordinary needs and were tutored by him. We have fascinating examples of such tutoring. He writes to one of them in ways that suggest his correspondent is on her way to flagrant prostitution....

> As you walk along, your shiny black shoes by their creaking give an invitation to young men. Your breasts are confined in strips of linen, and your chest is imprisoned by a tight girdle. Your hair comes down over your forehead or over your ears. Your shawl sometimes drops to leave your white shoulders bare... And when in public it hides the face in a pretence of modesty, with a harlot's skill it shows only those features which give men when shown more pleasure.[2]

In fact the letter is to one of these young women asking his advice about engagement and marriage. In many such letters Jerome rebukes women for their sexual attractiveness. Natural unselfconsciousness is reinterpreted by him as flirtation or lasciviousness. It seemed to him impossible for a woman to be youthful, beautiful, vivacious, with a good appetite and also spiritual. He counters their freedom at every turn, turning their lives into a permanent fast and their joy into weeping. A truly spiritual woman in his eyes could only be one who was "squalid with dirt, almost blind with weeping... continence... her luxury, her life a fast". Such a woman would spend all night long begging the Lord for mercy.[3] It is very evident to most readers of his letters that Jerome is haunted by repressed sexual fantasies and projects his obsessions onto his innocent enquirers. Unfortunately, posterity has not preserved their reply.

It is not fears of promiscuity which grip Jerome but fears of any expression of sexuality, even in marriage. He sees in marriage such an opposition towards our spiritual life that he argues it into the biblical text. Here he insists, not predominantly from St Paul's Letter to the Corinthians, but from the Book of Genesis that marriage was never part of God's intent. We have misunderstood sexual intercourse, it seems, for it could never have been intrinsic to our humanness or life in the Spirit. Jane Barr shows us how in curious exegetical gymnastics he finds his views reflected in some supposed biblical antipathy towards the number two. 'Two' equals couplings, union, sexual relationships, and consequently receives his condemnation.

There is something not good in the number 2. This we must observe at least if we would faithfully follow the Hebrew that while scripture on the first, third, fourth and sixth days, relates that having finished the works of each God saw that it was good, on the second day He omitted this altogether, leaving us to understand that 2 is not a good number because it prefigures the marriage contract. Hence it was that all the animals which Noah took into the Ark in pairs were unclean. Odd numbers denote cleanness.[4]

Now that kind of exegesis is going to get us into a lot of trouble as indeed it got Jerome into a great deal of trouble! Had he stayed merely one inconsequential Desert Father, rambling on his own, it would have had little import. But as history records he was also an extremely popular writer who translated the Bible and left his mark on scholarship; the Latin Vulgate was used for centuries after. Although the translation is well respected, there are those who accuse him of allowing his prejudice to affect his wording of particular texts.[5] Jerome also contributed volumes in theology and his legacy passed through the decades and centuries of the church.

In later centuries his views gave occasion for humour, especially when treated by literary satirists. In his *Canterbury Tales* Chaucer picks up some of the themes, playing around with them with wit and parody. In the Prologue to the Wife of Bath's Tale, there are generous reference to Jerome's anti-feminist work *Against Jovinian*. Jane Barr comments 'Chaucer, that master of irony, puts the words of one of the greatest anti-feminists of all time into the mouth of a woman who unashamedly advocates sexual enjoyment and licence.'[6] It is interesting that a thousand years after his death Jerome's work was still known enough to receive such parody. Today we still have access to some of his exegeses and the way he interprets the Fall and other parts of the Book of Genesis. In Genesis 3:16 the sense of the text changes from 'Your desire will be for your husband and he will rule over you' to 'You will be under the power of your husband and he will rule over you'. This error of translation, presumably deliberate, for Jerome was not incompetent, affected centuries of exegesis.[7]

Jerome was not alone in polarising sexuality and spirituality, and in making sexuality, particularly woman's sexuality, into an enormous problem. Through the writings and insistence of many early theologians, the 'spiritual' route was the only route towards God, for we could not serve God bodily in our sexuality. Spirituality itself became that to be accomplished in meditation, in quietness, in mortification of the flesh and in self-denial. And because we could only serve God in our minds, spirit and emotions once we had conquered the desires of the flesh, it is not surprising that for centuries afterwards people punished and abused the flesh. Nuns and others have since become canonised through this route to holiness. These saints were often the ones who mutilated and flagellated themselves, sometimes to great excess, starvation and near-death; yet it remained a mark of spirituality for women in the medieval period. To be a deeply spiritual woman was to be as far removed as possible from flesh and fleshly desires. Most of all, spiritual women had to ensure that they and their sexuality were not a hindrance to the spirituality of men.

Critics of these historic attitudes and practices within the church show how these attitudes hardened over time into not simple disapprobation but disgust towards women. In the eleventh century Pope Leo IX enforced a celibate priesthood, branding the wives of priests who were already married as concubines. Their treatment was harsh: imprisonment, flogging or banishment without subsistence.[8] In the thirteenth century St Bonaventure describing the kind and warm hearted St Francis showed great approval of his rejection of women:

> He said that one who held converse with women... could as little avoid contamination therefrom as he could, in the words of Scripture, go upon hot coals and his feet not be burned. He himself so turned away his eyes that he knew the features of scarce any woman.[9]

Two centuries later the notorious witchcraft trials and the general persecution of 'witches' which followed for more than two hundred years stand out as not unrelated to these kind of pronouncements. Many feminist writers in particular find it impossible to forgive the church for the oppressive attitudes towards women during this period which made them into scapegoats. They allege indeed that these are paradigmatic of the way in which the church have viewed women's sexuality throughout history.

Witch-hunts

The massive witch hunts have by now been fully documented.[10] They seem to have started in the Alps but quickly spread through Europe. In the year 1577 alone Toulouse, which did not have a big population, sent 400 witches to the flames. Between 1587 and 1593, 22 villages in the region of Trier burnt 368 witches. In England and

Scotland we were not ourselves without our witch trials. Scotland was rather more humane - witches were executed by hanging. But here again, as in Europe as a whole and in England, the trials were a mockery. Usually the trial was by drowning. If a woman was suspected of being a witch she would be sent into the sea or into a lake with a stone attached - if she drowned then she was not a witch. If she floated back to the surface then she was a witch. Since death was the outcome in either case, the verdict of 'innocent' did not benefit the accused. The allegation itself was almost synonymous with conviction.

One Scot, in 1602, was reported to have confessed before his own execution that he had been the cause of the death of two hundred and twenty women for whose exposure as witches he had been paid 20 shillings each. And a similar reaction occurred in New England in Salem in Massachusetts where a large proportion of the female population lost their lives in the witch purge in 1692. Incidentally, in Salem they have now become heroines. Monuments and plaques erected to these women make them also a tourist attraction. Not only have new witches' covens opened, but The Boston Globe reported in 1993 that a high priest of Wicca had become a member of the ecumenical circle of religious leaders.[11]

It is indicative again of our post-modern age that what in previous centuries was seen as fearful or shameful is now a celebration commodified for the leisure market. It also conveys a message about women's spirituality in the wake: that it must not be prescribed for them but that women have the 'right' to forge their own.

The Dominicans were among the first to become involved in the issue of witchcraft and the most authoritative manual written by two Dominican friars, namely Heinrich Heimer and Jacob Sprenger, was written in 1486 and it had gone through fourteen editions by 1520 and is actually still in print today: *Maleus Malificarum*, the 'Hammer of Witches'. It locates the causes of witchcraft as "women's carnality, women's sexuality". "All witchcraft comes from carnal lust which is in women insatiable". The friars catalogue some of the findings which have been reported. One of the chief activities of witches apparently was to collect male 'members' which they would keep together, as many as twenty at a time, in a little bird's nest or a box. These penises would then have a life of their own and would start to move around and eat corn and oats. We may laugh at that now and recall Freud's psychological theories of castration. Yet that there was deep anxiety over sexuality is an unavoidable conclusion, as is the fear that it is inevitably related to impurity, demonism and women. Male spirituality on the other hand seems to have been seen as pure yet fragile.

These are random examples of the split between sexuality and spirituality and its negative historic effect on women. The case here alluded to would not stand in an academic treatise; counter-evidence would need to be examined. Some study would also have to be made as to why these attitudes were apparently revised during the Victorian period when women were identified with purity and thus given the ideological task of safeguarding the nation's sexual morals. (Those women who failed in this however, were once again given punitive treatment. When Josephine Butler addressed the hypocrisy surrounding the Contagious Diseases Act she touched deeply into old fears of women's sexual potency.)

The methodology employed in contemporary feminist research on sexuality is not, however, one of delineating historical movements or dating events. Even less is it concerned with quantifying. It is more frequently qualitative: where case studies, specific periods or individual writers are the focus. Often it is narrative, where women's stories are relearned and relived. Feminist theological research is often episodic rather than systematic, allusive rather than dogmatic, value-laden rather than attempting to be value-free. Post-modern feminism in particular has lost interest in trying to find single (or even multiple) explanations for complex social phenomena. Yet, apart from the work of postmodern thinkers, there is still a strong consensus that the past yields many of the keys to the oppressive attitudes towards women in the present. In particular there is strong agreement that both mediaeval dualism and the later Enlightenment left legacies on our thinking which were both anti-sexual. They concurred in the belief that issues of the mind are key in our Western civilisation. So, in later Enlightenment thinking, the elevation of the rational, faith in the scientific, and the downplaying of emotions, will, passions, and body has been responsible for the continuing dismissal of women. For, whatever the era it seems women have remained identified with these characteristics.

2 Fusion: Contemporary writings on sexuality and spirituality

Tantra and New Age

One of the contemporary attempts to resolve the tension between spirituality and sexuality has been to draw on Eastern religions, especially some forms of Hinduism. New Age exponents have led the way in this. The resulting ideas and practices have been incorporated into some American 'alternative' communities. It rests on being able to put to sleep the 'sanity of reason', to 'kill the mind' which otherwise imprisons us. Capra explains:

> To free the human mind from words and explanations is one of the main aims..As long as we try to explain things we are bound by karma; trapped in our conceptual network. To transcend words and explanations means to break the bonds of karma and attain liberation.[12]

The teachings of the late Bhagwan Rajneesh, have become central in this new development, particularly those contained in his work *From Sex to Superconsciousness*. He identifies the mind as the 'chief villain' because it breaks up the unity of the cosmos, by recognizing objects only in their separateness from other objects. Rajneesh suggests that the whole Western enlightenment idea of categorising, of separating, of distinguishing, of differentiating between things, is actually distorting and perverting the true cosmic consciousness of the universe. Labelling and categorising denies reality, and the mind holds us in bondage. Therefore we have to find ways of both killing the mind and recreating the unity. One of the ways forward is the use of Mantras. A mantra is 'a deliberate annihilation of meaningful language by mechanical, non-personal repetition of a word or sound.'[13] Such repetition takes the person away from thought processes, from using language in a structured and meaningful way, and instead leaves us with vibrations. This enables us to achieve 'occult correspondence', to tap into the pure vibrations of the cosmos. For the cosmos is itself only vibration.

The focal issue for this chapter is how the New Age has used Tantric beliefs to affect understanding of human sexuality. In Eastern thinking human beings are microscopic versions of the cosmos, because we incorporate both fine 'consciousness' and gross 'body'. The gender division of male and female is therefore key to our human existence because it represents the polarity, the disunity, or bifurcation of reality. So the reunification of existence in the sexual intercourse of male and female is our point of contact with the cosmic powers. Our sexuality is ultimately one with our spirituality because it is the means of our direct connection with the Divine (where the Divine is the god-in-everything). Duality is a part of cosmic unity, but duality must be entered into and passed through to reach unity. In other words, reality is to be reached by embracing illusion and the illusion is our own body.

Shirley MacLaine adopts and adapts Tantric thinking from her New Age position. She emphasises not the polarity but the androgyny of the human self. For her, we comprise both feminine or spiritual energy and masculine or physical energy. But at heart we are androgynous. 'Therefore the more we each resonate to the perfection of the Higher Self, the more we are reflecting balance in ourselves, the more androgynous we are.'[14]

Although it is unity, not androgyny which authentic Tantra pursues, the rituals of Tantric sex often employ the processes of meditation or chanting. Through these processes sexual arousal occurs. But the aim of sex is not physical release or orgasm. The purpose is to immobilise semen, breath and consciousness, to hold them all at the point of maximum tension. So the sexual arousal is pursued until the point of tension is reached, it is then immobilised, maximised and released through a still mind. A 'spiritual orgasm' takes place as far as Tantric sex is concerned. Initially this may be between a man and a woman where the fusion of sexuality and spirituality takes place by immobilising the consciousness. But its aim is not to make a man and a woman one flesh, its aim is not sexual union at all but to go beyond that, to fuse a Tantric's own inner polarities into one. The desire is to gain the mystic experience of oneness, not to be in union with another. It therefore takes us away from the other person as a human being to the other person as an object or as a route for my achieving my own mystic sense of unity with my spirit and my body at the same time.

So according to Rajneesh, Tantra treats sex as simply a door: "While making love to a woman", he tells his disciples, "you are really making love to existence itself. The woman is just a door, the man is just a door."[15] Once *samadhi* or superconsciousness is achieved a man doesn't need a woman for sex, nor does a woman need a man. Men or women can have sex with anything, "with a tree, with the moon, with anything" because the aim of the sex is not union sexually. It is union mystically and spiritually with one's own oneness. It is to experience 'superconsciousness' and be released into this.

Although the language is obscure and the concepts quite foreign, the ideas involved in Tantric sex are beginning to have considerable impact on our Western world as part of the growing New Age spirituality. One curious example is in the process of self-fertilisation developed by women who want to have children without becoming involved in what they see as the patriarchal sexual relations of marriage and cohabitation. Donor sperm, provided by healthy men, and bought from sperm banks, is inserted by the women into their bodies whilst following something very similar to a Tantric ritual. Chanting, meditation, and the search for superconsciousness, for spiritual union with the cosmos, thus surrounds the conception of a new life.

Although Tantric sex is not, itself, supported or propounded by all New Age mystics, similar concepts lie behind the desire for mystic union within the New Age. The aim is the same. It is the fusing, or merging of the self with the cosmos through spirituality and sexuality. To be in spiritual union with the cosmos is the height of our sexual experience psychologies as well as in New Age. The chief technique is not now through mantras or through the repetition of words or chants or sounds, but through meditation on objects, 'cosmic fusion', until it is possible to become one with the object, and through that object become one with the cosmos. Particularly important is the 'merging' with objects of the natural environment. Ecology takes on a new meaning: the preservation of the planet becomes a spiritual task, not simply one of environmental conservation.

Many have written of this fusion with the trees or grass or flowers. It has been incorporated into many different kinds of rituals. I came upon a group of New Age women tourists in Greece at Delphi, or to be more precise on a wooded piece of grassland, below the ancient city. The leader was incanting "before the column was the tree", and a ceremony took place where they surrounded the tree, first holding hands, then winding a piece of ribbon around each of them and the tree. Thus attached both to each other and to the tree, they then quietly invited the tree into union with its human friends. The meditation was still in progress when I passed that way again an hour later.

What is happening is in keeping with what one writer insists is "the universally recognized need in our time for a general transformation of consciousness."[16] For Margaret Adler this transformation is to be found in the general re-emerging of paganism, especially in its fusion of the spiritual and the natural. She writes: "Most neo-pagans sense an aliveness and 'presence' in nature. They are usually polytheists or animists or pantheists or two or three of these things at once. They share the goal of living in harmony with nature and they tend to view humanity's 'advancement' and separation from nature as the prime source of alienation...They see ritual as a tool to end that alienation."[17] Robert Ogilvie Crombie writes of his own experiences. He describes his own union or fusion with Pan, the god of the woods, the flocks and pasture:

"He stepped behind me" - and he is in a forest - "and then he walked into me so that we became one and I saw the surroundings through his eyes. The moment he stepped into me the woods became alive with myriads of beings, elementals, nymphs, giants, fawns, elves, gnomes, fairies, far too numerous to catalogue."[18] In this passage, the spiritual experience of unity with the cosmos comes through the god Pan and calls up all the elemental spirits of the universe or the forest. This writer thus describes a New Age mystical union where the spirit's life of a human being is to become one with the spirits of the universe. The merging or identification involves mind, emotion, body and often sexuality. Yet again, this sexuality is generally experienced as non-gendered, non-differentiated sexuality. It is not male or female but 'one'.

New Age departure from traditional Western ways of understanding spirituality are evident amongst those who have had little contact with Christianity. I find it interesting to hear the questions about Gaia, or about experiences of heightened spiritual awareness, when I address university audiences on any aspect of spirituality. Sometimes the language used is mystical, subjective and non-public. There is usually no attempt at debate or discussion for no truth claims are being made. This 'experiential relativism' came out strongly for me at a meeting where I was explaining the relevance of Christ's life and death for people at the end of the twentieth century. One participant explained that she had no connection with Christianity, and she found this whole way of thinking too separate and logical. It seemed to be founded on distinctives, on some things being true and others being false. This, she felt, was out of keeping with her great desire for cosmic union and oneness. As a way forward she offered me the opportunity to embrace her idea of Jesus. She said she would be very happy to give the word 'Jesus' to experiences she enjoyed, which gave her the sense of peace and awe. As an example she offered the experiences of pleasure on watching the lapping of the waves on the sandy shore, or listening to the sound of the sea in a shell. If she could call these 'Jesus', then she said she could understand what Christians were talking about.

Feminist Spirituality

Another contribution to the contemporary discussion on sexuality and spirituality is offered by feminist writing. Drawing occasionally from both Eastern mystics and New Age subjectivists most feminists emphatically reject the dualism of the early mediaeval writers, and its dissociation of spirituality and sexuality. For such dissociation has inevitably penalised women, as we saw in the earlier examples. The elevation of men for their alleged inherent spirituality has been accompanied by the blaming and punishing of women for their sexuality. What is being stressed therefore by much contemporary feminist theology is the growth of 'women's spirituality' where women are invited to develop their own spiritual expressions and experiences.

This marks a departure from earlier models of feminist thinking. Then, the focus was on the equality of men and women, and consequently their equal acceptance by God. The attack was on centuries of stereotyping of women and the identification of women with nature and sexuality. Now, there has been a shift from equality, and its implied assumption of 'sameness' of men and women, to an embracing of 'difference'. But the difference is defined by women. Contemporary feminists now choose to identify themselves in terms of their own experience of connectedness and bodiliness. So in echoing this difference, women's spirituality will be a spirituality which is closely connected to sexuality.

Although there is broad agreement on the need not to divorce sexuality and spirituality there would however be a considerable diversity of views within feminism as to what this implies. One can identify at least five positions on spirituality within feminist theology although there is overlap and interplay between them. They might share a commitment to the eradication of stereotypes of women's sexuality and to a rejection of the long-standing dualist assumptions, but beyond that they differ considerably. For example, Evangelical feminists aim to stay faithful to the biblical text, although they may depart from some traditional interpretations of that text, and from many of the traditional teachings on gender. For them, spirituality is always linked with relationship with the Triune God and with the atoning work of Christ. Women's spirituality is not of an essence and nature which is separate from that of men, but it may embrace emphases which have been lost.

Those who espouse a 'hermeneutics of suspicion' de-code and contextualise much of the biblical narrative, and are suspicious both of traditional interpretations and exclusions. The recovery of women's stories behind and within the text goes along with a liberationist stance: where traditional Christian interpretations have not been 'liberating' for women, they must be treated with extreme caution. Women's experience and value provides its own hermeneutic, and gives the only real authenticity to the spiritual quest.

Eco-feminists have greater interest in Creation than in other areas of biblical revelation. They begin from the assumption of women's 'connectedness' with all life forms. Women's experience of pregnancy and childbirth bring us close to the earth our Mother, women's bio-rhythms are by nature in tune with the moon and the sea. Thus our spirituality must find its very basis in our earthiness and sexuality, and for some this means embracing Gaia, the great earth Mother, the spirit of creation.

Goddess feminists take this further. Beginning with women's experience of nature, they identify the Great Earth Mother as the Goddess, the ultimate religious feminine principle. The Goddess occurs not only in pagan, nature religions but comes also into Christianity as Sophia, wisdom, or even as the Virgin Mary in folk Catholicism. For them, the Bible would be a distraction rather than a vehicle of divine revelation. For it speaks only of male religion and embraces a male spirituality which excludes women. But when women authentically worship they experience goddess love, not necessarily as a personal encounter but as the dynamic force which helps women to know their own meaning. "Goddess is a symbol of the newfound beauty, strength and power of women."[19]

Finally, Post-Christian feminists are characterised by their overt rejection of Christianity, and of Christian spirituality. They may also be part of the goddess movement, or they may find the goddess symbol itself as still too close to a reified divine personal 'Being'. Accepting personal autonomy, personal divinity and personal responsibility for our own sexuality and spiritual power replaces any dependence on a god 'out there'.

There are feminists who blur the differences between these various groups and blend together many different characteristics. Amongst some of those who have stayed technically within the Christian Church, though on its very outer fringes, a theology has developed which has offered a radical and conspicuous way of breaking down old boundaries between spirituality and sexuality. However, 'theology' is somewhat redefined. It is now "about making connections- sensual and erotic as well as conceptual."[20] At the centre of theological thinking is the embracing of *eros*. The *agape* of the New Testament is rejected as being too sterile and masculine, and in its place *eros* has come to identify a more bodily-spiritual love. But *eros* is not what it was allegedly before: heterosexual lust, defined by men and imposed on women. It is now the blending of body, sensuality, spiritual yearning, justice and erotic love as articulated by women.

It has its fullest expression within 'lesbian theology'. In this spirituality, God also becomes identified with the erotic process, sometimes indeed god is envisioned simply as erotic love. For God is no longer Personal Being, but rather Verb, movement: "God is both the act of justicemaking/lovemaking and those who struggle for justice for themselves and others."[21] Where God is still referred to as Being, that Being is myself: "I found God in myself and I loved her passionately."

This concept of eros overturns what for centuries has been seen as biblical sexual ethics. New values are offered as substitute: "The first is the sacred value of our sensuality, our erotic power and our unalienated sexuality. We are embodied bearers of the erotic/God with one another, as she crosses over among us."[22] This replaces any rigid commitment to monogamy, for to be 'promiscuous' should not be seen as perjorative. "It may be rather a way of participating in the embodied fullness of different special friendships."[23] 'Faithfulness' is thus separated off from any notion of sexual exclusiveness. Being faithful means being prepared to "work with our sexual partner or partners in creating mutual senses of assurance that our relationships are being cared for"[24]; to act in "whatever honest ways we can." Sometimes, biblical passages are cited: "The erotic is the divine Spirit's yearning, through our bodyselves, towards mutually empowering relation which is our most fully embodied experience of God" (based on 1 John 4.7ff). "Regardless of who may be the lovers, the root of the love is the sacred movement between and among us."

Sometimes, 'Christa' is called upon: Christa can "touch many Christian women at embodied spiritual depths that Christ cannot." But Christa is not merely a female Christ. She is the sacred, erotic power - the symbol of a conjoined spirituality and sexuality as in this passage: "There is no greater delight than to celebrate and share the body of Christa. I praise her as both ground and figure of our lovemaking. She is in the power between us... I see her in you and I enjoy her in myself. I take her and stroke her playfully. I look upon her with immense tenderness. I take her and nibble a little. I take her and eat, take her and drink. I am taken, grasped and caressed by her power moving between us. Immersing myself in you, with you, through you, I move with you in the sensual wellsprings of her love."[25] As the spirituality of the celebration of eucharist becomes one with the sexuality of a lesbian love relationship, the old split is seen as finally ended.

3   Redemption and Wholeness:
Biblical perspectives on sexuality and spirituality

I have been arguing that the contemporary obsession with sex is part of a bigger search, for personal identity, meaning and spiritual integration. Whereas the mediaeval church saw our sexuality opposed to our spirituality, the latter part of the twentieth century seems determined to bring these together. From a Christian position, however, there are problems with each of these approaches. They have both been deeply influenced by pagan thinking. The early Greeks no less than the current New Age had at the heart of their conceptualising, ideas and theories which were fundamentally anti-biblical. And just as the *polarisation* of sexuality and spirituality of the Church Fathers was a major departure from a Christian worldview no less so is their attempted *integration* through pagan mysticism.

It is interesting how cultural history has made sexuality so much more confusing than is the Creator's own account. That account unfolds in the context of the great distinction between Creator and creation. Sexuality is a creature of God. Sex is not God, nor is God sex. In fact the Godhead is never defined or described in sexual terms. God is the great 'I Am', the relational Trinity, whose name is Love. When we use gendered metaphors for God this is because we need to speak of God as a person, not simply a force or a power or a verb. Sex, then, is something which God has breathed into creation; something God has placed close to our identity as humans. We have been given our sexuality as a way of procreating safely, of expressing intimacy, of experiencing excitement and mutual pleasure. And because sex is so powerful a reminder of our humanness, and our emotional needs of closeness and warmth it is also potentially dangerous. It can easily become an idol.

Because the biblical story is also a story about sin, sexuality is affected deeply by sin. Much of the Old Testament narrative describes broken sexual relationships, where power, patriarchy, lust, ownership or manipulation dominate rather than loving, trothful sex. The New Testament contains its own warnings about the dangers and problems which follow from promiscuous relationships. Marriage alone is to be the context for full body-giving of one to another. And that giving is to be mutual, respectful, honouring and full of love. But in placing these boundaries around the expression of our sexuality the Bible never implies that sex is sinful or dirty or repulsive. There is nothing intrinsically anti-spiritual about our body-lives.

Some problems occur in our modern thinking, however, because we are not clear about how to define sexuality. Frequently, people operate on a very narrow definition, where it simply means sexual relations, or more specifically, intercourse. Sometimes, people operate on a very wide definition, whereby sexuality means 'sexual orientation' - gay, heterosexual, bi-sexual - and where that sexual orientation then delineates who we are as persons. I believe that a Christian position is different. It never confuses sexuality with personhood (as I believe the latter position does) but nor does it reduce sexuality to sexual expression. It says rather that our sexuality is a created dimension of who we are, but only one dimension. Our sexuality is intrinsically connected to our creaturehood, our bodiliness, but also to our relationality.

Therefore, it is present in some way or another in all our relationships. Rather than deny that we are sexual beings, or be afraid of our sexuality, we need instead therefore to find appropriate expressions of that sexuality in our different relationships. This means that the way we express ourselves in friendship is different from the way we express ourselves in marriage, or in parenting or in work relationships. It does not mean that our sexuality does not play any part in our friendships. Our needs for bodily touch, warmth, affection, comfort, embrace may be met in a rich way by our friends.

Similarly, parents often express their fondness for their children physically. The problems arise when we blur the boundaries between the different relationships. When parental affection and fondling, for example, turns to sexual intrusion then this violates the relationship and becomes child abuse. Or when *inappropriate* expressions of our sexuality enter our friendships (namely those reserved for marriage) they blur the difference between marriage and friendship and become a threat to marital exclusiveness.

The problem with asceticism is that it fears human sexuality and denies it any legitimacy. It also fails to acknowledge the goodness of the body lives God has given us. The problem with contemporary 'inclusiveness' is that it makes every relationship sexual in the same way, and thereby fails to discern the wonderful variety of relationships which God has placed us in. It also fails to recognize their different normative structures.[26]

So because sex is such a powerful reminder of our humanness, and our emotional needs of closeness and warmth it is also potentially dangerous. It can easily become an idol. This is made very evident again in the Bible, for much of the biblical story is a story about sin.

Sexuality itself is affected deeply by sin. Many of the Old Testament narratives describe broken sexual relationships, where power, patriarchy, lust, ownership or manipulation dominate rather than loving, trothful, monogamous sex. The New Testament contains its own warnings about the dangers and problems which follow from distorting our relationships. And problems throughout the ages have resulted from the fact that we have not respected our sexuality or that of other people. Powerful tyrants have 'owned' the sexuality of others. Children have been sold into prostitution because of poverty and hardship. Troth has been replaced by deceit and unfaithfulness. People have become sexually obsessed, and it has destroyed them. Our contemporary commodification of sex is yet another chapter in the story of sin in our relationships and in the structures of our societies. When sex becomes god, then spirituality itself becomes focused on sex. And the warnings of St Paul to the early church about the power and potential destructiveness of sex are no less relevant today.

So, from a biblical viewpoint, marriage alone is to be the context for full, sexual body-giving of one to another. And that giving is to be mutual, respectful, honouring and full of love.[27] For whereas many expressions of our sexuality are appropriate in a wide range of our relationships, sexual intercourse is exclusive to marriage. But in placing these boundaries around sexual union the Bible never implies that sex itself is sinful, dirty or repulsive. There is nothing intrinsically anti-spiritual about our body-lives. For it is not our physical sexuality which is a problem, since this is given us by God. The problem is human sinfulness which can distort and pervert it.

That is why the biblical theme of redemption is a key one also for our human sexuality. Indeed, what can be more redemptive of human flesh than the fact that God took it. Jesus, the Word Made Flesh had a body. Jesus was fully human. He ate, drank, partied and slept, and when he washed or swam he was probably naked. Jesus touched and healed the bodies of others, and rejected the asceticism of his critics. He blessed the body of a woman with menstrual problems and accepted, physically, the kisses and tears of a woman with a doubtful sexual reputation. He challenged the hypocrisy of a crowd of self-righteous people who were ready to stone an adulterous woman, whilst ignoring their own sin. He asked for a drink at a well from a much-married Samaritan woman, ignoring the taboos of sex, race and hygiene which were imposed by his culture. And everywhere he showed that what was important in the worship of God was not good behaviour, or a legalistic spirituality, but a heart of love and an openness to God's Spirit of Truth. For the life of the Spirit is lived in the body.

Both our spirituality and our sexuality can therefore be redeemed. We can shake free from the pagan influences of our culture and from the brokenness in our relationships because Christ has died to release us from the bondage to sin. And that bondage is yet more powerful when it is the bondage of a whole society, rather than the struggles of any one individual. We can turn from our worship of the creature rather than the Creator, and develop a spirituality which centres on God rather than which centres on ourselves. We can reject the sexual unfaithfulness of our age, and work again at the meaning of marital commitment for a new generation. For we are people-in-relationship and even when those relationships have been damaged there is always hope for reparation. We can know broken relationships restored, young lives renewed and sexual distortions healed. For Christ's redemption is far reaching, and brings hope to those who are afar off, as well to those who are within the body of the Church. And when we can integrate our spiritual and our sexual lives in a way which holds them both in obedience to God's Word and God's Truth we are beginning to demonstrate what that redemption means.

We have to recognize, however, that this is not a generation for coyness. We cannot pretend either that there is no problem, or that there are no repercussions of the way in which people live. We do not yet know what effects lie ahead for a generation who have been encouraged to dispense with chastity. For no known culture has ever been so derisive about the dangers of promiscuity and survived intact. There is thus a great need to address the exploitation of sex and the confusion over spirituality with insight and faith. This might involve spending time with those whose relationships are in shreds. It might mean that the church must be ready to hear stories which distress and alarm, and work with people who are caught up in sexually distorted lives. For we need to know the culture of our age, and be adults in our response. Judgementalism is not good enough, and merely avoiding the issues will not help. What is certain is that the age of naiveté is past. And God calls his church not to innocence, but to wisdom and purity.

[1] Jean François Lyotard, *The Postmodern Condition: a Report on Knowledge*, Manchester University Press, 1986. p. xxiv.

[2] Jerome, Letter cxvii quoted by Karen Armstrong in *Gospel According to Woman*, Hamish Hamilton, 1986, pp. 57-59.

[3] Jerome, Letter XIV, *To Asella*.

[4] Quoted by Jane Barr, 'The Influence of St Jerome on Mediaeval Attitudes toward Women' in *After Eve*, edit. by Janet Martin Soskice, Marshall Pickering, 1990, p. 96.

[5] See Jane Barr, 'The Vulgate Genesis and Jerome's Attitudes to Women', in *Studia Patristica*, Vol. XVIII, Pergamon Press, Oxford, 1982.

[6] *After Eve*, p. 101.

[7] Ibid. p. 94.

[8] See Monica Furlong, *A Dangerous Delight. Women and Power in the Church*, SPCK, 1991, p. 22.

[9] St Bonaventure, *Life*, Chap 4, "Advancement of the Order", in E. Gurney Slater tr. *The Little Flowers of St Francis*, Everyman, 1963, p. 331.

[10] This section is taken from my article "Nuns, Witches and Patriarchy", *Anvil*, 1991.

[11] Lakshmanan: "Latter-day Witches Find a Seat in Salem" *The Boston Globe* 18 July 1993 23-4

[12] Capra quoted in Vishal Mangalwadi, *In Search of Self*, Hodder 1991 p 113

[13] *In Search of Self*, p. 114.

[14] Shirley MacLaine, quoted in *In Search of Self*, p.116.

[15] Rajneesh, *Isnio Sannyas*, Vol. 2.

[16] Preface to Marija Gimbutas, *The Language of the Goddess*, Harper and Row, 1898, p. XIV.

[17] Quoted in A.B. Spencer et al., *The Goddess Revival*, Baker Book House, 1995, p.24.

[18] Robert Ogilvie Crombie, quoted in *In Search of Self*, p. 130.

[19] Carol P. Christ, "Why Women need the Goddess: Phenomenological, Psychological and Political Reflections", *Womanspirit Rising; A Feminist Reader in Religion*. Eds. C.P. Christ and J. Plaskow, Harper and Row, 1979 p. 286.

[20] Carter Heyward, *Touching our Strength: The Erotic as Power and the Love of God*, Harper-Collins, 1989, p. 90.

[21] Dorothea Solle, ibid. p. 78.

[22] *Touching Our Strength*, p. 128.

[23] Ibid. p. 137.

[24] Ibid. p. 137.

[25] Ibid. p. 117.

[26] "Friendship and Intimacy", *The Search for Intimacy*, Hodder, 1995, pp. 140-163.

[27] This is developed very fully in Alan Storkey, *Marriage and its Modern Crisis*, Hodder, 1996.

Chapter 11 HOMOSEXUALITY - PREDISPOSING FACTORS

James B. Walker

This paper seeks to indicate some of the predisposing factors that may lead to homosexuality (this term being taken throughout as naturally inclusive of lesbianism).[1] The first part looks at the predisposition as it may arise from a biological basis for homosexuality, or at least where biological factors might play some part in determining predisposition to homosexuality. The second part indicates some of the psychological areas out of which homosexuality might develop. It is perhaps helpful to add that this paper does not tackle the moral and spiritual aspects of homosexuality which are always real issues for Christians, due to the Bible's unequivocal stance against homosexual behaviour.

Presuppositions

"Born or bred"? - considerable debate centres on this question. Much evidence is adduced, on both sides of the debate, and this evidence is presented through certain patterns of interpretation. The interpretation of the evidence tends to accord with the position the proponent wants to advance. By and large those who take a more liberal stance to homosexuality tend to be those who argue for a biological basis for homosexuality, those who take a more traditional viewpoint tend to argue that social, environmental factors are the key ones in determining orientation. Each side has a 'loaded' perspective, interpreting and advancing its position within its chosen framework. All such perspectives are 'loaded', but are not, because of that, necessarily wrong. We must always be aware of the perspective from which we come and which tends to colour our own interpretation. Christians, for instance, clearly interpret life and history from a Christian perspective, a perspective which differs radically from an atheist perspective. Although different, the Christian would still wish to claim his or her perspective is the right one.

BIOLOGICAL FACTORS

It is difficult to assess current research, and indeed, where claims are made counter claims tend to be advanced. Sexual orientation is a very complex phenomenon, involving many factors.

The Sexual Spectrum

All women and men appear to lie within a spectrum varying from heterosexual to homosexual, a small percentage being exclusively heterosexual or exclusively homosexual, with most women and men lying between the two extremes. The vast majority lie on the heterosexual side, with perhaps only 1-3% of people on the homosexual side[2]. For those predominantly heterosexual (or homosexual), but more than incidentally homosexual (or heterosexual), social and environmental factors may more easily cause such people to move from one side to another.

Sex and Sex Hormones

Magnus Hirschfield, the founder of the world's first Institute for Sex Research, suggested at the beginning of the century that there may be chemicals in the body that control our sexual development. By the 1930s a whole cluster of chemicals were seen to be involved, the male sex hormones being called *androgens*, of which *testosterone* is the most important, and the female sex hormones were called *oestrogens*. One cannot simply label the former as "male" and the latter as "female" for all these hormones are present in both men and women. However the male testis produces huge amounts of *androgens*, while the female ovary produces *oestrogens*. Hormonal sex is a matter of balance between male type and female type hormones.

Homosexuality from the 1930s through to the 1970s was held, by some who advocated a biological basis for homosexuality, to result, in men, from a deficiency of male sex hormones, and, in women, from a deficiency of female sex hormones. Injecting gay people with the appropriate male or female hormones was thought to be able to effect a cure. However, it was discovered that, while sex hormones could affect behaviour, they had in fact no direct effect on sexual orientation. Indeed most studies failed to find any connection between adult hormone levels and sexual orientation.[3] The answer to homosexuality thus did not lie, at least exclusively, in hormone deprivation.

Attention then moved through the work of Gunter Dorner in the late 1960s to examining exposure to sex hormones during early development. While previously it had been thought that production of testosterone began at puberty, research showed that the male testicles actually started making testosterone during the baby's development in the womb. The critical period was perceived to be between three months after conception to two years (if not four years) after birth, overlapping with the period of male/female brain differentiation. Without the hormone the male baby would develop to the female body pattern, but with the testosterone the physiological balance would be tipped towards the male 'foetus' developing along male lines.[4] The idea here is that exposure or lack of exposure to sex hormones during early development determines sexual orientation.[5] Thus fluctuations, at times very small, in early hormone levels are thought to affect the way the nerves of the brain are "wired up" as the brain develops. Different parts of the brain may be sensitive at different times to sex hormones.

Anatomic Difference in the Brain

In 1991 Simon LeVay published research which purported to show that there was a difference between the brains of homosexual and heterosexual men, specifically in the hypothalamus, which is thought to be the centre for the brain's sexual activity.[6] His study was based on brain tissue obtained from routine autopsies of 41 people who had died at hospitals in New York and California. 19 of these were homosexual men, all of whom had AIDS; 16 were presumed heterosexual men, 6 of whom had been intravenous drug abusers and had died of AIDS; and 6 were presumed heterosexual women.

LeVay concentrated on the volumes of four cell groups in the anterior hypothalamus of the brain, an area which regulates male/ female sexual behaviour. He claimed:

No differences were found between the groups in the volumes of INAH[7] 1,2, or 4. ... INAH 3 was more than twice as large in heterosexual men as in women. It was also, however, more than twice as large in heterosexual men as in homosexual men. This finding indicates that INAH is dimorphic with sexual orientation, at least in men, and suggests that sexual orientation has a biological substrate.[8]

Further evidence of difference was advanced by Swaab and Hofman, who claimed that in the hypothalamus another cell group called the suprachiasmatic nucleus (SCN) varies with respect to sexual orientation in men. Evidence was presented that the SCN is larger in homosexual than heterosexual men.[9] It must be added however that in men and women the SCN is usually the same size, which suggests that the brains of homosexual men have some unique aspects.[10]

There are problems with both Swaab and Hofman's and also with LeVay's studies. The former has yet to be corroborated, but, as Byne and Parsons comment, "even if corroborated, this finding would not support the prenatal hormonal hypothesis, because in humans the size of the SCN does not vary with sex. Furthermore, existing evidence does not suggest a primary role for the SCN in the regulation of sexual behaviours."[11]

LeVay's' study is problematic for the following reasons:[12]

(a) His sample size was small - 41 people, 19 known homosexuals, 16 supposed heterosexual men and 6 supposed heterosexual women, although he never bothered to check that the heterosexuals were in fact heterosexuals. His failure to identify one of the control groups meant that some of the supposed heterosexuals might have in fact been homosexuals, a fact that would have affected his data.

(b) It can be conjectured that the presence of AIDS might account for the differences in sizes. The heterosexual men who died of AIDS might have died earlier in the course of the disease, due perhaps to their being intravenous drug uses, and so likely to have had lesser health care than the homosexual men.

(c) Although the argument for differentiation centres on the mean cluster sizes for heterosexuals and homosexuals, there were a number of significant data exceptions. "Three of the 'heterosexuals' had clusters smaller than the mean size for homosexuals. Three of the homosexuals had larger clusters than the mean size for 'heterosexuals'."[13]

(d) The INAH 3 and the SCN are only a couple of millimetres big, and it is conceivable that the differences could arise *because* people are homosexual over a reasonable period of time, rather than being a cause of homosexuality.

Chandler Burr comments:

> Even if LeVay's hypothalamus study stands up to scrutiny, it will not justify drawing extravagant conclusions. Establishing a distinction is not the same thing as finding a cause. Anatomy is not etiology, but it may offer a starting point for a journey backward in search of ultimate origins of sexual orientation. That journey takes us into the realm of hormones and genetics.[14]

Recent research in 1992 by Allen and Gorski offered another example of brain difference between homosexual and heterosexual men. The *anterior commissure* (AC), a bundle of nerve fibres that carries messages between two halves of the brain, was found to be similar in size in both women and homosexuals but in both larger than in heterosexual men. As these fibres are fixed within a few months of birth the conclusion was drawn that difference in the brains of homosexual men must arise very early in life.

This study has yet to be replicated and indeed another similar study has found that the *anterior commissure* is larger in men than in women.[15] Byne and Parsons point out that there are technical flaws within Allen and Gorski's study.[16] (a) Due to the considerable overlap in AC size between heterosexual and homosexual men ("the size of the AC of 27 or 30 homosexual men fell within the range established by 30 heterosexual men"), the size of the AC yields nothing about sexual orientation. (b) The fact that Allen and Gorski relied on brain tissues of men who had died of AIDS leaves their study open to the "same interpretative difficulties" as LeVay's.

Genetic Studies

Bailey and Pillard conducted research on homosexual males, published 1991, and homosexual women, published 1993.[17] Their research involved 56 homosexual male identical twins (71 female identical twins), 54 homosexual male non-identical twins (37 female non-identical twins), and 54 brothers adopted into homosexual families (35 sisters adopted), and 142 non-twin biological brothers (71 non-twin biological sisters). The studies purported to show that 52% of male identical twins were both homosexual (for women the figure was 48% being both lesbian); 22% of male non-identical twins were both homosexual (for women the figure was 16%); 11% of adoptive brothers were homosexual (for women the figure was 6%); 9.2% of non-twin brothers were homosexual (for women the figure was 14%). Bailey and Pillard concluded in the earlier study (paralleled in the later study), that "Heritabilities were substantial under a wide range of assumptions and ascertainable bias"[18]. Their main argument is this: because the role of environment is the same for all the brothers (and sisters) and because identical twins share the same genes, the higher number of identical twins who are homosexual, compared with non identical twins and the others, suggests that the difference lies in heritable factors, in the genes.

The study however is questionable in several ways, and the following points are drawn mainly from Byne and Parsons.[19]
(a) If the identical twins share the same genes, why are not all of them homosexual, instead of only 52%? The large numbers that do not fit into the heritable thesis (48%!) reveal clearly our ignorance of the factors that are involved in sexual orientation.
(b) The percentages for adoptive (non-genetically related) brothers and biological (genetically related) brothers is about the same, 11% and 9.2%, yet a genetic hypothesis would expect a higher rate among the biological brothers. As Horgan puts it, "Bailey and Pillard found more concordance between unrelated, adopted brothers than related (but non-twin) brothers"[20]. To account for this anomaly, Bailey and Pollard suggest that the figure of 9.2% for non-twin brothers may be

artificially low and result from their sample material. Nevertheless from their own results it is at least arguable that, with both the non-identical male twins (22%; women 16%) and the non-twin brothers (9.2%; women 14%) sharing the same proportion of genetic material, and also being closer to one another in percentage terms than to the percentage of identical twins (52%; women 48%), differences are more likely to arise from environmental factors than from genetic factors.

(c) The unique psychological relationship between twins, in particular identical twins, is nowhere taken into consideration.

(d) The subjects in both studies were recruited through advertisements in homosexual publications, and it may be that a bias is thereby introduced, for those who are inclined to read such periodicals and who volunteered for the project might have a point to make in advancing the homosexual rights movement.

(e) No account was offered of the possible effects that environment and family setting might have on the subjects. It is impossible to separate out genetic and environmental factors for those who grew up in the same household.

In 1993, Hamer with others published results of research purporting to show:

> DNA linkage analysis of a selected group of 40 families in which there were two gay brothers and no indication of nonmaternal transmission revealed a correlation between homosexual orientation and the inheritance of polymorphic markers on the X chromosome in approximately 64 percent of the sib-pairs tested[21].

In other words, if brothers, both homosexual, turn out to have in common specific DNA sequences on their X chromosome (a chromosome inherited solely from the mother), these sequences can be considered to be genetic markers for homosexuality. Hamer arrived at his conclusions thus. Following the discovery that, for some homosexuals, the homosexual trait is passed through female members of the family, Hamer found that, of 40 pairs of homosexual brothers tested, 33 pairs shared a set of five markers located near the long arm of the X chromosome, in a region called Xq28. The linkage of homosexual orientation to these markers indicates "a statistical confidence level of more than 99 percent that at least one subtype of male orientation is genetically influenced"[22].

It is notable that these results have yet to be replicated, but as they stand they contain some serious flaws. Of the small sample tested, 18% did not have these markers. This may however be due to the fact that, as Hamer suggests, homosexuality may arise from a number of causes, both genetic and environmental. Nevertheless the figure of 18% is high. Further Hamer never checked for the presence of these markers among the heterosexual brothers of the homosexual men they studied.

Conclusions from the biological evidence

To assume that there are hard and fast results from biological evidence is, certainly at this point in time, false. Equally it is important to note that biological evidence may well be forthcoming in the future and cannot be dismissed at this stage. Of course even if biological differences are found, it is still a big jump to claim that behaviour is linked to brain organisation.

Burr, who believes that one day a biological cause will be found, underlines the difficulty and complexity of the study:

> What makes the science in this case so problematic, quite apart from the usual technical difficulties inherent in biological research - particularly neurobiological research... - is the ineffable nature of our psychosexual selves. This encompasses a vast universe of stimulation and response, of aesthetic and erotic sensibilities. There are those who see an element of hubris in the quest to explain such things in biological terms. Others see not so much hubris as hype... It is undeniably true that neurobiological research is often pursued in a context of great ignorance. The brain remains an organ of mystery even in general, not to mention with regard to specific functions.[23]

Byne and Parsons, following their survey of past and current claims, conclude:

> There is no evidence at present to substantiate a biological theory, just as there is no compelling evidence to support any singular psychosocial explanation. While all behaviour must have an ultimate biologic substrate, the appeal of current biological explanations for sexual orientation may derive more from dissatisfaction with the present status of psychosomatic explanations than from a substantiating body of experimental data. Critical review shows the evidence favouring a biologic theory to be lacking.[24]

PSYCHOLOGICAL ROOTS AND NEEDS

Homosexuality can appear to develop without genetic or hormonal factors being determinatively operative, and this section outlines some of the psychological roots and needs which may predispose towards its arising. These psychological factors may serve to produce hormonal imbalance and changes in the brain that can affect sexuality, but equally they may have no effect on hormonal imbalance or brain changes. The factors involved in homosexuality are very complex indeed. In the list that follows it is crucial to remember that each item *may* lead to homosexuality and equally it *may not*. Many of the following points are drawn from Leanne Payne's book, *The Broken Image*.[25] Payne has herself come across these factors and readers may wish to consult her book for fuller details. She, and others, have found that in many instances and in certain circumstances and conditions homosexuality is reversible.

LONELINESS

A person may choose a homosexual relationship out of a deep desire for intimacy and for exploration of personal identity.[26]

TRAUMATIC EXPERIENCES IN CHILDHOOD

Incidents such as rape (homosexual or heterosexual) can cause a badly wounded self-image, an overwhelming sense of guilt and considerable confusion over one's own identity. This can leave an inability to relate to both males or females in general, depending on who effected the rape, and depending also on who connived at or did nothing to prevent the rape occurring. Where molesting is particularly severe, confusion and guilt can intensify the sense of brokenness and result in separation from normal human relations. A person may attempt to overcome this separation and discover love through tentative sexual exploration with another person.[27]

BIRTH TRAUMA

It is surmised that birth trauma can lead to a 'hurting' infant, fearful of being outside the womb, and hence lead to a repression of one's true self. This can create an inability to think of oneself as a true person, if one is always fearful of the 'outside' world.[28]

EXCESSIVE SELF-LOVE; or perhaps, EXCESSIVE INSECURITY

A person who thinks very highly of himself or herself, or indeed who is very insecure, may engage in considerable masturbation and fantasy, in an attempt either to reinforce his or her own sense of perfection, or to seek desperately to find security in his or her sexual identity.[29]

ARTISTIC ABILITY

There is a public myth that gifted artistic ability is connected to homosexuality, but this can be a self-fulfilling prophecy.[30]

REBELLION

Gaining one's identity in rebellion can lead to homosexuality, as a way of more rigorously rejecting accepted mores.[31]

DEPRIVATION OF A MOTHER'S LOVE

Deprivation can lead to a child not separating himself or herself from his or her mother's identity (for true love enables separation and acceptance of oneself and the other), and hence result in a confusion of who the self is. It must be noted that at times a mother may be actually unable to give love, perhaps through exhaustion, through psychological problems, through strictness of upbringing, through hospital treatment, and through divorce.[32]

POSSESSIVE AND DOMINATING MOTHER

The child is not enabled to develop as a real person, but always must accord with the demands of his or her mother. The person may be constantly craving the approval and affection of his or her mother, and be unable to develop his or her own identity in distinction from his or her mother.[33]

SUPPRESSED MASCULINITY

Lack of paternal affirmation may lead to a less developed view of one's own identity. "A man is not a man until his father *tells* him he is a man."[34] Suppressed masculinity may also occur where there is a weak or absent father.

DISAPPOINTED FATHER/MOTHER

A father or mother who may have desired a child of the opposite sex can treat a girl as a boy or a boy as a girl, and so give rise to confusion over identity.[35]

BITTERNESS, HATRED AND FEAR

Bitterness and hatred of others can lead to rejection of normal relations of acceptance and love, added to which can be the determination to be very different from what other people expect, in order to hurt.[36] Bitterness and hatred of oneself can lead to thinking always the worst of oneself, and, through inability to relate naturally to others, to conceiving of oneself as strange, ill-fitting and rejected by society (a conception of some homosexual [and heterosexual!] people).[37] Fear of men or women can lead to extreme feminist or masculinist attitudes, with the belief that acceptance and warmth in relationship can only occur with persons of one's own sex.[38]

FAILURE TO ACHIEVE AN ADEQUATE SENSE OF BEING

Through not accepting and loving oneself, relations with others can become distorted and frustrating, leading to loneliness and a craving for love. Such a person may feel on the fringes of society and so assume he or she is homosexual. Through not knowing a mother's love a person can fail to achieve both a sense of well-being and also of being itself. This can result in a person identifying himself or herself with a sense of non-being.[39]

Conclusion from the psychological evidence

It is worth repeating that the above factors *may* lead to homosexuality, equally they *may not*. Where a person is homosexual, the above factors are believed by Payne and others to form the reasons why a person, who has come to them for help, is homosexual. Such reasons are, they have found, often buried very deep within those seeking help, often at sub-conscious or barely remembered levels. In their experience a number of people have had their orientation changed through counselling and prayer, some change occurring quickly but others over a lengthy period of time. It must be added however, as a challenge to this claim, that some counsellors and psychotherapists have claimed that only in a very few instances have lasting changes occurred to homosexuals in their orientation and lifestyle. Payne's claim, for which there appears to be clear evidence, directly challenges the claim that homosexuality derives from hereditary factors which exert a determinative influence. This however is not to deny that heritable factors may have some predisposing, if not determinative, influence as to why a person develops as a homosexual rather than a heterosexual.

There is, it must be underlined, considerable mystery as to what makes a person develop as he or she does, and research is under way to seek to understand why a person becomes, for example, schizophrenic or depressed or whatever. It is a puzzle why two people from the same home and facing similar problems can yet react in such different ways to tension and stress, one facing them positively, the other becoming depressed and lethargic. What is it that makes one react in one way and not the other? Does the answer lie only in environmental circumstances, in family background, in personality traits, and can these really be disconnected from all hereditary aspects?

CONCLUSION

Burr quotes a conversation he had with LeVay:

'You shouldn't draw such a distinction between biological and psychological mechanisms,' he chided me at one point during our conversation. 'What people are really getting at is the difference between innately determined mechanisms and culturally determined mechanisms, but people screw that up and say that's the difference between biology and psychology. It isn't. It's two different approaches for looking at the same thing: the mind. Biologists look at it from the bottom up, from the level of synapses and molecules, and psychologists are looking at it from the top down, at behaviour and such'.[40]

Whether LeVay is correct is a matter for debate, but it should lead to a greater openness to, and genuine critical dialogue concerning, the multi-form causes that appear to underlie homosexuality.

It is quite possible that, as Knight comments

Someday, scientists may find a hereditary condition that makes some people particularly susceptible to the environmental factors that may tend to produce homosexual orientation. But this is a far cry from finding a 'gay gene'.[41]

As was quoted earlier from Byne and Parsons, thus far "critical review shows the evidence favouring a biologic theory to be lacking", but it must also be added, thus far "there is no compelling evidence to support any singular psychosocial explanation".[42] Byne and Parsons are careful to insert the word "singular" here. There is no *single* psychosocial explanation, but rather there are many and varied psychosocial explanations, each interweaving with others in differing degrees in different people.

There are thus a whole variety of possible facilitating influences that may dispose a person towards homosexuality, and the phenomenon cannot be accounted for or embraced within one particular theory. All sorts of things - personality, temperament, family background, hormonal aspects, heritable features - may help nudge a person one way or another. Obviously genetic and hormonal factors play some part, for we are all biological beings. Nevertheless, and it needs to be reiterated that at present there is a lack of decisive evidence from the biological side, any part genetic and hormonal factors may play is undoubtedly influenced by learning, culture and mixing in family and society.[43]

[1] It should be noted that the meaning of the term 'homosexual' is not as clear as one might think, and indeed no clearly acceptable definition of the term exists which embraces all disciplines, including the medical and psychosocial. Further, the way in which homosexuality is perceived varies considerably across cultures and can embrace orientation and/or practice, states of the mind and/or physical behaviour.

[2] A C. Kinsey, et al, in *Sexual Behaviour in the Human Male*, W.B. Saunders Co., Philadelphia, 1948, and in *Sexual Behaviour in the Human Female*, W.B. Saunders Co., Philadelphia, 1953, argued, on the basis of 12,000 individual interviews that 10% of the male population is homosexual, with 5% of women being lesbian. This figure is now reckoned by the scientific community to be far too high. Kinsey had gleaned a considerable part of his evidence from criminals, including sex offenders, and extrapolated his findings to the general population. More recent estimates tend to put the figure at just under 3% for men and just over 1% for women (D. Forman and C. Chivers, "Sexual Behaviour of Young and Middle-Aged Men in England and Wales," *British Medical Journal*, 298, 1989, pp.1137-1142, and G. Remafedi, et al, "Demography of Sexual Orientation in Adolescents," *Paediatrics*, 89, 1992, pp.714-721, which involved a study of over 36,000 teenagers in Minnesota.)

[3] W Byne and B Parsons, "Human Sexual Orientation: The Biologic Theories Reappraised," *Archives of General Psychiatry*, 50, 1993, p.228, "the relevant literature includes only three studies that suggested lower testosterone levels in male homosexuals, while 20 studies found no differences based on sexual orientation, and two reported elevated testosterone levels in male homosexuals."

[4] Ibid., "Advocates for the primacy of biologic determinants might conclude, 'the prenatal hormonal history is strongly implicated in the genesis and ultimate differentiation of a homosexual, bisexual, or heterosexual status,' while advocates for the primacy of pyschosocial factors would counter that 'biological factors exert at most a predisposing rather than a determining influence.'"

[5] G Dorner in the 1980s advocated the theory that hormonal imbalance in a mother could be caused by stress, thus causing homosexuality in her child. His research was based on people born in the later years of World War II, whose pregnant mothers suffered under the allied bombing blitz.

[6] S LeVay, "A difference in Hypothalamic Structure between Heterosexual and Homosexual Men," *Science*, 258, 1991, p.1034-1037. "Sexual differentiation of the hypothalamus of the human brain is generally believed to take place around midpregnancy and thought to be related to the development of sexual orientation and gender identity," D Swaab and M Hofman in "An enlarged suprachiasmatic nucleus in homosexual men," *Brain Research*, 537, 1990, p.141.

[7] Interstitial nuclei, the cells which are part of the anterior hypothalamus.

[8] Ibid. p.1034.

[9] Swaab and Hofman, op.cit, p.141-148.

[10] If Swaab and Hofman's conclusion is correct, it is not therefore the case, as used to be thought, that a homosexual male brain is basically a female brain which has not developed through male hormones along male lines. There is no evidence as yet of the size of SCN in lesbians and whether this differs from heterosexual men and women.

[11] Byne and Parsons, op.cit., p.235.

[12] Ibid.

[13] R Knight, "Sexual Orientation, Faulty Research in the Homosexual Debate", *Family*, 1993, p.4.

[14] C Burr, "Homosexuality and Biology", *The Atlantic Monthly*, 1993, p.58.

[15] S Demeter, et al, "Morohometric analysis of the human corpus callosum and anterior commissure", *Hum Neurobiol*, 6, 1988, pp.219-226.

[16] Byne and Parsons, op.cit, p.235.

[17] J M Bailey, R C Pillard, "A Genetic Study of Male Sexual Orientation", *Archives of General Psychiatry*, 48, 1991, pp.1089-1095; "Heritable Factors Influence Sexual Orientation in Women", *Archives of General Psychiatry*, 50, 1993, pp.217-223.

[18] Ibid, p.1089.

[19] Byne and Parsons, op.cit., p.229-230.

[20] J Horgan, "Eugenics Revisited", *Scientific American*, 1993, p.131.

[21] D H Hamer, et al, "A Linkage Between DNA Markers on the X Chromosome and Male Sexual Orientation", *Science*, 261, 1993, p.321.

[22] Ibid.

[23] Burr, op.cit., p.47-8.

[24] Byne and Parsons, op.cit., p.228.

[25] L Payne, The *Broken Image*, Kingsway, Eastbourne, 1988. Similar points are made by M. Bergner, *Setting Love in Order*, Monarch, Crowborough, 1995. See also the articles by Dennis Wrigley and Linda Stalley in this book.

[26] Payne, p.65.

[27] Ibid., pp.76, 82, 85.

[28] Ibid., p.80.

[29] Ibid., p.85.

[30] Ibid., p.93.

[31] Ibid., p.98.

[32] Ibid., pp.101-2.

[33] Ibid., p.102.

[34] Ibid., pp.66, 72, 109.

[35] Ibid., pp.108-9.

[36] Ibid., p.102.

[37] Ibid., p.103.

[38] Ibid., p.113.

[39] Ibid., pp.121-2.

[40] Burr, op.cit., p.52.

[41] Knight, op.cit., p.5.

[42] Byne and Parsons, op.cit., p.228.

[43] See S L Jones and D E Workman, "Homosexuality: The Behavioural Sciences and the Church", *Journal of Psychology and Theology*. 17, 1989, p.221), quoted in C Townsend, "Homosexuality: Finding the Way in Truth and Love", *Cambridge Papers*, 3, 1994, p.3.

Chapter 12 HEALING AND WHOLENESS

(1) IDENTITY AND SEXUALITY

Dennis Wrigley and Linda Stalley

Introduction

Strong and permanent relationships based on mutual trust, respect and love undoubtedly strengthen society. Relationships which are temporary, shallow, debased and exploitive clearly weaken society. Relationships in which there is indifference and detachment are not neutral, they can be positively destructive.

The breakdown of relationships is a characteristic of contemporary society and with the obvious breakdown of marriage and the destruction of so many family units the issue of sexual relationships is increasingly the subject of public debate. Simultaneously with changes in legislation, the consequent alteration in behaviour patterns and the emergence of the AIDS crisis have also placed the issue of homosexual relationships in the arena of public discussion. This has undoubtedly caused much pain and deep divisions whilst partisan protagonists seek to normalise what others regard as abnormal behaviour.

Much of the debate has sadly been driven by aggressive 'gay' pressure groups which have used considerable public influence to obtain both platforms and funds for their movement. Their activities frequently involve coercion, threat and occasionally violence although doubtless the vast majority of homosexuals, being ignorant of these activities, would themselves disapprove of this behaviour.

On the other hand however it can be argued that many homosexuals, lonely and unhappy, have felt vulnerable and rejected. The emergence of a strident gay subculture often driven by commercial and political interests has tended to create exclusively gay ghettos and thus to separate homosexuals from the rest of the community. It has tended to divert attention away from the need for an understanding, caring and loving approach to the whole issue of male or female homosexuality.

What is Homosexuality?

Homosexuality is essentially a confused condition and therefore there is confusion in its definition. Lawrence J. Hatterer in his book

Changing Homosexuality in the Male defines the homosexual person as "one who is motivated, in adult life by definite erotic attraction to members of the same sex and who usually, but not necessarily, engages in overt sexual relations with them". To have a pre-disposition or propensity for members of one's own sex may not be a permanent situation. J.J. West in *Homosexuality Re-examined*[1] stated, "Few people pass through life without at some stage experiencing homosexual feelings". He emphasised, "Like other aspects of human behaviour, sexual orientation is the outcome of a complex interplay of different factors". He pointed to these being mostly environmental, including general cultural habits and expectations, family upbringing and personal circumstances.

In one sense the homosexual through his or her orientation is expressing a profound psychological need or deficiency. Hence, according to Dr Elizabeth Moberley to stop 'being a homosexual' means "to stop being a person with same sex psychological deficits".

Our starting point in considering homosexuality therefore must surely be that God does not put labels on anyone. All human nature is wounded and in need of healing and the one who is called 'a homosexual' must primarily be seen as a human being to be loved and treated with the same respect as any other person. The fact that one aspect of their life differs from the norm must never be an excuse for them being robbed of their dignity, worth and uniqueness.

Christians believe that every man and woman is created in the image of God. In spite of weaknesses and problems we are each of inestimable value in His sight. We believe that our relationships with each other are of immediate concern to God. They are directly influenced by the nature of our relationship with Him. The current debate about homosexuality must be seen in the context of the rapid growth of promiscuity, the devaluation of marriage and in the encouragement of child sex instanced in the distribution of condoms to young schoolchildren.

Driven by commercial interests which are ruthless and amoral we have become a sex-obsessed society with a totally unnatural emphasis upon the sex act, often in the context of violence, as distinct from normal, healthy, loving human relationships. Bruce Gyngell, Managing Director of Yorkshire/Tyne Tees Television, speaking to the Royal Television Society, asked, "What are we doing to our sensibilities and moral values and, more important, those of our children when, day after day, we broadcast an unremitting diet of violence, extremes of sexuality and negative behaviour?". As these commercial interests have become stronger they have become more greedy and have not hesitated to debase, degrade and devalue the relationships which should be valued for their gentleness, dignity and modesty.

Children, in particular, have had ugly and sometimes frightening sexual images imposed upon them by irresponsible adults. The so-called "National Condom Week" Report boldly proclaimed "serial monogamy is the buzz phrase for the 1990's" and there is no doubt that there are now heavy pressures militating against life-long partnership in marriage. These pressures are of course generating immense human suffering, particularly amongst children.

Jesus comes to put right our relationships with God, with ourselves and with others. He specifically says, "Whatever you did for the least of these brothers of mine, you did for me".[2] A judgmental attitude can be deeply wounding and highly offensive, but on the other hand, a desire for good relationships should not blind us to the truth. In the emotionally charged debate on homosexuality which is currently taking place both in society at large and in the Church there is all too often a readiness to compromise the truth in order to be politically correct.

The first truth emphasised is that the incidence of homosexuality is far lower than we are led to believe. In the U.S. Government General Social Survey of 1989, Professor Tom Smith of the University of Chicago undertook a survey of sexual behaviour. This showed that 98.5% of adults were exclusively heterosexual. Studies carried out in other countries show a remarkable consistency. A survey in the United Kingdom sponsored by the Welcome Trust reported 1.4% of males having had a homosexual partner in the previous five years and 1.1% in the previous year. The Report claimed that the results were "consistent with those from other recent studies in Europe and the United States".

The second truth emphasised is that a high proportion of homosexuals are deeply unhappy in their condition and would wish to change. In the 1992 SIGMA study funded by the Medical Research Council and the Department of Health no fewer than 34% of homosexual men expressed regret at being homosexual. Possibly more than this proportion felt regret but did not express it. 17% "had considered giving up being gay" and 9% "would take a pill today to make them heterosexual (if one were available)". Recognition of this is important in really meeting the needs of those who are caught up in the 'gay' scene.

Homosexual practice for many participants creates in its own right a stress level which makes the homosexual hypersensitive to criticism and to competition. Therefore, homosexual relationships are fraught with jealousies and angers and these are made worse by the promiscuous practice of multi-partnering. For the Christian the sex act is sacred and not to be taken lightly. Yet, sadly for many male homosexuals the physical sexual encounter is ephemeral as a result of encounters while 'cruising'. This in itself is a devaluation of relationships and inevitably has a high exploitive content. Love is about giving and receiving, not taking and dominating.

Promiscuity and multi-partnering robs the participant of their human dignity and debases sexuality. During this century we have seen countless examples of the way in which the value of individual men and women has been swept on one side. Privacy has been invaded. Modesty, a fundamental ingredient in civilised society, has been ridiculed. The gentleness and beauty of sexual relationships in marriage have been scorned and torn apart. The process of dehumanisation has continued apace assisted by the media and militant secular humanist influences. We, by omission and apathy, encourage our children to have sex. Moreover, we teach them about sexuality without any real guidance on spiritual and moral factors, frequently imposing upon them the dogmas and doctrines of a very bigoted and intolerant humanistic minority.

The Background

The predisposing factors and circumstances which may give rise to homosexuality are complex and numerous. The current debate about homosexuality centres largely upon basically whether it is genetic or acquired. If it is the former there ought to be considerable evidence available to show that it is genetic and/or organically determined. This evidence does not exist. As Laurence Hatterer, the American psychiatrist states, "homosexuals are not born but made and genetic, hereditary, constitutional, glandular or hormonal factors have no significance in causing homosexuality"[3].

Dr Frank Lake, who pioneered clinical theology, discovered considerable evidence of the significance of disorders in infant years being directly related to the homosexual condition. All 50 male homosexual patients to whom Lake and his colleagues administered LSD between 1950 - 1966 relived a traumatic incident or painful period of babyhood in which life in the woman's care had been horrific.[4]

Dr Charles W. Socarides of the Albert Einstein College of Medicine in New York states that homosexuality is not innate, it is learned, acquired behaviour. Even Masters & Johnson in their book

Human Sexuality have written "the genetic theory of homosexuality has generally been discarded today". Dr John Money of the John Hopkins School of Medicine and Director of the Psycho-hormonal Research Unit states, "Whatever may be the possible unlearned assistance from constitutional sources, the child's psychosexual identity is not written, unlearned in the genetic code, the hormonal system or the nervous system at birth".

There is a remarkably high success rate in leading homosexuals into heterosexuality through Christian healing. Countless examples of this are to be found in the ministry of Leanne Payne. Revd John Hampsch has given much evidence of the healing of homosexuals through the work of *Desert Stream*, one of twenty-five groups listed in the central referral agency of Exodus International. The way in which we perceive ourselves and others is fundamentally changed when a person grows in Christian faith.

All the evidence points to the fact that homosexual orientation in adult life is the result of pre-birth and early childhood experiences.

As Dr Elizabeth Moberley states, "From the present evidence it would seem clear that the homosexual condition does not involve abnormal needs, but normal needs, that have abnormally, been left unmet in the ordinary process of growth. The needs as such are normal; their lack of fulfilment and the barrier to their fulfilment is abnormal".

There is Hope

Many people who are wrestling with problems of homosexuality and sexual identity come for help feeling hopeless, trapped and guilty. They are often hypersensitive to what they perceive to be other people's critical attitudes. Their hurts - and the arrogance that sometimes flows from these - must be treated with great sensitivity and love, not judgement. Often they are very lonely or alternatively have been dragged reluctantly into a sordid 'gay' scene. This environment may have temporarily enabled them to put on a cloak of respectability and public acceptance but this rarely enables them to escape from a sense of degradation, despair and guilt. The task of the Christian is not to intrude upon other people's personal lives but rather to respond to them constructively and in love when they cry for help. We are called to give hope to the seemingly hopeless, and to share deeply and confidentially with all the inner conflict and turmoil which afflicts the homosexual. We must do this in the full knowledge that most of us experience conflict and turmoil of equal magnitude in various other aspects of our lives.

When homosexuals discover that their condition is not irreversible and that Christ's power to heal covers every part of their being, they may expect to experience a new self-worth and self-esteem. The radical change they will encounter may be quite sudden or spread over a period of months or even years. It is our experience that God leads those he is healing along the path which is right for them. He never demands more of us than we are able to give. His grace is truly sufficient for all our needs. It must always be recognised, however, that the Gospel demands change and many of us are afraid of change. In this respect the homosexual is no different from any one else. We all need to hear and receive Jesus' words, "Behold I make all things new".[5]

What is Healing?

The subject of healing has been exposed to much debate and controversy within the Christian Church. When faced with the evidence, however, it is beyond doubt that Jesus heals today and the main channel for his healing is his Church - his Body on earth. In looking at the subject of healing, therefore, we are in the same position as the early writers in the church who stated simply, "We proclaim to you what we have seen and heard, so that you also may have fellowship with us".[6]

Many of the misconceptions and disagreements about healing seem to be related to differences in the interpretation of its meaning. Some confine healing to the proven cure of a physical or mental condition, but this definition is damaging in itself, leading to the conclusion that someone who is physically or mentally ill is unable to attain greater wholeness without the curing of their physical or mental condition. This disappointment in turn has a negative effect upon the individual's understanding and experience of the love of God in their lives, and thus damages faith.

For this reason, some have decided that the healing ministry was only seen during the life of Jesus. This interpretation denies the healing ministry given to the disciples, both when Jesus sent them out in twos and as reported in the Acts of the Apostles following Pentecost. It also denies the experience of the Christian Church throughout the years and the promise of Jesus that "anyone who has faith in me will do what I have been doing. He will do even greater things than these, because I am going to the Father".[7]

So, what is healing and how is it seen in lives today? Very simply, healing may be described as putting right what is wrong. Healing is bringing wholeness in place of impairment. Healing is bringing peace in place of disturbance. Healing is bringing equilibrium in place of imbalance. Healing is not just an isolated or even spectacular event, neither does it simply relate to one area of our lives. Healing is a continuous process. Healing may perhaps best be described as a journey upon and during which we come closer to God. In coming closer to him we become the fullness of the person he created us to be and are gradually transformed into a greater measure of his likeness. This is wholeness.

On our journey God is at the same time both the Father who accepts us just as we are yet who awaits us at the end of the road, calling us to our true home, and our companion Jesus who seeks to share in every pain and joy along the way.

We can only come closer to God when, in the depth of our being, we desire to do so. This desire in itself comes from his presence within us, his imprint, his Spirit planted within each being at their creation, the source of the love which so naturally flows from the heart of each member of humanity. Our desire to come closer to God and to be at peace with him is our response to his call to us. As St. John wrote, "This is love: not that we loved God, but that He loved us...".[8]

The Healing Ministry of Jesus

The way of Jesus is in stark contrast to the way of the world. He comes to serve, not to be served. He comes to give and not to receive. He points to the way of forgiveness, not retribution. His way is the way of total love, a love which is without condition or limit. His way is the way of peace.

Followers of Jesus were initially called people of the Way. They were called to serve, to give and to love. Followers of Jesus were called to be ministers of reconciliation, leading others on the path of forgiveness, bringing peace into a troubled world. The same applies to his followers today.

The ministry of healing was central to the life and teaching of Jesus and this ministry was basically about changing people's lives. All of the miracles reported in the Gospel narratives were signs of an encounter with the Son of God. The physical cures were the direct consequence of the authority of Jesus exercised upon a person's life and pointed to a far deeper healing of mind and spirit. Jesus came to announce the Kingdom, the place where God rules, and claimed to have all authority in both heaven and earth. Thus, wherever Jesus went there was healing. What was wrong was put right.

Jesus chose to become one of the people. He did not remain separate from the sick and the outcasts. He deliberately sought out the company of prostitutes, tax collectors and those considered to be 'unclean'. He touched the leper, He allowed a Samaritan woman to give him a drink, He stood by the woman caught in adultery, He welcomed the children. His whole life demonstrated love for the loveless - healing for those who knew they were sick.

The hallmark of Jesus' ministry was that he knew the real need of each individual who came to him. Their encounter with him was an encounter with the Truth and they were set free. To the man who was lowered through the roof of the house by his friends, Jesus said, "Your sins are forgiven".[9] He was set free from the paralysis of guilt, not simply the dysfunction of his legs.

Similarly, the woman who had suffered bleeding for 12 years needed to know that she was accepted and loved by God. The cessation of her bleeding which made her an unclean outcast was not sufficient to bring her the deeper healing which she really needed. Jesus sought her out to meet that need.

Today Jesus comes to each man, woman and child in the person of his Holy Spirit. To each of us he announces, "Here I am! I stand at the door and knock. If anyone hears my voice and opens the door, I will come in and eat with him and he with me".[10] Today, Jesus still chooses to eat with sinners, bringing healing to those who recognise they are sick. There is no difference in Jesus' offer to those with problems of sexuality than for any other individual. As St Paul said, "...righteousness from God comes through faith in Jesus Christ to all who believe. There is no difference, for all have sinned and fall short of the glory of God, and are justified freely by his grace through the redemption that came by Christ Jesus".[11]

The person who experiences homosexual tendencies is an individual, unique in the sight of God and loved by him, who needs his healing in body, mind and spirit. The healing of sexuality is a facet of the healing which is needed for the whole person, not a problem to be addressed in isolation. When real needs are identified by God, the healing and fulfilment of sexuality follows. The healing process for the homosexual, as for all of us, flows from a fuller understanding of forgiveness and love.

The Healing Body of Christ

The Church of Christ - that is Christians of all traditions throughout the world - is Christ's Body on earth today. Jesus still lives, and his Spirit gives life to his Body, bringing his presence, his love, his light and his peace wherever his followers gather together. Just as God's power to heal was seen in the earthly ministry of Jesus, so the Body of Jesus is used by God to bring healing here and now. The miracle is that God chooses to use sinful men and women with all their faults and failings to bring his healing love to the world. The only requirement is that those who would be used by God have the same attitude as Jesus, who "made himself nothing, taking the very nature of a servant".[12]

The power of the Church to heal comes only through the name of Jesus. When he is acknowledged as Lord, he gives believers authority to heal the sick and cast out demons, just as He did when He sent out His disciples.[13]

Healing, therefore, may also be described as the recognition that God loves us and calls us to himself. Healing involves an admission that we are damaged, impure and incomplete and that we need God. Healing is the recognition that wholeness comes from God. Perhaps most importantly healing is accepting the authority and rule of God in our lives. Thus on the journey of healing, which leads to ultimate wholeness, we invite God to rule over more and more of our lives and so we become more like him.

Broken Relationships

From this definition it is easy to recognise that we all need healing. We live in a sick world and we all contribute to its sickness because we are all sinful. The sickness in our world is a sympton of human alienation from God. It is the result of the rule of man rather than the rule of God in our individual lives, in our nations and in our societies. Alienation from God is the source of all discord, disturbance, disease and imbalance.

Our refusal as individuals to accept God's authority and his rule means that we inevitably submit to other powers or that we endeavour to exert authority over others. Our rebellion against God means that we are alienated from others whom we perceive to be different from us, whether by class or colour, race, belief, or attitude. Alienation and separation inevitably cause pain in our relationships with others, in our societies, and within ourselves, whether in body, mind or spirit.

The fundamental healing which we all need is in the relationships which make up our lives. Namely, our relationship with God; our relationship with ourselves; our relationship with others and our relationship with the whole of creation.

The evidence of broken relationships is to be found in a world experiencing separation and pain. We are surrounded by casualties as broken relationships have become the most dominant characteristic of contemporary society.

It is always in the midst of need that we discover Jesus.

Wrong relationships are manifestations of sin - such as selfishness, intolerance, pride, greed and lust. They are characterised by inhibition, guilt, anger, resentment, fear, sadness and sometimes violence. Wrong relationships generate a distorted understanding of the value and role of people. This, in turn, may lead to destructive processes such as ruthless exploitation or unhealthy subservience.

History proves that the cost of continuing wrong relationships is very high. Inner city deprivation, class division, colonial exploitation, racial hatred and religious bigotry are all evidence of this. We are alienated from God, estranged from each other and in conflict with God's creation.

Jesus came to restore all broken relationships by offering to each individual the opportunity of reconciliation with God. This surely is the meaning of the word righteousness - to be in a right relationship with God. This is why Jesus taught, "Seek first his Kingdom and His righteousness, and all these things will be given to you as well".[14] By "these things" Jesus meant everything that we ever need in life. God's Kingdom is the place where his rule and authority is accepted by everyone. Jesus urges us to seek the Kingdom of God in our own lives, characterised by a right relationship with him, and promises that everything else will follow. Thus by pursuing God's righteousness, our relationships with ourselves, with others and with creation will also be put right. This is the path of healing which leads to wholeness. It is a path of reconciliation leading to peace.

Identity and our Search for Peace

Most people, when asked the question, "What do you want most in life?" respond with the simple answer, "peace", but the peace that humanity is searching for is not simply the absence of conflict and war, it goes beyond this. Because we are damaged people we often find it difficult to accept ourselves, love ourselves and forgive ourselves. We need to recognise that as well as being damaged by the world, we have damaged ourselves. In a restless world, the peace that every man and woman is seeking is that which comes from the knowledge that each one is accepted and loved unconditionally. Jesus teaches us about our value - "You are of more value than many sparrows".[15] God gives us our identity - "I have summoned you by name, you are mine".[16] The Hebrew word *shalom* describes a state of well-being in which a person is at peace with God, at peace with themselves and at peace with others. It is this peace that Jesus promises to his disciples, clearly indicating that it is not available by worldly means. "My peace I leave with you; My peace I give you. I do not give to you as the world gives".[17] Only God can bring peace and fulfilment in the heart of our being, the place which has been reserved for him since our creation. This is healing.

The peace for which humanity is searching is the peace which comes from the establishment of right relationships. Firstly, a right relationship with God, but also a right relationship with ourselves. Our attitude to ourselves should be neither lauding nor condemning. We should think of ourselves neither too highly nor too lowly. We are called to see ourselves as God sees us - as children, who need the love of a Father, as sinful men and women who need the redeeming love of a Saviour, each one known and called by name. Above all, God wants us to love ourselves as he loves us. When we accept and love ourselves as we are, then we discover a new peace in the depth of our being.

From the earliest moments of our lives we set out on a journey of self-discovery, or as the teenager may term it, "my search for my identity". This search is frequently seen as an adolescent phase and indeed its intensity is often greatest during these years of change. However, the process of self-discovery and the formation of self-image begins even in the womb and continues into late adult life. In posing the question, "Who am I?", the teenager soon affirms, "I am not the person others think I am" but it perhaps requires the hindsight of greater maturity to recognise, "I am not even the person I think I am".

Our walk through life in development and self-perception - our identity - is not a walk that can be made in isolation. We discover our identity through our relationships with others, initially within the family, but also within the many realms of experience and people which influence our life.

Our identity is to be found in our uniqueness. There is no-one with the same identity as another. The world paints a picture of individuals based upon skills and attributes, their status in society and place in the family. The world defines identity in terms of physical characteristics and behavioural tendencies. We perceive one another on the basis of categories. Thus, a person may be described as the conscientious accountant who is kind-hearted, giving much of his time to charity work, the son of the university professor and husband of the vicar's daughter. The accountant's wife's description of her husband would doubtless suggest a completely different person and his description of himself would be different again.

Our relationships with others are governed by the category in which we place them or, put another way, the label which we apply to them in relation to ourselves. We may regard them as superior or inferior. We may regard them as a potential threat or as a potential benefit. We may enjoy their company or dislike them.

The danger in categorising people according to their condition, disposition, race, colour and nationality is that the labels which we apply prevent us from seeing the person who is in need of healing as a person with God's imprint upon him or her, with his or her uniqueness and great value. Thus we refer "to the person who displays homosexual tendencies" or "to the active homosexual", with all the preconceptions which we would attach to these labels.

We must recognise that the homosexual experiences a personal identity crisis of enormous magnitude and tends to be in conflict with himself or herself and often with society. Many researchers believe that same-sex love is itself a striving to complete the discovery of identity.

For the homosexual, as for all of us, the healing love of God can restore and bring to fulfilment that true identity for which each individual is searching. This brings about a new self respect.

Our Perceptions

It is important to recognise that the perception we have of ourselves and others, which we believe to be identity, is based upon and influenced by our own observations, our knowledge of the person from the accounts of others and our relationship with that person ourselves. It is also important to recognise that this is only a perception of a person's identity - the view of one human being through the eyes of another - and not the true identity of that person which is usually hidden and actually still being discovered.

It is not difficult to recognise that our perception of someone changes as we get to know them. This is achieved through repeated and varied encounters with them. Our perception of someone whom we have never met is formulated in our imagination and is subject to the reports we have heard about them from others, who, for their part, have already made their own assessment of the person based upon their encounter or experience.

We readily believe the stories of the boy in the next street who must be very wicked to have done the things that our neighbour reports. We are also quick to comment upon the character of national figures based upon what we read about them in the press, not stopping to reflect that the politician whom we thought to be so praiseworthy a few months ago on reading a certain magazine, has now become, in our eyes, a devious scoundrel according to what we saw on the television today. Our perception of a person changes frequently, almost with the change of direction of the wind, if it is based solely upon reports and speculation.

Personal encounter brings us closer to an individual, but even then our perception is coloured by the situations in which we meet and the roles which we play. A child, who has only encountered the teacher in the classroom has a fixed and narrow perception of the teacher's identity. He or she exists simply as a good or bad teacher, a nice or nasty person, perhaps confined to a knowledge of only one subject and limited to a certain style of dress. On a school field trip, this teacher is suddenly transformed, almost as if another person. He or she becomes a younger person who wears trainers and is nice to talk to. He or she plays rounders rather well and knows a lot about cars.

In a similar way we are deceived into thinking that the club treasurer is honest and diligent. He or she is always very pleasant and quick to help anyone in need. When he appears in court for defrauding his company we question whether this is really the same man. Our perception of his character is not in keeping with the reality of a new situation.

When we encounter someone in only one situation, our perception of them is restricted to the role which they play. We do not see the person they really are. Similarly, our perception is governed by the role which we play. The way in which we perceive another person is governed literally by "the glasses" that we wear, the eyes through which we see. An Englishman, seeing an African, sees a black man. An African seeing the same man, sees a man from another tribe. A man from that tribe, seeing the same man, sees a brother.

Varied personal encounters with a person broaden our perspective, and certainly more intimate encounters as in family relationships deepen our understanding of an individual, but even then our perception of them is coloured by our personal interpretation of what we see, which in turn is entirely influenced by our own life experience.

When we are damaged, through emotional trauma in our own lives, it is as if we wear broken glasses and our perception of others is distorted. Failure to recognise our dignity and worth as unique individuals robs us of our full humanity and blinds us to God's love and to that of others. This impedes our ability to communicate and share with them. Wrong perceptions cause separation as restricting as any physical disability..

This separation is especially evident in relationship to God in a society in which many have dismissed this relationship as being non-existent and irrelevant. Their perception of God is governed by what they think they know about God and also by their perception of those who claim to be his followers.

If we perceive God to be absent and believe that there is nothing beyond our temporary earthly existence, the value of our life is diminished. If we perceive God as severe and punishing, we view ourselves as unworthy. When we encounter God personally, as a loving Father, we are overwhelmed by his intimate care for us as children.

Self-discovery

Our perception of others is coloured and influenced by our own experience of life. Our perception of ourselves is governed by the nature of our relationships in early childhood. Contrary to the belief of some, we do not discover very much about ourselves in isolation from others. In fact the truth is that we will never discover our true identity except through the eyes of God.

Despite all our 'learning' and understanding we are left with the statement "I am not the person I think I am". Despite all our techniques and therapies, we cannot arrive at that place of peace and wholeness by ourselves or even through others. We are left in the position of the psalmist who simply states, "O Lord, you have searched me and you know me..... For you created my inmost being; you knit me together in my mother's womb. I praise you because I am fearfully and wonderfully made..... When I was woven together in the depth of the earth, your eyes saw my unformed body...".[18]

The only person who knows us through and through, who knows our true identity, is the one who created us - God himself. He created each human being out of the expression of his own creativity, each a unique work of art, or as one lady put it, "each one is the dream of God". If we regard ourselves purely as the result of a biological event, we deny our true identity which goes far beyond the description of our characteristics and attributes. Our identity goes beyond our membership of a tribe, race or nation, beyond the colour of our skin, the language we speak and even the gender that we are. We are firstly unique beings made in the likeness of God. We are secondly human beings with physical bodies, still unique, but taking on human traits from the moment of our conception. It is from this moment that we develop our own individual personality. This is the expression of our identity.

Most psychologists would agree that our personalities are largely formed by the age of 10 years. The way in which we behave and respond to situations during the majority of our living years is governed by the full range of our life experiences before our tenth birthday. Our personalities are most strongly influenced, therefore, by the situations which we face in early childhood, but, more importantly by the relationships which make up this foundational period of our life. Our experience of family is central to the expression of our identity. Healthy relationships affirm our true identity and generate personal security. Unhealthy relationships mar our true identity and create personal insecurity.

(2) UNDERSTANDING HOMOSEXUALITY

Bonds and Bonding

In order to understand the way in which our relationships in life affect us physically, emotionally, mentally and spiritually, we need to understand a little of the way in which bonds are forged.

In the context of relationships a bond may be described as a connection between one person to another. This bond is primarily a spiritual connection and is like a rope with many strands representing the different areas of mutual sharing. This is, in essence, a sharing of attitudes and experiences which may be reinforced through gifts and physical expression. Thus the bond between two people who have experienced infrequent and superficial encounters is weak, whereas the bonds between close friends and especially family members are strong. The varied encounters between two individuals have either a constructive or destructive effect upon their relationship. Thus bonds may be described as good or bad, positive or negative.

In the context of the healing of relationships good bonds need to be strengthened. Bad bonds need to be broken.

Positive bonds have a beneficial effect on the lives of both the individuals involved encouraging personal growth. They are characterised by love, trust and freedom. Negative bonds have an adverse effect on the lives of the individuals involved and inhibit, or sometimes even destroy, personal growth. They are characterised by resentment, unforgiveness and a lack of freedom.

Bonds are not only established between individuals who know each other but between those who have any kind of connection. This is most obvious in the generations of families where the bond of connection between family members who have never met is visible in physical features, mannerisms or temperamental characteristics common to the family.

The strong bonds in a family influence the attitudes and beliefs of subsequent generations. Where these beliefs and attitudes are positive and constructive, they provide a foundation of security. Where, however, there are negative or destructive practices or beliefs, they operate to taint future generations which may be held in bondage. This is particularly true when there has been allegiance, by a family member, to a secret society or an occult grouping. In a very real way, the family is subject to the power or god worshipped by its forbears.

A negative bond between two people is not simply a relationship in which there is discord. A strongly negative bond, such as that between an abused child and their abuser, is actually a relationship in which one person controls and limits the other - this is bondage.

Negative bonds between people can be very destructive and can be the root cause of physical and emotional disease. Bondage is a sure sign of a wrong relationship.

We have not been created to live in isolation. God has created each individual to live in relationship to him and others. His intention is that all the bonds in our lives are good and strong so that we are secure and fulfilled in our relationship with him, with ourselves and with others.

The Unborn Child

From the moment of conception within our mother's womb, we become part of a family, itself the product of the union of our mother's and father's families. Physical features, temperamental characteristics, strengths and weaknesses become a part of our very being. We cannot be separated from the parents who conceived us. Neither is the relationship a purely physical one. We are literally born out of the union of two people. A union which goes far beyond the physical act of intercourse. It is a union which is primarily spiritual.

The unborn child is not merely an appendage to the mother's anatomy, but, literally, a part of her being, and whilst not physiologically joined to the father, is already strongly bonded to him also.

The growth and development which takes place in the child within the womb is strongly dependent upon inherited genetic factors, but, is also affected by environmental influences. Although the unborn child is well protected within its mother it is vulnerable to her experiences during pregnancy. What the parents do the child does, where the parents go the child goes, what the parents feel the child feels.

It is medically proven that the child in the womb responds to both external stimuli, such as loud noise or physical assault, and the emotional state of its mother. Strong maternal feelings of fear or shock provoke a reaction in the child which is measurable on scans. A strong desire or unsuccessful attempt by a mother to abort the child which she is carrying also appears to produce a reaction in the infant, planting a sense of rejection. A similar sense of rejection may also be planted in the child whose parents, before its birth, had expressed a strong desire for a child of the opposite sex. There is considerable evidence pointing to the existence of foetal memory from a very early age.

The Childhood Years

It is easy to see the way in which some situations in childhood influence future behaviour. For example, the child who has a frightening encounter with a dog, may go on to fear dogs during their adult life. Similarly, the child who has to undergo unpleasant tests in a hospital may experience nervousness in hospitals as an adult.

Our experiences in childhood not only influence our future reactions to events but they also mould our perception of associated places and people. The person admitted to hospital as a child may hold to the perception that all doctors are cruel or that all hospitals and medical establishments are places of fear.

It is important to recognise that what is traumatic for a child is not necessarily a major event in the eyes of an adult and therefore, in looking for reasons for a child being withdrawn or disobedient, a rational deductive approach is often unproductive. Similarly, when as adults we search for reasons to explain our fears or misgivings, we are often unable to find satisfactory explanations.

Just as events and encounters in childhood leave their imprint upon us, so too do words and phrases. The words spoken to us during childhood have at least the same, if not greater influence upon our perception of ourselves as those of our later life experiences. The spoken word is a powerful tool, especially when it is delivered by someone whom we recognise to be in a position of authority over us. Therefore, the words of parents, close family and teachers are especially important in childhood. They have the capacity to build up or destroy the fragile personality which is emerging. The child who is repeatedly told and showed that they are loved, irrespective of their wrongs, will grow up with a sense of personal security. The child who is only allowed rewards for good behaviour may grow up feeling the need to please people. The child who is told it is stupid is less likely to achieve good results at school, whereas the average child who is encouraged is more likely to perform to its maximum potential.

Conversely, the child who is smothered with inappropriate affection, and the child who is urged to achieve beyond his or her capability also suffers as a result of adults seeking to fulfil their own needs through their children.

The effect of the spoken word is often related to the circumstances in which it is spoken. Hence the child who is reprimanded by a teacher in front of the class will react in a different way to the same words spoken in private. The association of words with a feeling of shame or guilt remains as part of the imprint made upon them.

It is an interesting exercise to ask a room full of adults if they can recall a word or phrase spoken to them in childhood. Our experience is that within 15 seconds approximately 70% of those present are able to recall such a word or phrase and it is always in the negative. We all carry within us the unhealed hurts of unjust or unkind words spoken to us many years ago. Contrary to popular belief, time does not heal.

The power of words is perhaps most clearly demonstrated by the way in which some people, most notably satanic and other occult groups, use specific words to 'programme' a child to react in a certain way. This may be in the form of inducing a hypnotic state in order to require the child or adult to do certain things without subsequent memory, or by the use of word associations which alienate the child from good things and especially God. It is a common experience, therefore, for those born into such a setting to have had pain inflicted upon them whilst being told, "this is love". Another example is the speaking of a name such as 'Jesus' in association with being burnt by a cigarette. The pain associated with the word spoken goes far deeper than the physical pain inflicted and is consistently reproduced even years later when the same word is spoken.

Childhood is the time when we observe, absorb and adopt role models. Our adult perception of specific role models, such as those of mother and father are formed during this time and these role models may be subconsciously accepted or rejected during childhood and adolescence.

Wrong sexual role models can cause considerable suffering. With the growth of more single parent families a child may be completely deprived of the influence of an adult of the opposite sex.

Not only is the perception of role models significant in childhood, even more important is the child's relationship with the people who have that particular place in their life. Thus, the child who has an apparently good role model in an upright father may actually have a poor relationship with him. Similarly it is possible for a child to have a warm and loving relationship with a father who gets drunk every night.

The relationships between key members of the family influence a child's understanding of interpersonal relationships in the world and especially the relative roles of men and women. A boy brought up in a family which is cruelly dominated by the father may seek to dominate women as he progresses into adult life. Conversely, he may subconsciously reject the role of the man (as he has experienced it) and, in later years, pursue a relationship with another man, seeking the love of which he has been deprived by his father. There is no predictable behavioural pattern because each child is unique and will react and compensate for their childhood situation in different ways.

Undoubtedly, our relationships with our mother and father are the most important and the most influential in the whole of our life. Our relationship with both parents begins at the moment of our conception; this is our foundation in life. Our relationships with each of them individually and with both of them as parents are the basis upon which our identity is either built up, diminished or even destroyed. These two relationships are fundamental to our sexuality and to our self-discovery and expression.

Gender and Sexuality

The term gender refers to the biological sex of an individual and is determined by the chromosomal make-up of the fertilized egg at the point of conception.

The sexuality of an individual is the expression of their identity in the context of their gender. It is not confined to sexual practices, although this is an obvious expression of sexuality. It includes physical attributes, attitudes and the manner of relating to other people.

The human body produces both male and female hormones which vary both in quantity and relative balance throughout life from conception through to early adulthood. At the same time the developing individual is subject to a varying balance of male and female influences through key relationships.

The gender of the individual is fixed, but, the expression of their identity and sexuality is dependent upon the interaction of three main influences which themselves are variable and interdependent. These are firstly, their intrinsic hormonal balance, secondly, the relative male and female external influences upon their lives and thirdly, the surrounding environment of family, culture and society.

The personal and sexual development of the child begins in the womb where there is obviously a dominantly feminine and maternal influence.

The unborn child is inextricably bound to the mother and totally dependent upon her for life. At birth, when the umbilical cord is cut, the child emerges as a small person in its own right and sets out on its road of self-expression and self-discovery. Although set free from total dependence, the child is still heavily dependent upon a maternal relationship for the first five years of life. Any event which causes an interruption of this early bonding by separating mother and child is a threat to the fundamental security of the infant. This insecurity often persists in the grown adult.

Damage may be inflicted upon a child unwittingly, even in the moments after its birth. Parents may express disappointment at the arrival of a son when they wanted a daughter and vice versa and may subconsciously and sometimes even consciously superimpose their preconceived sexuality upon their child. Sadly we have encountered a number of men who were dressed up as little girls during the first few years of their lives, with disastrous consequences. Ambiguity of identity at this early stage inevitably leads to confusion in later years.

When the process of birth itself is difficult, dangerous or traumatic, a variety of fears may arise, and even a basic denial of life and identity. The sexual consequences can be highly destructive and life-denying. An example of the physical expression of one who has experienced trauma early in life is found in the man who, still seeking the security of his mother's womb, dresses in women's clothing, often in secret.

Although the influence of mother is especially important during infancy, the presence of father is also important in a variety of ways, particularly in bringing a balance to male and female influence and in the creation of stability in the home. Different parts of our personality need to be affirmed at different stages of development by those in key relationships.

Early childhood is the period in which the affirmation of mother is needed for the development of personal identity and security. It is during adolescence that the role of father is most important in the affirmation of the sexuality of both boys and girls. Most would agree that adolescence is the time when the child develops the independence of a young adult by being fully weaned from maternal dependence through the influence of father. Affirmed in their own identity, both personal and sexual, the young adult goes on to seek out new adult relationships.

The absence of mother and/or father during any part of childhood may be compensated for by the presence of other female or male role models but such a relationship must be permanent and secure in order to meet the need of the child for both maternal and paternal influence and affirmation. Insecure or temporary relationships only exaggerate the unmet need, rather than fulfil it. New partners and step-parents inevitably have a disturbing influence upon children, particularly in threatening the security of the relationship with their natural parent.

When the closeness, gentleness and security of an early maternal relationship has been lacking or absent, this unmet need is carried by the child into adulthood and becomes almost like a vacuum demanding to be filled. Conversely, a child who has been smothered by maternal love may remain dependent upon this type of relationship and fail to fully enter adulthood, remaining unaffirmed in their own sexuality. Similarly, the child who has not experienced a father-child relationship, for whatever reason, will subconsciously seek to meet this need in future adult relationships.

Every child has a natural need for same-sex love. He or she, in this way needs affirmation and acceptance. The homosexual condition is a continuing and usually unconscious attempt to compensate for earlier unfulfilled needs and these same-sex deficits lead to impermanence in relationships especially of a sexual nature. One man told of his ongoing deep yearning to be held by a man. Despite many homosexual relationships his yearning was never satisfied. His real need was to be held by his father as a child. Dr Elizabeth Moberley states, "There is no basis for permanence in this structure of the homosexual condition". Men are often cut off from their masculine identity because of lack of affirmation as children.

There are parts of our being which need to be affirmed by the influence of someone of the same sex and if this affirmation is not effected during childhood, same-sex relationships become important in early adulthood.

'Crushes' upon school teachers or older pupils in secondary schools have been well-recognised for years, particularly amongst girls. There is no evidence to suggest that any of these bonds are in any way precursors to a homosexual orientation in adult life and, hitherto, have been accepted almost as a normal part of adolescent emotional development. In single-sex establishments such as boys' boarding schools, where there is an unnatural absence of family life, same-sex encounters may include sexual activity which may or may not set a pattern of sexual relations for life. Such imposed patterns of behaviour may, sadly, convince an immature boy that he is homosexual, particularly if this is reinforced by others such as gay 'help-lines' or an adult abuser.

A factor which seems to have a direct influence upon sexual orientation is early genital interference or sexual activity, initiated by an adult. This may be in the form of childhood sexual abuse which is readily recognised by most as being a traumatic event. Equally traumatic, however, is the sexual approach to a child in early teenage years by an older person, especially if of the same sex. The mixed sensations of sexual arousal associated with an unnatural situation causes intense confusion and the need is for the child to be affirmed and set free from the associated fear and shock.

A young woman who has been subject to sexual assault by a man may reject future male relationships and seek the companionship of women. This may be compounded if, coincidentally, she rejects, consciously or subconsciously, the female role as encountered in her mother.

Similarly exposure of the child or adolescent to pornography, which sadly is a rapidly increasing occurrence in contemporary society, causes confusion and damage to their future relationships. The period of life from childhood to adulthood has at each stage a varying male or female emphasis. Any significant traumatic event occurring during a period of female emphasis in the life of a boy, or male emphasis in the life of a girl may cause 'freezing' of further development. This means that their normal and healthy maturation process is halted or distorted, resulting in damaged sexual identity. When this interruption happens during adolescence, the person may remain for many years in a state of excessive self-consciousness and introspection.

The tragedy of many homosexuals lies in the fact that, having experienced a trauma and its consequences, they put themselves into a fixed position which, consciously or unconsciously, they believe to be permanent and this precludes any hope of a progression towards a normal process of sexual maturing. Sadly, homosexual militants may, quite wrongly, confirm homosexual orientation in the lives of young, impressionable teenagers and consequently inhibit and impair their natural growth to sexual maturity. If this uncertainty is compounded by a physical homosexual encounter the resulting confusion may lead them into a variety of abnormal sexual experiences. A considerable number of men who have been guilty of sexual offences against children and young people have themselves entered into an unnatural homosexual relationship during their teenage years through encounters with people or by fantasy through pornography. They subsequently go on to express their immature sexuality by sexual encounters with those younger than themselves and who are often under their authority, although this expression does not always necessarily take on an overtly physical nature.

Deep within every human being there is a basic need for intimacy. From the moment of conception, the child is in a deeply intimate relationship with its mother. The intimacy continues after birth with feeding, touching and cuddling and, in healthy family relationships, continues through childhood, not just with the mother but also with other family members. We need to be understood, accepted and loved in the context of trusting self-disclosure.

A considerable number of people enter into homosexual activity because of a fundamental identity crisis, often rooted in an insufficient closeness and healthy bonding with the same-sex parent. The desire in the adult to compensate for what he or she appears to have been deprived of as a child is a very powerful influencing factor in sexuality. This being the case, the question arises as to whether this compensation can be achieved retrospectively. It is the experience of many within the Christian healing ministry that this is certainly the case.

The personal identity of every human being bears the fruit but also the scars of their life situations. Each of us, on our journey through life is in a process of 'becoming'. Our sexuality is but a part of the expression of our whole developing personal identity. When we allow our sexuality to have a dominant influence upon our life we are robbed of our true selves.

(3) HEALING AND WHOLENESS FOR THE HOMOSEXUAL PERSON

The Truth

The starting point of all healing is the acknowledgement that there needs to be change, whether in attitude, lifestyle, or physical or mental state. And without the recognition of the truth of the situation, there is no recognition of the need for change.

Jesus promises, "the Truth will set you free".[19] We live in a society in which we are sold the fundamental lie that truth is relative and not absolute. It is this creed which leads to the assertion that it is acceptable to hurt or even kill someone in certain circumstances and it is the same creed which reduces God to the person, being or power that you want him to be. Absolutes have been rejected in favour of personal preferences, especially when it concerns what is right and wrong. The distinction between what is understandable and what is normal has become blurred, as has the difference between what is forgiveable and what is acceptable.

To deny the truth of humankind's sinfulness is to deny the opportunity of healing. Put more simply, the person who denies they are hungry will not receive food or eat it. In the context of the homosexual person, the denial that this is an unnatural sexual orientation is a denial of the need for personal healing.

The Spirit of God, the Holy Spirit, is by nature Truth and Love. It is God's Spirit who leads us into all truth. He reveals the absolute truth in any given situation. Those who listen to the Holy Spirit are given an understanding of the Truth which is not relative to circumstances or dependent upon human knowledge. God always reveals his Truth in love. Jesus stated that he did not come to condemn the world but to save it. In revealing Truth, God's purpose is to see creation set free, not to bring judgement. The Holy Spirit comes to convict the world of guilt in regard to sin. Put another way, the truth is that we live in a world that is sick. The truth is that as individuals we are sick and each of us contributes to the sickness of the world. The truth is that God can and wants to heal our sickness. With specific regard to homosexuality, the truth is that genital homosexual acts are biologically unnatural and damaging.

The majority of sexually active homosexual people have had more than one partner and often have many. The truth is that God loves every human being, regardless of their sinfulness and that He can heal any damaged area of our identity, including our sexuality.

The Bible points us to the truth, but even here, the interpretation of passages referring to genital homosexual activity has been subjected to distortion or open denial by those who seek to justify their lifestyle. The reason that homosexual acts are forbidden by God is because they cause damage and disorder. This is the basis of all God's law - not to simply be a moral code, but, more importantly, to provide guidelines for avoiding sickness and disease of body, mind and spirit.

Homosexual orientation, in itself, should not be seen as inherently sinful, but there can be little doubt that Biblical teaching both in the Old and the New Testaments clearly warns that homosexual activity is against the will of God. The Church has consistently taught and endorsed Biblical teaching on this matter. Archbishop Runcie, speaking at the Synod of the Church of England was very clear about this when he said "I do not deny, and cannot, that homosexual acts are condemned in the biblical and Christian tradition".[20]

As a whole, St Paul's teachings repudiate homosexual behaviour. It is presented as a vice of the Gentiles in the letter to Romans. It is seen as a bar to the Kingdom in the letters to Corinthians. It runs contrary to the basic precepts of the rabbis and was seen by the early church as in direct conflict with the Christian way of life.

There can be little doubt that those Christians who deny the immorality of homosexual acts, do so on the basis of discarding the relevance and authority of biblical teaching to life today. An example of this was seen in 1977 when an Episcopal Bishop in the United States justified his decision to ordain a practising lesbian by saying: "There is a timelessness to the message of God's love that outweighs the datedness of so many biblical injunctions rooted in ancient societies".[21]

The Old Testament quite clearly depicted homosexual activity as sinful in itself. The problem confronting society today is the phenomenal degree of promiscuity which is associated with homosexuality. This, beyond doubt, was a major factor in the early spread of AIDS. In this respect it is interesting to note the views of Cardinal Basil Hume of Westminster, "AIDS is neither the problem nor the central issue. It is a symptom of something deeper and more deadly. AIDS is but one of the many disastrous consequences of promiscuous sexual behaviour. Promiscuity is the root cause of the present epidemic. It has always been sinful; it is rapidly becoming suicidal".[22]

In responding to the needs of the homosexual it is important to recognise that promiscuity, as such, inevitably inflicts deep and lasting damage upon the emotional and spiritual well-being of the person concerned. The damage inflicted by promiscuity, in many cases, overshadows the initial problem of homosexuality. Wrong relationships between people reflect a wrong relationship with God.

The Bible points to the truth that Jesus comes to set the prisoner free and to lead us into a right relationship with God, ourselves and others. He clearly stated "I am the way, the Truth and the life. No one comes to the Father, except through me".[23] We have a simple choice - either we follow him or we go our own way. Similarly, we can choose to receive his healing and transformation in our lives or we can attempt to satisfy our needs and desires by other methods.

The point currently being asserted by the militant homosexual movement is that their condition is not one of disorder or abnormality, that it is not a condition of un-wholeness. This conclusion is often reached for reasons of self-defence and self-justification.

The way of Jesus is the way of healing. Whether homosexual or not, we all need healing. We fall perhaps into three categories - firstly, those who recognise their need for healing, secondly those who do not recognise this and thirdly those who recognise it but refuse to receive healing.

The truth is - we cannot encounter Jesus and remain unchanged.

The Healing Power of God

It has been our privilege and the experience of many involved in the healing ministry to see men and women discovering and expressing their identity through the power of healing prayer. This has not been by inward-looking self-analysis but by the simple yet profound encounter with the healing love of Christ for them personally. Jesus draws us out of our introverted individualism into the recognition and experience that we are all a part of God's creation with a unique role to play, not as isolated individuals but joined together by relationships in families, communities, societies and nations. Thus our personal healing brings healing to our family, our community, our society, and the world in which we live.

The following are examples of the way in which we have personally encountered God's healing in the lives of some of those who have come for help over several years.

Deprived of Father

A distraught young man approached us because he felt a strong and what he considered to be unnatural attraction to men. He also had a fear of women whom he envisaged as being interfering and intrusive. It transpired that he had been brought up in an over-protective and virtually all-female environment both at home and at school. He had been deprived of a father who could have been a male role model for him in his early teens. He had been severely punished and publicly embarrassed by a rather cruel woman teacher. After much struggling he was able to forgive the teacher in the name of Christ for the suffering she had caused him. He was brought to a real understanding of the role various women had played in his childhood years and he was set free from what he recognised to be an unnatural attraction to men. In particular he was able to establish a loving relationship with his parents. He soon established a rapport with women and, in due course, entered into a happy and fulfilling marriage with the joy of children. He now recognises the need for a male role model for his children.

Domination and 'Consumption'

A twenty-five year old man came in great distress because he had been drawn into the gay scene in such a way that he had become emotionally unbalanced and he was riddled with guilt and fear. On three occasions he had gone through the experience of believing that he was HIV positive. He described about how he had been searching for a hero figure. Whenever he met a man whom he admired or envied he had a deep desire to exercise power over him and to possess the qualities which he had. In a very real sense he was seeking to consume that which he liked. In praying for the roots of this disorder it became clear that his father had treated him brutally and had therefore been rejected as a male-role model and, to some extent, he had been searching for a father substitute ever since. After considerable prayer he recognised this and gave his searching to God. He also in the name of Christ forgave his father and within a very short period of time abandoned his homosexual behaviour. There was a fundamental change in his attitude and although he did not have or seemingly want to have a girlfriend, he was seen by all his friends to be liberated and at peace.

Cleansing of Memory

A man came for help because he had totally lost confidence in himself and shared that many of his friends considered him to be 'gay'. It transpired that both his parents died when he was a baby. In his teens he had been indecently assaulted by a group of male homosexuals and after this he had developed a deep revulsion towards all sexual matters. He was very confused, lonely and afraid of women. He was wary of men but nonetheless experienced some 'pull' towards them. On forgiving his assailants in the name of Jesus he was immediately set free from many of the inhibitions which had plagued him for more than ten years. He went through a delayed and adolescent period for about two years and gradually developed a natural and a healthy attitude towards women. He also experienced a cleansing of what he considered to be his soiled and unworthy self.

Gender Affirmation

A young man, filled with anxiety and lack of self confidence, came to us urgently seeking help. He was actively homosexual and over several years had had numerous partners. When he was born his mother was disappointed because he was not a girl and repeatedly told him so in his early childhood. He received little affirmation as a small boy and, indeed, was dressed as a girl until he was four years of age. Not unnaturally he had a profound desire to escape from women and yet felt effeminate. In his early uncertain teenage years he became involved with two older homosexual men who, as often happens, superimposed their wills upon him. He freely admitted that he was searching for his real identity and that his homosexuality was, in fact, a cover for his real emotions. He began to realise that what had been presented to him as normal was not so. In prayer he forgave his mother for what she had said to him and he gave to God all the years of promiscuity. As he did this he discovered his true manhood, turned away from homosexuality and within eighteen months had fallen in love with a girl and was engaged to be married to her.

No Relationship with Parent

One man recounted to us how he had been interfered with by a scoutmaster when he was in the scouting movement. The man responsible convinced him that he was homosexual by birth and that nothing could change him. For two or three years he was shown gay pornographic videos and introduced to other friends of his scoutmaster in the gay scene and also to drugs. He went through a period of intense sexual activity with many partners. Looking considerably younger than his age he seemed to attract older homosexual men who clearly exploited him. For a short period he was virtually a 'rent boy'. By this time he had lost all self-respect and was totally confused about his identity. Offering his life back to God in prayer, he realised that he had virtually 'frozen' at a particular stage of adolescent development. He recognised that his relationship with both his parents had been distant and cold and that he had responded to the first affection ever shown to him. He reaffirmed his love in Christ for his mother and father, forgiving them for being distant from him. He forgave the scoutmaster, after considerable heart-searching. He forgave all who had exploited him. He then went through a painful process of emotional maturation, and reached a point of spiritual self-discovery in which, as he put it, his 'disorientation' disappeared and he rediscovered his manhood. His entire lifestyle changed. The tensions disappeared.

Broken Trust in Mother

A middle aged lady confided in us that she had been involved with a series of lesbian relationships over a period of years and was extremely unhappy. She was very possessive by nature and had gone through the pain of successive rejections. It transpired that she had been sexually abused as a young child over many years both by her own father and other male relatives. Understandably she had a deep antagonism towards all men and she experienced fear and unease in their presence. She was also resentful of the fact that her mother had failed to protect her and felt she had been searching for a mother substitute. After a considerable period of intimate sharing she was able, in the name of Christ, to forgive by name each of the men who had so cruelly assaulted her. She was able to give to God the circumstances and places of the assaults and to affirm his presence then and now. She was able to break the negative bonds forged with the various sexual partners. Her lesbian activities ceased and the tension so evident in all her relationships came to an end.

Childhood Traumas

One lady recalled how, as a nine year old girl she had arrived home one day and experienced the trauma of confronting her own mother in bed with a strange man. She was immediately filled with repulsion and developed an antagonism towards all men. As time went on she began to search for trustworthy love from other women. In her late teens she was drawn to a woman whom she later discovered had lesbian tendencies and with whom she soon established a close physical and emotional relationship. On her own admission she had great unease about this and came to us seeking help, because she felt she had a dangerous dependence upon her partner who was exerting increasing control over her. In identifying and acknowledging her continuing anger towards her mother and her mother's male companion she was able to forgive both of them in the name of Jesus for what they had done to her through their action. Empowered to do this by the Holy Spirit she had an immediate and radical change of attitude towards men and towards her mother, with whom she developed a belated but deeply loving relationship. She began to see men in a different light and her lesbian relationship ended within a short period. Forgiveness was at the heart of her healing.

Corruption

From the age of eight years, a young boy had been regularly shown pornographic films by his uncle while his mother was out working in the evenings as a barmaid. These films depicted male homosexual acts and soon became the prelude for repeated sexual attacks. His uncle then introduced this boy to other homosexual men who also drugged and repeatedly abused him. By the age of fourteen he had grown to accept this as normal, because virtually all the men he met were practising homosexuals. Eventually, he became suicidal and alcoholic and approached us in great despair. He rediscovered motherly love from an elderly lady who took him into her home. After experiencing the cleansing of his memories in prayer, he became able to relate to women in a normal way for the first time in his life. His homosexual desires gradually diminished as he found his faith and was eventually set free at the age of twenty from those influences which had plagued him since childhood.

Broken Home

A young boy of four was confused and deeply hurt when his mother married to a man with a drink problem left home with him to live with another man. This man repeatedly beat both him and his mother, who eventually ran away with him and proceeded to live with a succession of different men, living in squalor. At the age of fourteen he was totally bewildered and depressed. A wealthy businessman befriended him, showing him great understanding and affection and showering him with presents. Eventually this man abused the boy and after having been initiated into homosexual acts he was led into a homosexual lifestyle. He was injured in a sado-masochistic act and the shock of this, together with the discomfort of suffering a series of sexually transmitted diseases, led him to question his lifestyle. After considerable heart searching he sought forgiveness and reconciliation with God and was given the power to forgive all who had damaged him. He found his faith and got married at twenty, although it took a further two years before he was set free from occultic bonds which had been formed during the years of promiscuity.

These examples have been given in order to illustrate the ways in which God both identifies and heals the roots of the homosexual condition. The process of healing may be very quick or may progress slowly over a period of months or even years. In ministering to many of those who have been caught up in a homosexual lifestyle, there is usually a need to deal with other associated problems.

Hurting people frequently look for ways of soothing their hurt and supporting themselves in their weakness. Thus, some homosexuals who have been traumatised in their childhood become involved in alcohol and drug abuse and the occult, although it should also be recognised that all these influences themselves may activate a latent homosexuality or predisposition to abnormal sexual behaviour. It is well known that in many occultic ceremonies such as meetings of witches' covens, abnormal sexual acts frequently take place which disorientate and even traumatise the participants.

Homosexual neurosis frequently leads to the desire to own, to control and consume another or to be owned, controlled and consumed by another. Frequently, homosexuals subconsciously seek out partners with specific attributes which they feel they lack, for example sporting ability or certain physical features. Subconsciously there appears to be a desire to possess these qualities by possessing or 'consuming' the person.

Sometimes this insatiable appetite leads to sexual practices including physical bondage and forms of sado-masochism which involve the receiving or inflicting of pain. In a very real sense these physical practices are the acting out of an underlying compulsion to devour and be devoured, to hold and be held in bondage.

The bonds of love which God forges through Jesus have the power to destroy all chains of bondage. The demonic powers behind obsessions, compulsions and the acting out of fantasies are expunged and a new and exciting gift of freedom is given.

Cross dressing and transvestism are becoming more apparent in contemporary society, largely due to commercial exploitation. The man who wears women's clothes actually seeks to experience excitement and this may become a fetish. It is rooted in his failure to establish a healthy relationship with his mother. This relationship can be restored in prayer. He is usually heterosexual.

The homosexual who cross-dresses (the transvestite) attempts to relate to men by wearing women's clothing. Transsexuals believe themselves to be a male held prisoner in a female body or vice versa. Their inability to satisfactorily identify and confirm their gender and sexuality inevitably leads to extreme depression which is rarely helped and often exacerbated by surgery.

The basic question "Who am I?" remains unresolved. Those who have been held captive to this condition have usually found their healing in what, to them, is a startling discovery that first and foremost "I am a child of God", not in the first instance a son or daughter. They recognise that it is God who created them and that he calls them by their name which reflects their character and personality, not their gender.

The condition of homosexuality can be changed. There is considerable evidence to show that homosexuality is not a fixed all-life condition. Many heterosexuals have been drawn into homosexuality through a variety of different influences and encounters, often reverting with considerable pain and guilt to their original condition.

Many homosexuals have spent years searching for an alternative life-style and for a release from what they perceive to be an incurable state. When they discover that it is God who is searching for them, and when they acknowledge his desire to find them, they frequently experience a total change of inclination, attitude and belief. The concept of a passive God is revealed in its falsity. They experience, first hand, a sharing with God in their deepest feelings, fears, hopes and aspirations.

The only way in which we can be fully set free from past events, traumas and perceptions is through the healing love of God. It is only he who can heal the scars of the past because Jesus Christ is the same yesterday, today and forever.[24] God's healing is not limited by time. Past guilt and hurts may be dealt with today. Forgiveness for past wrongs can be given and received today. Wrong relationships from the past can be put right today.

Praying for Healing

There are different ways of approaching a person who is in need and seeking help. We may adopt a 'professional' approach and maintain our distance from them, or we may follow the example of Jesus and love them as a brother or sister. We may depend upon our acquired skills and attained knowledge or we may simply pray to be filled with God's Spirit who will guide us into all truth.

We may help the person intellectually to understand the basis of their need and help them to address it, or, we may support and encourage our brother and sister to welcome and receive the healing of Jesus.

In responding to the cry for help, there is a need to listen and pray. The listening skills learned through courses on counselling can be helpful, but, only prayer can bring about true healing. The counsellor may be able to help identify and manage negative emotions and harmful patterns of behaviour but only prayer will heal the roots of these problems.

Counselling may achieve some understanding of the roots of the homosexual condition, but, only prayer, guided by the Holy Spirit, will reveal the hidden and often subconscious memories from the time in the womb and early childhood of the individual man or woman who has sought healing.

The starting point in praying for healing is our readiness to be used by God as a channel of His love and peace. This means that we put to one side the human tendency to analyse and discuss in favour of a quiet waiting in openness upon God.

In praying for and/or with anyone in need, including the homosexual person, we must recognise that we too are in need. The basis of our praying is sharing as equals not as people who are superior to others. In a very real sense we are beggars telling other beggars where there is food. Jesus knelt and washed His disciples' feet. His teaching is that we are all of equal value in God's sight and that those who seek to be first will be last.[25]

To pray for and with someone is a privilege and requires those ministering to put aside all pre-conceived ideas, being literally emptied of all but love. Just as we need to be loved for who we are, so we must love others as they are, rather than as we would like them to be. The one with whom we are praying must be assured of total confidentiality and of our love and respect for them as individuals, irrespective of what is revealed.

Our attitude is one of awareness, listening and loving - awareness of God's immanent presence, listening to the voice of God through His Holy Spirit, loving and responding to the person to whom we are ministering unconditionally. Whenever possible it is better not to minister alone and preferably in a mixed-sex team of two or three people.

Listening in Prayer

Our praying always commences with a time of silence followed by prayers for peace in body, mind and spirit. It is often helpful to use scripture such as Psalm 139 or Psalm 23.

We ask for the gift of God's Holy Spirit both for ourselves and the one for whom we are praying. Together we ask the Lord how to pray for our brother or sister, relying totally upon his direction. In praying we give God the opportunity to speak to us. In a world of distraction, noise and confusion, the Lord wants us to wait upon him. He says, "Be still and know that I am God".[26]

We listen to God by firstly focusing the whole of our attention upon him, having placed the one for whom we are praying into his care. Each of us 'hears' God in a different way, some are given visions, some may hear a voice. Some may have a physical sensation, or, even be able to smell a particular scent. A word of knowledge may be given as a gift of the Spirit. In this instance, a word comes into the mind of one who is listening which is not understandable to the one who receives it, but which is immediately recognised by the one for whom it is given. A word of knowledge and other sensations or images are all pointers to a particular memory or relationship which God wants to heal.

A person who believes that God is speaking simply shares what they have heard with those present. That which is of God is confirmed through another of those praying and most often through the person who is receiving ministry. We all accept that we may hear wrongly, therefore any prompting which is not confirmed is simply left to one side.

By listening to God together, the direction of prayer is revealed step by step through the individuals present.

Life Prayer

There is one particular pattern of praying which has been greatly used by God to bring healing to the whole of a person's life. We have simply called it Life Prayer. It is not a technique but, rather, a spiritual discipline. It is primarily a prayer of thanksgiving for a person in which we place before God, in prayer, every part of their life from the moment of their creation. In doing this we ask the Lord to identify any events, situations and relationships in their lives that need his healing touch.

The first step towards healing is giving ourselves in our entirety to God, placing all our experience and feelings in his hands. The second step is giving the situation, image or memory which has been identified to God for him to receive and transform.

When an area of need is identified, there is invariably a recognition by the brother or sister with whom we are praying of buried pain, fear, anxiety, anger or guilt. We support our brother or sister in the giving of their negative feelings to God, encouraging them to loosen their grip on the hurt, holding on to nothing. This is often helped by the posture of holding up their hands with palms upwards so that having released the burden carried they might physically express their freedom and receive the healing which God wants to give.

This first step may be likened to the cleansing of the wound which then needs to be healed.

Second, therefore we ask God to heal the root cause of the wound. This deep healing usually involves the giving and receiving of forgiveness and love, in prayer, for those who have caused hurt.

After first praying for peace and the gift of God's Holy Spirit, we thank God for the gift of our brother or sister. In recognising that we are the fruit of the generations of our family tree we offer to God the entire family and ancestry of our brother or sister. We thank him for all the good they have inherited and we ask him to strengthen those bonds with our forebears which are good and honourable.

We offer to God all that they have inherited which is tainted and ask him to purify and cleanse the family tree breaking any bonds with forebears which are negative and destructive. We do this in the name of Jesus. During this period of prayer we also silently ask God to identify any person in the family with whom our brother or sister has a negative bond or wrong relationship, and to reveal any patterns, attitudes or beliefs by which they are held in bondage. At each stage of our praying we ask God to heal wrong relationships and bring freedom from bondage in the way he directs. Having thanked God for the whole family of our brother or sister we quietly uphold them before the Lord with reverence and love thanking him for the gift of their life. We acknowledge that our brother or sister is created by God and that he knew them before even their parents knew of their existence.

We thank God for our brother or sister's parents offering their relationship to him, and especially the moment of our brother or sister's conception.

We thank the Lord for each month of our brother or sister's development in the mother's womb, thanking him for the security and love of this special place. We recognise that the child in the womb senses the feelings and reactions of the mother and responds to many outside influences and so ask him to remove any trauma our brother or sister may have experienced through any shock or other negative experience of their mother.

We offer to the Lord all the relationships during this period and all the words spoken. We ask the Lord to identify and heal anything which has caused damaging feelings such as rejection, pain, fear or insecurity.

We particularly pray that God would affirm the special moment of their birth, thanking God for this event. We acknowledge that Jesus is present every moment of our lives, from the very moment of our conception and because for Him 40 years ago is as today, we ask him to bring healing into those situations in the past when we were unaware of his presence. We offer to God all the years of childhood and relationships both at home and at school. We offer to him all the years of adolescence and adulthood. As, step by step, we offer these years in thanksgiving, God identifies the roots of any disorder, including that of homosexuality.

Both before birth and in all the subsequent years, we recognise that there are things which need to be healed - attitudes inherited from parents and family, words which have been spoken, actions which have been hurtful, situations producing guilt and fear.

We recognise that in looking back over our brother or sister's life, we are not just relying upon their memory, we are asking God to identify that which needs healing through his Spirit of Truth. In each instance brought to mind we simply ask him to put right what is wrong.

In sharing Life Prayer there may be laughter and tears, but, as we support our brother or sister gently and lovingly we find the Lord gives to us his sensitivity and discernment which is then shown in words and actions.

Our experience is that at almost every crucial stage of healing there is a relationship which needs to be put right. This can only be done through forgiveness in the name of Jesus. The giving and receiving of forgiveness requires the help of the Holy Spirit. In purely human terms to forgive those who have deeply hurt us is sometimes impossible - but in the power of God all things are possible.

In the context of Life Prayer, God identifies the people whom He wants us to forgive by reminding us of situations where there has been hurt, separation or division. The forgiveness is always specific to this event. Thus we are not simply asked to forgive someone for everything they ever did to hurt us, but for that one word or deed of unkindness which God brings to light. Sometimes during a Life Prayer the same person needs to be forgiven several times for different situations which caused hurt and sometimes there is a need for the person who is receiving ministry to ask forgiveness of someone whom they have hurt.

The giving and receiving of forgiveness in prayer is through Jesus. We ask him to be the reconciler of the two parties. In this way it is possible to be reconciled with someone who may have since died for a hurt inflicted in childhood simply because Jesus is the same yesterday as he is today and forever.

On identifying the need for our brother or sister to forgive someone, we first ask God to give them the desire to forgive. It is impossible truly to forgive unless there is the desire to do so. This is the most important stage of the prayer of forgiveness and in situations where there has been grave hurt, such as sexual abuse, it may be necessary to pray for some time before our brother or sister is able to receive that desire in their heart.

When there is a desire to forgive, we pray that God would give our brother or sister the power to forgive and this is spoken by them aloud, addressing the person concerned by name, in prayer saying, "I forgive you in the name of Jesus".

The next stage in the healing of relationships is the release of Christ's love into each situation which has been identified, and we pray that God will give to our brother or sister the desire to love the person who has hurt them. If they are able, there and then, to receive from God the desire to love, we ask for God's Spirit to give them the power to say to the person in prayer, "I love you in the name of Jesus".

The declaration of love for a person who has hurt us may happen weeks, months or even years after the first stages of forgiveness but once this process is started, God will bring it to completion if we continue to seek his healing.

Life Prayer is gentle and unhurried and emotional expression such as tears are often an outward sign of God's healing grace at work. It may be that God will move rapidly over a period of years until a particular need is identified, whereas on some occasions we do not even progress beyond the day of birth. We ask the Lord to show us when to close our prayers. The Life Prayer may continue for one or two hours after which it is important to thank and praise God.

On some occasions a person has had their Life Prayer in stages, seemingly to allow the effect of one area of healing to be deepened before going on to the next. When praying for someone with problems of sexuality, there is frequently a change in attitude and practice which is recognised and welcomed by the person.

The experience of the person having Life Prayer ministry varies, but, is always positive. Some experience a sudden and radical change in their life, others experience a more gradual transformation over weeks or months, but without exception everyone who asks for healing receives healing. It may not be in the way that they expect, but always in the way that God knows they need.

The average length of time to pray Life Prayer is around two hours and following this we would often pray a prayer of abandonment. It accords with the mainstream of Christian traditions of praying over the centuries.

Abandonment

The Prayer of Abandonment is an act of total surrender to God, offering to him all our senses, our minds and our hearts. In praying this prayer we desire to be as clay in God's hands and we specifically put ourselves into a position of being vulnerable to Him, relinquishing all power and control to him.

The act of surrender to God is reflected in the chosen posture of lying on the floor, facing upward, with hands upturned in an attitude of giving and receiving. Out of respect for the person, only those of the same sex would usually pray this prayer together.

We begin by affirming that God's love is all-powerful and everlasting and that our total security is in him. Those praying then gently touch in turn the parts of our brother or sister related to the five senses. We offer to the Lord everything they have ever seen, whilst touching the eyelids, asking God to cleanse and heal anything which has caused harm. We then pray that they will be given the eyes of Christ. We pray for their ears and offer to God everything they have ever heard, asking for this cleansing and healing and that they be given a new gift of hearing. In similar fashion we offer to God all memories associated with the sense of smell, taste and speech and then pray for their hands and sense of touch.

The cleansing of the senses is especially significant for the homosexual who frequently has sensory associations with past events which distort their understanding, perceptions and feelings.

We would then offer to God all the thoughts, dreams, imagination of our brother or sister, whilst gently placing a hand on their forehead. Having asked for cleansing and healing we pray that they would have the mind of Christ.

We offer to him all their emotions and feelings whilst placing a hand on their chest, over their heart, praying especially that God would heal all the wounds of their lives, giving to them the heart of Christ.

Finally we place a hand on the abdomen of our brother or sister, symbolising the place where fear is experienced and pray that the perfect love of God would cast out all fear, bringing deep and lasting peace in body, mind and spirit.

This prayer, in itself, has been a means of great healing and blessing and has been especially powerful in praying for those who have suffered any kind of abuse.

When praying for someone who has been involved in wrong sexual relationships, there is frequently a need for prayers of deliverance. These prayers are in two parts. Firstly, there is always a need to pray for the severing of the negative and controlling bonds which have been forged. Secondly, there may be a need to pray for the removal of demonic entities, together with a prayer for the cleansing and protection of all present.

Where there has been deviant sexual behaviour and where pornography has been viewed, there is almost certainly a need for deliverance from specific demonic entities such as lust which are associated with these practices. This requires the renunciation of all evil by the person receiving ministry and the verbal confession of the Lordship of Christ. This process of cleansing through deliverance may take many months to be completed.

It is often appropriate after prayer for healing to use oil to anoint the one who has received ministry.

Conclusion

A culture which manifests abnormal and excessive emphasis upon sex is in need of healing. If we see sexual relationships primarily in terms of a physical act, we are degrading and diminishing a relationship upon which society depends for its health and well-being. If, as in our society, an obsession with coitus is so actively and unnaturally encouraged, we will inevitably witness the collapse of loving, respectful relationships and the fall of our culture into a chasm of degradation.

The recognition that sexual instinct is given to us by God must also be matched by an admission of our personal responsibility to use that instinct for His glory and not merely our personal gratification. Contemporary society is characterised by a lack of real intimacy. We have substituted shallow physical encounters for deep spiritual relationships. The experience of intimacy with God inevitably means that we can establish close and loving relationships with others without inhibition and fear.

The person who has received little or no love as a child, will constantly seek love, affection and security offered from any source. These individuals are open to abuse and are extremely vulnerable to homosexual advances. The security of a same-sex relationship does not carry the personal threat or challenge of the heterosexual encounter. The real love and security which the vulnerable need is within family relationships. This is one of the basic roles of the Christian church - we are the family of God, caring for the orphans and outcasts of society. We are ourselves adopted into this family. Sadly even this has sometimes itself been a place of abuse.

When people discover their true identity as children of God, they generally develop a clear perception of their sexual identity and role. While recognising basic sexual preferences they also recognise that God gives them, through His Spirit, a very real power over their sexual desires and drives. This is not to be confused with inhibition and frustration but rather to be seen as fulfilment.

God's confirmation and affirmation is the foundation of our physical, emotional and spiritual maturity. Without this we cannot accept or love ourselves.

As Christians we are called to give hope to a hopeless world. We are called to be the Body of Christ, ministering healing to a broken world.

[1] Duckworth 1977
[2] Matt.25:40
[3] Quoted in *The Church and Homosexuality* - Green, Holloway, Watson
[4] Quoted in *Christian Attitudes to Homosexuality* by Peter Coleman, SPCK
[5] Rev.21:5
[6] 1Jn.1:3
[7] Jn. 14:12
[8] 1 Jn.4:10
[9] Matt.9:2
[10] Rev.3:20
[11] Rom. 3:22-24
[12] Phil. 2:7
[13] Lk. 9:1
[14] Matt.6:33
[15] Matt.10:31
[16] Is.43:1
[17] Jn.14:27
[18] Ps.139:1 and 13-16
[19] John 8:32
[20] *Gay Christians* by Peter Coleman pub. SCM.
[12] Quoted in *The Church and Homosexuality* by Green, Holloway, Watson. pub. Hodder and Stoughton.
[22] *The Times* 7th Jan. 1987.
[23] Jn.14:6
[24] Heb.13:8
[25] Mt.20:16
[26] Ps.46:10

Message from LADY LOTHIAN

Journalist, Broadcaster, Author,
Patron of the *Scottish Order of Christian Unity*

Currently all over the world there is increasing concern as to how best to strengthen the family as an indispensable social component for community stability.

In this book the contributors provide caring consideration and, above all, Bible based advice on how to recover and establish a firm foundation for family living.

The collection of opinions held by Christian men and women, whose work in the community has earned respect and recognition, gives their individual advice on Christian priorities for the family. The subjects under review include contraception, divorce and homosexuality. When the advice given is denominationally oriented it may become open to challenge from those who adhere to different Christian disciplines, particularly on subjects such as divorce and homosexuality. But this will encourage Christians to ask themselves sincere questions and to find sincere answers in the light of the teaching of Jesus Christ.

Discussion and dialogue, both within and without the Christian Church, concerning modern family problems is urgently necessary. The informed contributions on current controversies in *God, Family and Sexuality* raise questions whether or not to accept prevailing and varied Christian attitudes.

This book should inspire all who care about the family to look into their own hearts to find Christ's way to save the family.

CONTRIBUTORS AND MEMBERS OF THE STUDY GROUP

William D. Brown is a minister of the Church of Scotland, who has served in Linlithgow, Edinburgh, Wishaw. Prior to entering the ministry he was a teacher of English and a journalist. He is secretary of the Scottish Church Theology Society and the Scottish Order of Christian Unity.

Alison Dickson is a graduate of Aberdeen University. She worked with Grampian Regional Council, then with a firm of solicitors for ten years.

Graham Dickson is a graduate of Aberdeen University first in Economics, and then in Theology. He is a minister of the Church of Scotland. While in Aberdeen he met and married Alison. In 1985 they moved to Glenluce where Graham was the minister of two rural parishes. He is now minister of St. Stephen's Comely Bank Church, Edinburgh.

Brigid Cecilia McEwen, widow of Sir Robert McEwen of Marchmont, baronet and barrister, is an active member of the Roman Catholic Church, and of the SOCU. She was educated in convents in Cambridge and Mayfield, Sussex, and read modern languages in St. Anne's, Oxford. She is the author of *Birth Regulation: the Non-Contraceptive Method of Family Planning* and lectures on N.F.P. and Fertility Awareness to schools, engaged couples and Colleges of mid-wifery.

Donald McLeod was minister of Kilmallie Free Church from 1964 to 1970, and then minister of Partick Highland Free Church, Glasgow. He is now Professor of Systematic Theology at the Free Church College, Edinburgh. He was Editor of the *Monthly Record of the Free Church of Scotland* between 1977 and 1990, and is a member of the SOCU.

David C. Searle is a minister of the Church of Scotland, who has served congregations both in Scotland and in Northern Ireland, and is a member of the Scottish Order of Christian Unity. He is now the Director of Rutherford House in Edinburgh, and is the Editor of *The Rutherford Journal of Church and Ministry*. He is regularly involved in preaching workshops for ministers, and conducts residential seminars in practical theology throughout Scotland and Ireland.

David Short, a member of the Christian Brethren, was trained in medicine in Cambridge and Bristol, and served with the RAMC during the war. After being a Consultant in Bristol and London, and lecturer in medicine at

Middlesex Hospital in London, he became Professor of Clinical Medicine, University of Aberdeen. He was a former Chairman of the University and Grampian Health Board Committee on Medical Ethics; he is Physician to the Queen in Scotland; and a past President of the Christian Medical Fellowship.

Linda Stalley is an active member of the Church of England and of the Maranatha Community. She is a Medical Practitioner in an inner city practice and is part of a voluntary medical team for the Barnabas project for the homeless which operates in Manchester. She leads training courses and is involved in all areas of the Christian healing ministry.

Jock Stein is a graduate of Cambridge. He and his wife Margaret studied theology in Edinburgh, and together served as missionaries of the Church of Scotland in Kenya. On their return to this country Jock became minister of a large city centre congregation in Dundee. Since 1986 he and his wife, who are members of the SOCU, have served as joint wardens of Carberry, a Christian Conference Centre. He is also editor of the Handsel Press.

Margaret Stein has diplomas in art and religious education from Edinburgh colleges, and a degree in theology from Edinburgh University. She is an ordained minister of the Church of Scotland and serves as warden of Carberry along with her husband, with a special interest in healing and spiritual direction.

Elaine Storkey is Director of the Institute for Contemporary Christianity, and teaches for the University of London, Birbeck College Centre for Extra-mural Studies. She is a visiting lecturer in King's College, London, having previously lectured at the Open University, Oak Hill College, Stirling University and Manchester College, Oxford, chiefly in the areas of Philosophical Theology and Sociology. Her main book *What's Right with Feminism?* has been printed many times. Her latest book is *The Search for Intimacy*. She is a member of the General Synod of The Church of England and has served on the Crown Appointments Commission and a wide range of other Councils and Trusts.

Howard Taylor taught Mathematics and Physics in the University of Malawi. After graduating in theology in Edinburgh he was ordained by the Church of Central Africa Presbyterian, where he served for a further ten years. He is now minister of a Church of Scotland city congregation and lectures part-time for Glasgow Bible College. His subject relates theology to the frontiers of science. He has written and published on such subjects as Israel, the relationship between modern Science and Belief, Prayer and the Uniqueness of Christ. With Jock Stein he wrote *In Christ all Things Hold Together*. He is a member of the SOCU.

David W. Torrance like his brothers was born of missionary parents in China. He studied in Edinburgh University and in Basel. He has served as a Church of Scotland minister in three parishes. He co-edited with his brother Tom a new translation from Latin to English of Calvin's commentaries on the New Testament and edited *The Witness of the Jews to God*. He has served on various medical ethical working groups within the Church, and is a member of the SOCU.

James B. Torrance served as a Church of Scotland parish minister in Invergowrie, Dundee. Thereafter he taught Theology for sixteen years in New College, Edinburgh before becoming Professor of Systematic Theology in the University of Aberdeen. He has been chairman of the Church of Scotland Panel on Doctrine, co-chairman of the British Council of the Churches Commission on the Doctrine of the Trinity and of the conversations between the World Alliance of Reformed Churches and the Lutheran World Federation.

Thomas F. Torrance, is Professor Emeritus of Christian Dogmatics at New College, Edinburgh after serving as a parish minister for ten years. He was Convener of the Church of Scotland General Assembly Commission on Baptism, 1955-1961: Moderator of the General Assembly, 1976-1977: awarded the Collins Religious Books Prize, 1969 and the Templeton Prize for Progress in Religion, 1978. He was editor of the *Scottish Journal of Theology*, 1948-82, a Member of the Faith and Order Commission of the World Council of Churches, 1952-60, and of the Reformed/ Orthodox Dialogue of the Doctrine of the Trinity, 1979-83 and 1986-90. He is the President of the Scottish Order of Christian Unity.

Kevin J. Vanhoozer a doctoral graduate of Cambridge, is Senior Lecturer in Theology and Religious Studies at New College, Edinburgh. He has written extensively on hermeneutics and Biblical interpretation. He is a member of the Church of Scotland, in which he serves on the Panel on Doctrine, and is a member of the American Academy of Religion, where he co-chairs the group in Systematic Theology.

James B. Walker is Chaplain to St Andrews University. Born of missionary parents in Malawi, Africa, he is a graduate of Edinburgh University and gained his Doctorate from Oxford University. He has served in two Church of Scotland Parishes, Mid Craigie and Wallacetown, Dundee, 1975 to 78 and in Old and St. Paul's, Galashiels 1978 to 87. From 1987 to 93 he was Principal of The Queen's College in Birmingham where he taught Systematic Theology, Ethics and Christian Discipleship.

Robert B.W. Walker born of missionary parents in China was educated at Chefoo school, N. China. He graduated as a medical doctor at Edinburgh University. After studying Theology at New College, Edinburgh he was ordained as a minister of the Church of Scotland and served for several years as a medical missionary in Nyasaland (now Malawi). On his return to Scotland he was until his retirement minister of the parish of Abbeygreen, Lesmahagow. He is the treasurer of the Scottish Order of Christian Unity.

Dennis Wrigley, a Methodist, is leader and co-founder of the Maranatha Community, a movement of Christians in all the churches committed to Christian healing, unity and renewal. As a lay preacher he has been deeply involved in politics, youth work and broadcasting. He worked for many years in senior management in industry.

Two fairly recent books, published in the USA, support the positions argued in this publication, and are recommended for further study:

Reparative Therapy of Male Homosexuality - a new Clinical Approach, by Joseph Nicolosi (1991)

Homosexuality and the Politics of Truth, by Jeffrey Satinover (1996)

Some other books by Handsel Press, which deal with fundamental issues from a basic Christian point of view:

John Wilkinson: CHRISTIAN ETHICS IN HEALTH CARE
(a case bound text book, now available at £17.50)
Heinz W. Cassirer: GRACE AND LAW
(a book of theological testimony, £7.50)
T.F. Torrance: THE CHRISTIAN FRAME OF MIND *(£3.50)*
T.F. Torrance (ed.): BELIEF IN SCIENCE
AND IN CHRISTIAN LIFE *(£5.25)*
Reid, Newbigin and Pullinger: MODERN, POSTMODERN
AND CHRISTIAN *(£4.95)*
T.F.Torrance: THE MINISTRY OF WOMEN *(£2.50)*

(and forthcoming)

John Wilkinson: THE BIBLE, MEDICINE AND HEALING
George Knight: CENTRED ON CHRIST
- a Biblical Theology of the Incarnation
Fearghas MacFhionnlaigh: RAINBOW IN THE NIGHT
(an epic Christian testimony on suffering, in Gaelic and English)